FIELD & STREAM

THE TOTAL KNIFE MANUAL

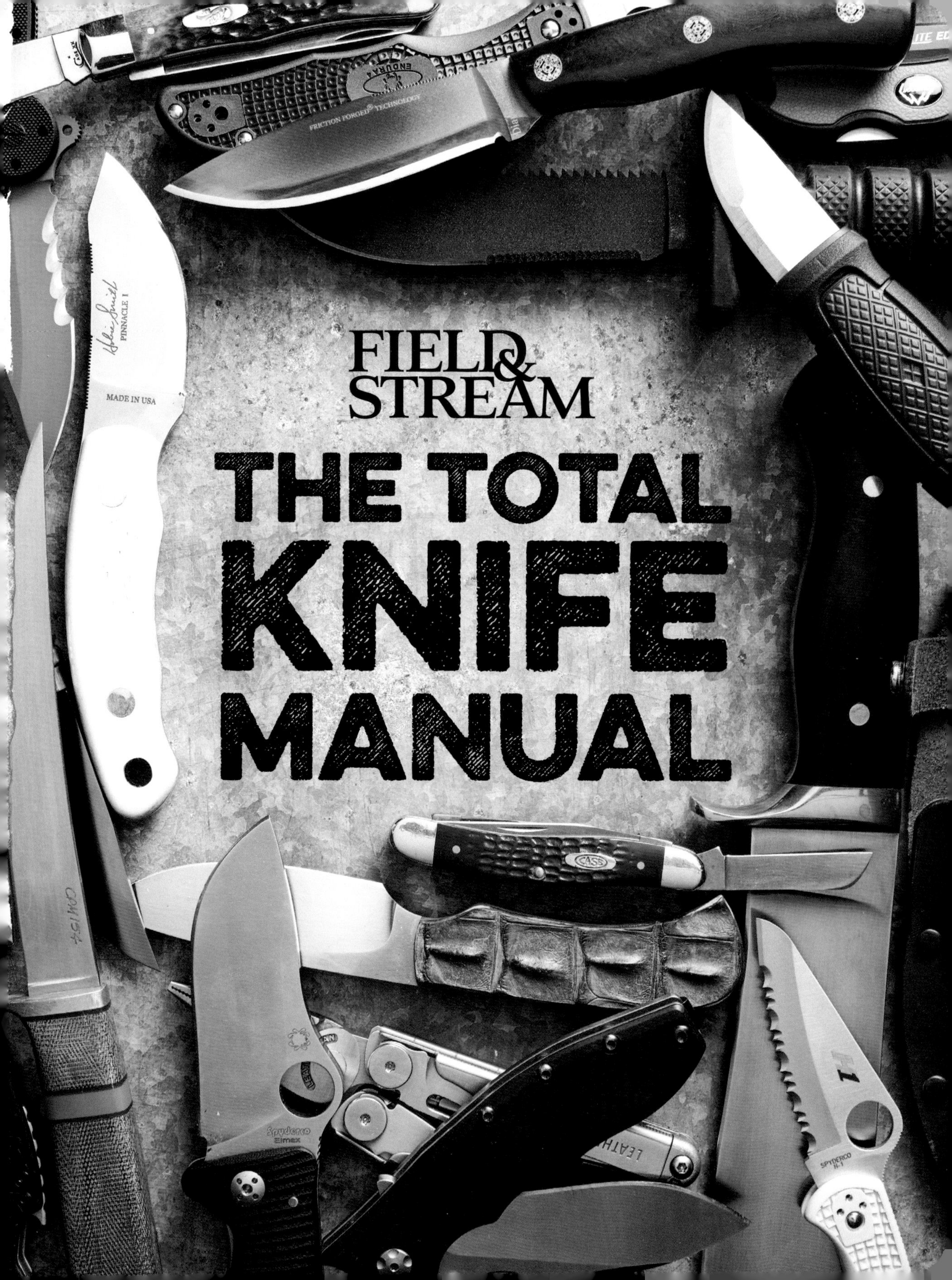

FIELD & STREAM

THE TOTAL KNIFE MANUAL

T. EDWARD NICKENS
AND THE EDITORS OF
FIELD & STREAM

weldonowen

KNOW THE KNIFE

KNIFE DESIGN

KNIFE TYPES

MULTITOOLS

CUSTOM KNIVES

USE THE KNIFE

AXES, HATCHETS & SAWS

FROM FIELD & STREAM

The most recent addition to my always-growing collection of knives is a Swiss Army Champ, a Christmas gift from my mom. The Champ is really too bulky to be considered an EDC knife, but that doesn't keep me from using it as one. In fact, it's sitting on my desk as I write these words. I love this knife too much not to carry it everywhere.

During the first few weeks I owned it, I looked for any opportunity to use one of the 33 tools in that iconic red handle. (For the record, I've now deployed just about every one, although it's safe to say I'll probably never need the parcel carrier, because... who the hell needs a parcel carrier?) When I have this knife in my pocket, I feel like there's no job I can't handle, because there's no job it can't handle.

And in the years I've been working with him, I've come to feel the same way about T. Edward Nickens: There's no job he can't handle, no adventure he'll turn down. He hunts, fishes, and camps. He's a naturalist, conservationist, gear junkie, river rat, and *Field & Stream*'s resident Total Outdoorsman. Nickens is also the most enthusiastic knife nut I know, as well as a gifted writer—both of which you're about to see for yourself in the following pages. Which is why I'm going to keep this introduction short, because I don't want to keep you from enjoying the rest of this book.

And what a book it is. It's packed with timeless stories of the knives we love and rely on, photo galleries of blades so beautiful they're works of art, and skills and tips to give you an edge in the wild. Master them all and there's nothing you won't be able to handle.

Colin Kearns
Editor-in-Chief, *Field & Stream*

AUTHOR'S NOTE

The knife is one tool—the only tool, really—that cuts across the entire sporting spectrum. Hunting, fishing, camping, and survival—you simply can't do without a knife. Or two. Or 50. You could choose a single smartly designed, well-made knife that could adequately perform every outdoor task imaginable, but where's the fun in that?

This book is for people who obsess over the details of the knife in their pocket or on their belt. The same folks who fuss over how to properly sharpen an ax or replace the handle on a hatchet. It's for people who can't stand a dull knife and who are always looking for new ways to gain an edge. After all, this is a golden age for knife nuts. Advances in steel metallurgy are bringing to market new steels with incredible properties of strength and edge-holding ability. A growing network of custom knifemakers is thriving. The advent of tactical-style equipment is expanding the world of edged tools in ways few could have imagined.

This book will help you navigate these new worlds of field cutlery and remind you of the fascinating heritage of bladesmithing. It's packed with details on every aspect of knife design, construction, and use—from steel composition to how to throw a knife to how to choose between carrying a folding knife tip-up or tip-down in your pants pocket. One thing I hope comes through, particularly in the anecdotes about famous knives and influential knifemakers, and the testimonials from *Field & Stream* editors, is the way certain knives take on a life of their own when they are imbued with the power of story. Often, it's not how a knife is made or what kind of steel comprises the blade that makes a particular knife such a beloved tool. It's the story the knife tells. The story of a cherished relative. An accumulation of memories shared with a blade in hand. Or perhaps a single moment, when life and death was balanced on the very edge of the blade.

So dive in. Every page is crammed with knife know-how, knife stories, and fabulous photos of some of the finest knives, axes, hatchets, machetes, and saws on the planet. I hope you learn a few things. I bet you'll disagree with a few opinions, and that's fine by me. If you have strong opinions about knives, you're my kind of reader.

In *The Adventures of Tom Sawyer*, Mark Twain wrote about Tom receiving a singular gift—a bone-handled pocketknife. Tom knew a swell present when he saw one.

"Mary gave him a bran-new 'Barlow' knife worth twelve and a half cents," Twain wrote, "and the convulsion of delight that swept his system shook him to his foundations."

Tom and I would have had a lot to talk about. Since you've gotten this far, I bet you'd have plenty to say, as well. Enjoy.

T. Edward Nickens

Editor-at-Large, *Field & Stream*

KNOW THE KNIFE

THE RIGHT KNIFE

I remember when I lost the knife. I was climbing a narrow ladder that led to the top of a river lock on the Santee-Cooper Lakes in South Carolina when I felt the familiar weight of it suddenly leave my pocket. Ten feet below, the knife plopped into the water of the lock chamber. My stomach turned. I knew instantly it was gone forever.

I've mourned that knife for years, not because it was the best knife I've ever owned, but because it was the first one that helped me understand what a knife could be. It was a Gerber Model 5866—the original Air Ranger II. It was larger and beefier than the current version, but, sadly, it's been out of production for years. It was fastidiously designed by a famed knifemaker named Bill Harsey, and it was packed with wonders of knifesmithery. Its nearly four-inch blade forever ruined me for smaller EDC knives. The handle, built on an open frame so I could hose it clean, had checkered aluminum scales with chamfered edges that never gave me a hotspot. The clip point blade had jimping on the spine ramp, though back then I could not have defined either "jimping" or "spine ramp." Nor did I understand the value of the rotolock that backed up its liner lock, or how to sharpen its partially serrated blade. But the more I used it, the more interested I became in knife design—an interest that would blossom into obsession.

I loved everything about that knife except its AUS-8A steel, which could barely gut, skin, and quarter a piddling coastal-plain whitetail without needing a touch-up. That helped me hone my sharpening skills, though, and I carried that folder constantly. When I inadvertently carried it to a pro hockey game, I buried it under a bush near the entrance metal detector, only to leave the game early to retrieve my baby before someone else discovered it. Once, in the span of a single weekend, I used that knife to clean several squirrels and a deer, brush up a duck blind, slice meat loaf at a church dinner, and cut a wedding cake.

I'd carry it still if it hadn't sunk out of sight. Every mechanical detail of that knife fit my hand, my style, my life, and I miss it every day.

In the following pages, you'll read about how a blade's performance is derived from a combination of its steel, geometry, and edge characteristics; the differences between increasingly elegant locking mechanisms; how to enter the heady world of custom knife collecting; and what it is about a knife—the right knife—that can add grace and security to everyday life.

KNIFE DESIGN

→ IN THIS SECTION →

FIXED VS. FOLDER:

KNOW THE COMPONENTS OF EACH

BOB LOVELESS:

THE MAN BEHIND THE DROP POINT

LOCKED UP:

PROS AND CONS

OF 6 LOCKING MECHANISMS

GRIND CONTROL:

IT'S ALL ABOUT THE EDGE

PROFILING:

CHOOSE THE RIGHT BLADE STYLE FOR EVERY TASK

GET A GRIP:

11 POPULAR HANDLE MATERIALS

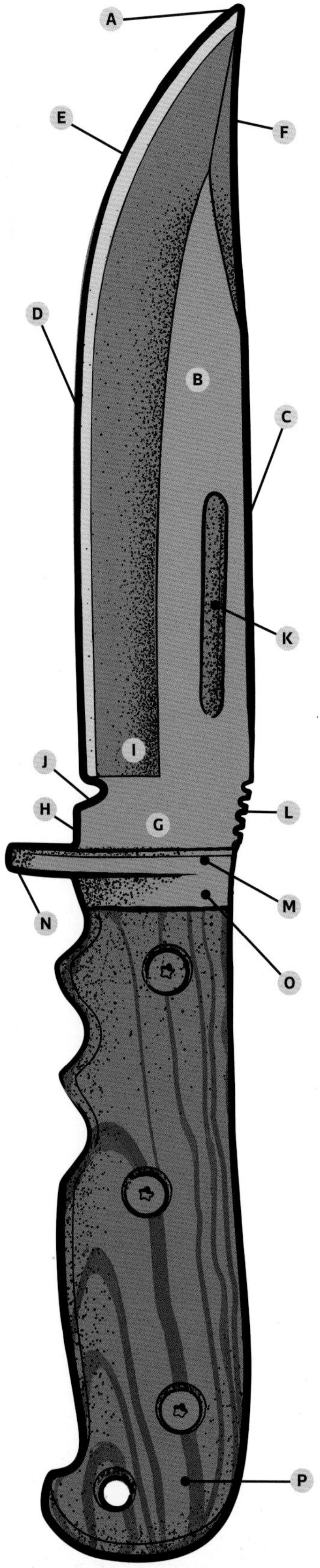

001 ANATOMY OF A FIXED-BLADE KNIFE

The sleek lines of a fixed-blade knife speak to the essence of outdoors competence. Fixed-blade knives consist of a blade, a handle, and a tang, which is the extension of the blade that carries into the handle. They are easy to clean and quick to deploy, with no moving parts to break or become gunked up. A strong fixed-blade knife can be batoned (struck on the spine) through wood. It can be twisted and torqued. Its strength comes from its seeming simplicity–although a cheaply made fixed-blade is no bargain at all. No fixed-blade knife is built with all the elements listed here, and many of them are found on folding knives, too. How designers choose among such a broad menu of options is what makes knives so endlessly fascinating.

A POINT Also called the tip. The sharper the point, the better a knife's piercing ability—though at the expense of tip strength.

B CHEEK The side of the blade, also called the face.

C SPINE The unsharpened back of the blade.

D EDGE The sharpened cutting surface.

E BELLY The curved section of the edge. A knife with lots of belly is useful for long, sweeping cuts like those used for skinning animals.

F SWEDGE A ground edge on the spine near the tip. A sharpened swedge increases piercing ability. Most are unsharpened and purely decorative.

G HEEL A general term for the section of the blade where it meets the handle or guard.

H RICASSO The short, unsharpened part of the blade between the edge bevel and the handle or guard. The ricasso allows for sharpening of the full blade without risk of marring the handle.

I PLUNGE LINE Where the cheek's grind meets the edge bevel.

J CHOIL An unsharpened, scalloped indent where the blade meets the handle. A large choil can be handy as a finger grip. Smaller choils serve as a stop for sharpening devices to protect the guard or handle.

K FULLER Often called a blood groove, this channel runs parallel to the spine. The fuller functions like an I-beam, reducing weight and adding strength.

L JIMPING Ground notches in the blade spine, and sometimes the handle, that provide traction for the user's finger.

M GUARD Designed to keep the hand from slipping onto the blade. Guards range in size, though many modern designs lack them.

N QUILLON An elongated point on the guard that provides added protection. Fighting and tactical knives often have double quillons, one on each side of the blade.

O BOLSTER A thick metal shoulder at the front of the handle, or separate pieces that sandwich the tang. Bolsters can be either separate pieces of metal or part of the blade and tang.

P POMMEL Also called the butt, this is the end of the handle. A stout pommel can be used to pound stakes.

002 MEET THE TANGS

With a fixed-blade knife, what you see is only part of what you get. The extension of the blade into the handle is called the "tang," and the design of a knife's tang is a major factor in the overall strength and durability of the knife. There are two broad categories of knife tangs: full tangs and partial tangs, with lots of variation within each approach.

FULL TANG Unquestionably the strongest design, a full tang extends the full length and width of the handle. In many knives, a full tang is tapered toward the butt to reduce weight. Less common is a skeletonized tang, which has portions of steel removed. Skeletonized tangs are most typically found on lightweight tactical knives used for survival.

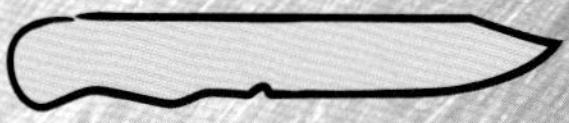
Full Tang

Skeletonized Tang

PARTIAL TANG A partial tang doesn't extend the length of the handle, or is narrower than the handle. While not as strong as a full tang, a well-made partial-tang knife is still a great choice for tasks that don't involve pounding and hard use. Many skinning, camp, and general-use knives have partial tangs, of which there are several different designs. A hidden tang is narrower than a full tang and may or may not run all the way to the pommel. A push tang is less rigid than a hidden tang and is simply pushed with adhesive into the handle material during construction. Rat-tail or stick tangs can be a thin extension of the handle or a piece of metal welded to the rear of the blade itself. This is the weakest tang design.

Hidden Tang

Push Tang

Rat-Tail Tang

DESIGNERS WHO CHANGED EVERYTHING

R.W. "BOB" LOVELESS

After witnessing a number of knife fights in foreign ports as a merchant marine, Bob Loveless became increasingly intrigued with knife design. In 1953, with his tanker docked in New York City, Loveless visited the city's preeminent sporting goods store, Abercrombie & Fitch. When he learned there was a nine-month wait for a custom blade by famed designer Bo Randall, Loveless decided to try his hand at the craft and forged his first knife blade from the leaf spring of a 1938 Packard. Within a year, he sold his first knives to Abercrombie & Fitch for $14 a piece.

Loveless went on to chart a new course for American knife making. He used 154CM stainless steel, developed for jet-engine exhausts, in his lustrous, tough, and virtually rustproof blades. The tapered tang he employed, winnowing to as narrow as $^{1}/_{16}$ inch, lent his knives incredible balance and a deft touch. But it was really the development of the drop point blade–so-called because the tip of the knife drops below the plane of the spine–that made him a legend.

Loveless grew up in Ohio during the Depression, and it always irked him that the collector's market drove up the price of his knives. "A knife is a tool, and I make 'em to be used," he told the *Los Angeles Times* in 1981. "It burns me up that most of them wind up in velvet boxes and display cases, priced so high your average deer hunter or cowboy can't afford 'em."

Thankfully, Loveless' influence was wide-ranging. Today there is no shortage of high-quality drop point knives available for nearly any budget.

003 ANATOMY OF A FOLDING KNIFE

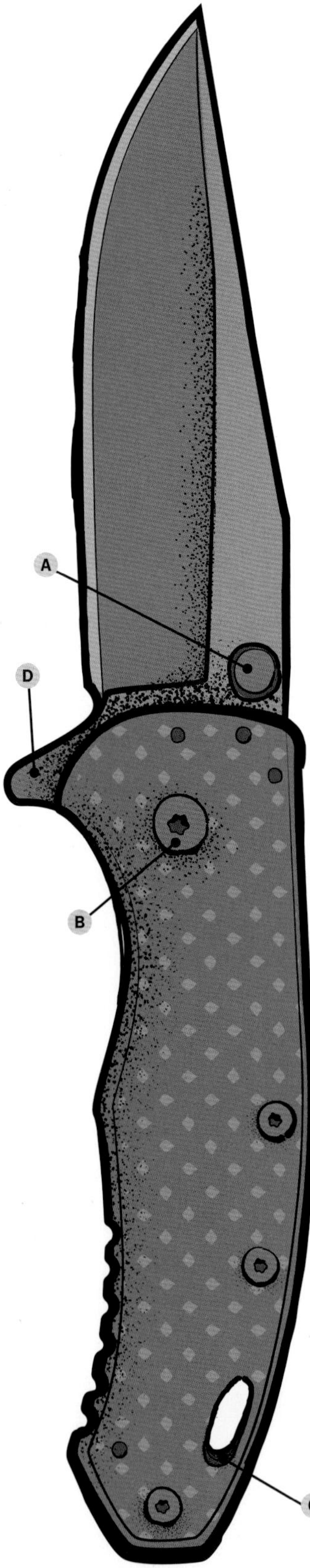

In a folding knife, the blade swings around a pivot at one end of the handle. When open, it is locked into position. When closed, it is nestled inside the handle scales for safe carry in a pocket or pouch. From there, folding knife design varies widely. Much of a folder's design is centered on its greatest inherent weakness–the reliability of the lockup when open. Other aspects include speed of opening, beautiful handles, and sleek interior parts.

Manual folders are still the most common type, which require the user to open the blade. Assisted-opening folders, in which spring mechanisms complete the opening process once the blade is partially opened, have joined the scene in recent years. Automatic folders–in which a spring mechanism exerts opening pressure on the blade with the mere press of a button–are growing in popularity as more states loosen knife restrictions.

The advent of the pocket clip ushered in a new way of thinking about carrying knives, complete with its own acronym: EDC, for "everyday carry." EDC knives are highly functional models designed to be clipped to a pocket or belt.

Fixed-blade and folding knives share plenty of common ground, but in many respects they're different species entirely. Here's the engineering behind the flick.

A THUMB STUD A metal stud or opening near the knife's pivot. By pressing or hooking a thumb onto the stud or opening, the blade can be swiveled open with one hand. Thumb studs are typically found on both sides of the blade, to allow for ambidextrous opening.

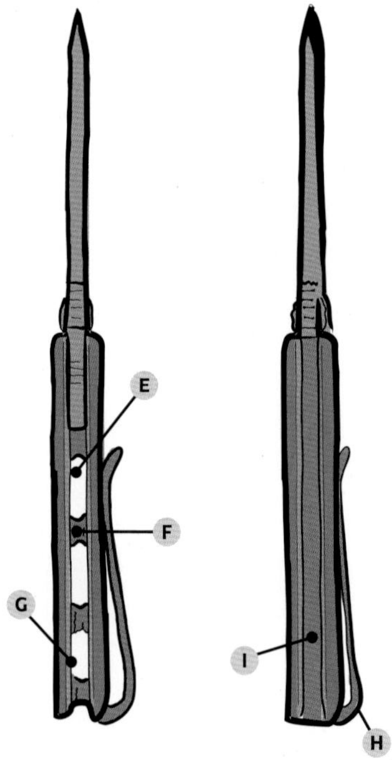

B PIVOT The joint around which the blade swings. On some knives, the pivot can often be manipulated to adjust the tension of the action.

C LANYARD HOLE Allows for the attachment of paracord or other cordage.

D FLIPPER A triggerlike protrusion on the blade that allows the knife to be flipped open with a finger. Not found on all knives.

E OPEN FRAME An open-frame folder has no backspacer. It can be cleaned easily, but the blade edge is exposed to loose change, keys, and other hard objects in a pocket.

F STANDOFF A metal pillar that provides the proper interior spacing for operation of the knife.

G LINER Thin plates, typically of steel or titanium, on the interior face of the handle slabs. The liners reinforce the handle; on liner-lock designs they serve as the locking mechanism.

H POCKET CLIP A metal clip that enables the user to clip the knife to a pocket for comfortable carry and quick deployment.

I BACKSPACER A strip of metal or tough synthetic material, such as G10, that spans the interior of the two sides of the knife handle. Metal backspacers are sometimes intricately filed.

004 CATCH A WAVE

Designed by Ernest Emerson for Navy SEALs, the "Wave" is a hook ground into the base of the blade spine. On a tip-up carry knife, a user can draw the knife from a pocket while hooking the Wave on the corner of the pocket fabric, opening the knife with the speed and flair of a gunslinger.

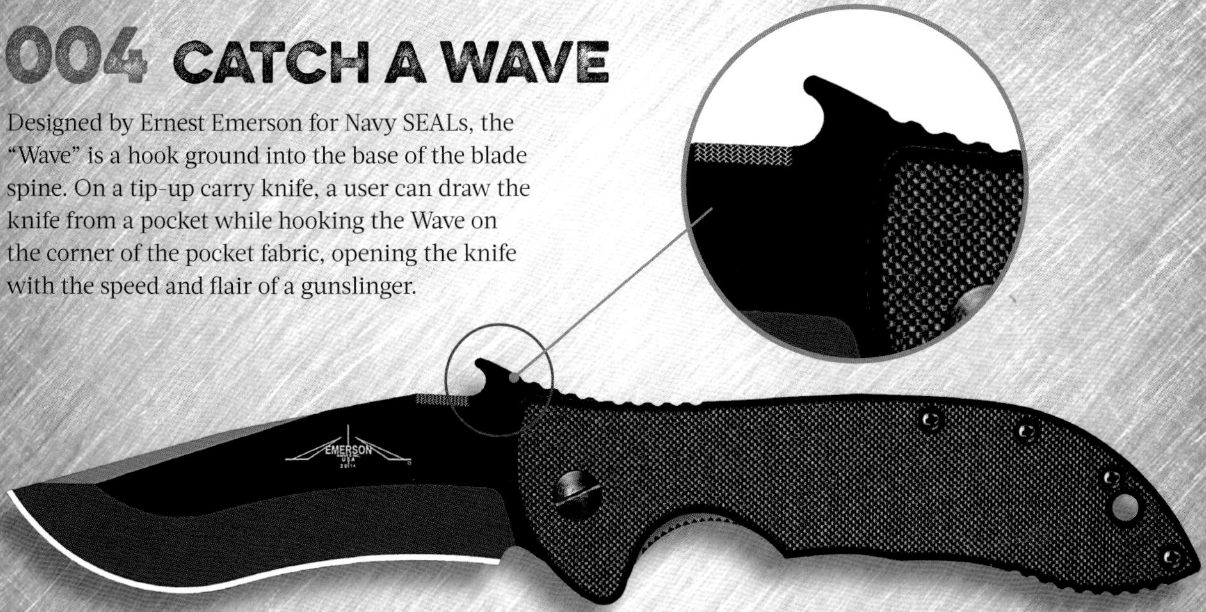

DESIGNERS WHO CHANGED EVERYTHING

ERNEST EMERSON

Ernest Emerson's own custom CQC-6 (Close Quarters Combat) helped kick off the knife world's tactical revolution. One of the first, and considered among the finest, of the true tactical folding knives, it was developed for U.S. Army Special Forces and other elite fighting units. In 1994, Benchmade began producing the CQC-7, a somewhat smaller production version of the CQC-6. It quickly became the industry's most sought-after production tactical folder.

Emerson made his first knife–a balisong–as a student at a full-contact fighting school, the Filipino KALI Academy. He continued to hone his craft and was soon working with the British SAS, U.S. Navy SEALs, and other tactical fighting units. Waiting periods for his handmade knives stretched out to 10 years.

Emerson's tactical knives are devoid of gimmicky blade and handle shapes, reflecting his philosophy that close-quarters combat is often won simply on "violence of action." One of his most famous design features–the Emerson Wave–is incorporated into many of today's EDC knives.

In the mid 1990s, the U.S. Navy SEALs had requested a knife with a blade-catcher on the spine to prevent an attacker's blade from running up the spine and onto the operator's hand. Emerson designed a small hook that served the purpose well. The feature also provided a useful secondary purpose. The Wave, when caught on corner of a pocket as the knife is drawn, allows for nearly instantaneous deployment.

005 PICK A LOCK

These are the most common locking mechanisms available, each strong enough for most cutting tasks. Well-made knives with these lock types are staples in the outdoors, but each has its strengths and weaknesses.

LOCKBACK

The lockback system uses a lockbar between the scales that runs the length of the handle and is pinned in the middle. When the knife is open, a spring bar in the rear of the handle presses on the lockbar, pivoting it around the pin. This presses a hook in the forward end of the lockbar into a cutout on the tang's end. To close the knife, you press on the bottom of the lockbar to release the hook. A midlock knife is a lockback with the lock in the middle of the handle instead.

PROS Simple; few moving parts; ambidextrous.

CONS Prone to inadvertent release when gripping the knife; clumsy to close with one hand; prone to gunk buildup in the lock mechanism.

LINER LOCK

Simple but strong, a liner lock uses one of the knife's liners as a kind of leaf spring. One liner is cut and angled toward the handle's interior, butting against the blade tang to keep it from moving. The best liner locks have a stop pin in the scales to guide the blade tang to the correct open position; a small detent ball on the liner keeps the blade in the closed position.

PROS Easy to use; inexpensive to manufacture.

CONS Clumsy to close with one hand; possibility for wear on the tip of the liner where it engages the blade.

FRAMELOCK

Beefier than the liner lock, a framelock uses the knife's frame to engage the open blade and lock it in place. A channel is cut into one of the handle scales; this part of the scale angles inward to engage the blade tang and lock the knife open. To close the blade, the frame must be pushed back with a thumb to release the lock. Many framelocks have extra features to bolster them. Inserts are bolted to the end of titanium framelock bars since titanium can wear faster than some steels. LionSteel of Italy's Rotoblock has a disk in the handle liner that can be turned with a fingertip to keep the lockbar closed.

PROS Very strong; less prone to gunking up.

CONS Not ambidextrous; prone to wear on the blade tang and tip of the lock and tends to cost more.

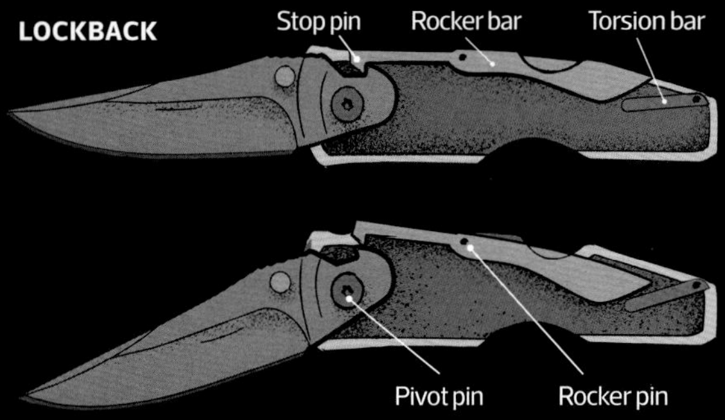

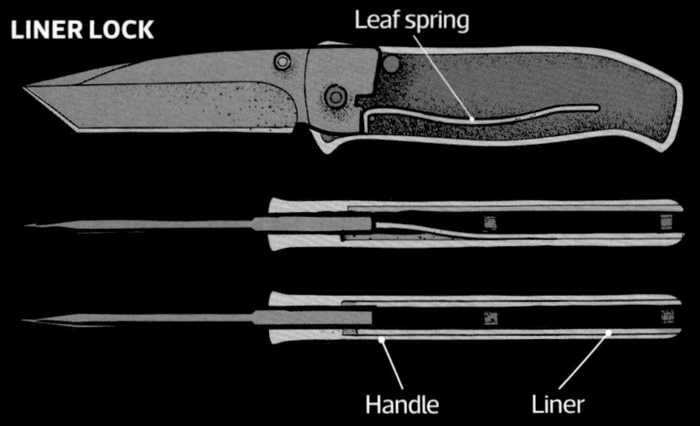

006 KNOW THE NEXT-LEVEL LOCKS

Often proprietary to specific brands, more-complex locking mechanisms seek to close the gap between fixed knives and folders, and illustrate the engineering beauty hidden inside an elegantly designed lock.

AXIS LOCK

One of Benchmade Knife Company's finest achievements, the AXIS debuted in 1998 and is still considered very advanced. A spring-loaded bar spans the handle's width, and rides forward and backward in a slot cut out of both liners and scales. When the knife is opened, the bar slides in the slot and locks into place in a notch in the back of the tang, wedging the tang between this locking bar and a stop bar.

PROS Completely ambidextrous; fingers stay out of the way of the blade when closing; very strong.

CONS Plenty of moving parts to attract dirt, blood, and gunk; springs can fail, though this is rare.

TRI-AD LOCK

Cold Steel beefed up the traditional lockback by adding a stop pin to redistribute force pressure from the blade to the handle frame and liners. In this midlock design, the deeply notched lockbar butts against the stop pin, and the lockbar and blade tang mate almost completely.

PROS Rarely needs cleaning; slightly oversized rocker-pin hole allows for self-adjustment as metal parts wear.

CONS The lock can be released by torque and grip on the handle.

TRACK LOCK

Designed in partnership with U.S. Special Forces, FirstEdge Knives and Tools employs a specialized lock in which a heavy steel pin rides transversely through the blade tang and the handle liners. This steel pin moves with the blade to lock into the 440C liners.

PROS Very simple to use; just press the button.

CONS The thumb button could be inadvertently pressed during hard use.

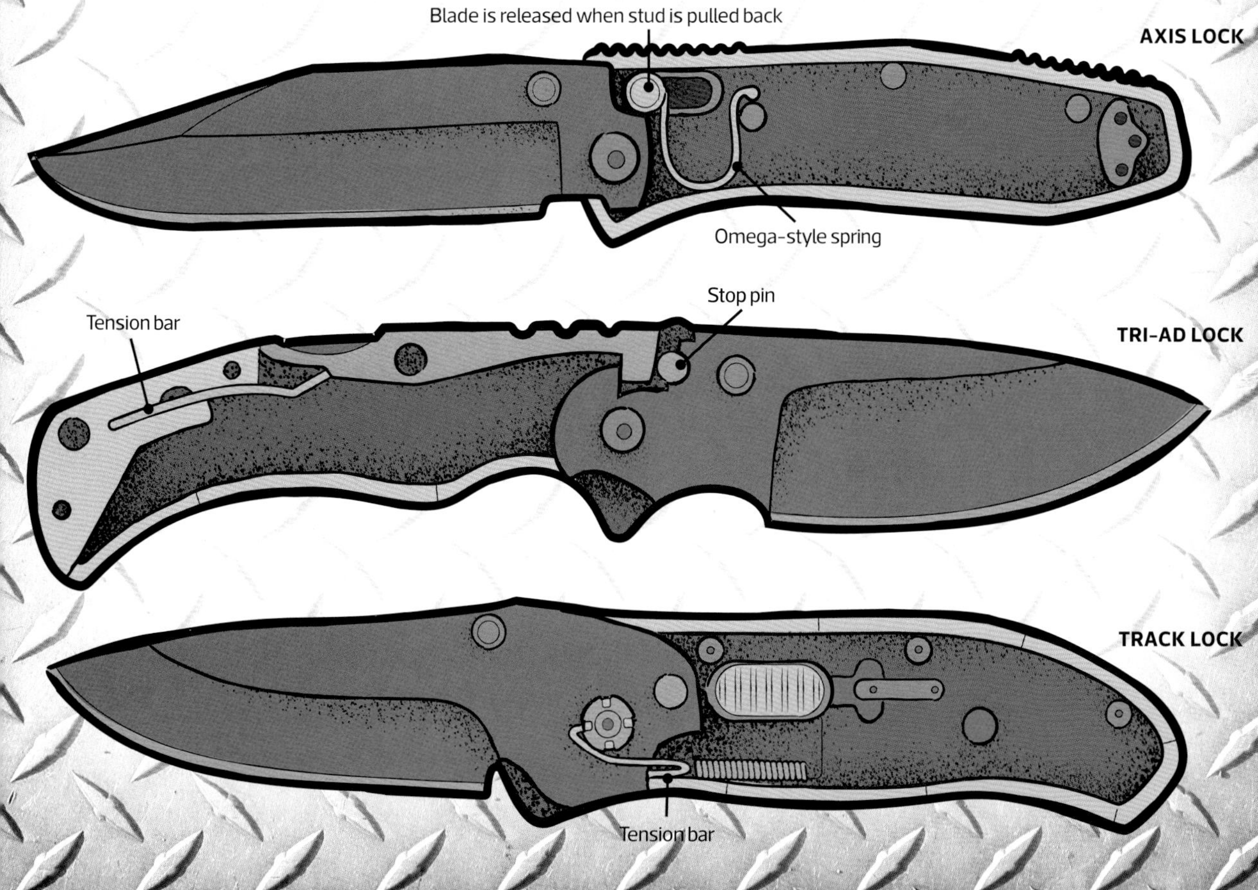

007 STEEL 101

Determining which blade steel best suits your needs can be confounding, but few factors are as important to knife function as a steel's pedigree. Some steels are harder than others; some are easier to sharpen. Some are known for holding an edge well; others are more resistant to corrosion. Each attribute typically comes with a tradeoff. For example, a blade that is hard and holds an edge might be prone to chipping. Knowing a bit about metallurgy will help you make the right decision when choosing a steel, whether you're shopping for an inexpensive, general-use knife or a high-dollar custom blade.

Basic steel is nothing more than iron and carbon, but that's just the beginning of the story. We've used steel for some 4,000 years; ancient pieces of ironware have been found at an archaeological site in Anatolia that dates back to 1800 B.C.E. Over the ages, steel makers learned that a pinch of cobalt or a dash of chromium–not to mention a smidge of more exotic compounds such as vanadium and molybdenum–changes a steel's character.

Which is best for you? 1095 or D2? 8Cr13MoV or AUS-8? H1 or ZDP-189? These are just a few of the more common varieties of steel available today among thousands of options.

The least you need to know is that the higher the carbon content, the harder the blade and the better it will hold an edge–but too much can make a blade brittle, reducing toughness. Blades with a higher carbon content also rust and corrode more easily; adding chromium prevents rust (stainless steel usually has at least 12 percent chromium) but can soften the steel. After you decide between carbon or stainless, you'll be faced with a series of tradeoffs between hardness and toughness, more or less corrosion resistance, higher or lower wearability, and more. But don't be overwhelmed. The choices are what make this so much fun.

CONSIDER CARBON STEEL

All steels contain carbon. A medium-carbon steel blade might be 0.4 to 0.7 percent carbon, while high-carbon steel contains at least 0.8 percent carbon, and some contain as much as 2 or 3 percent. Carbon steels often include various other elements that give them specific properties, but chromium (the key to stainless steel) is either absent or present in very low amounts. Carbon steel knives are more brittle than stainless blades, and require cleaning and oiling. On the plus side, proponents point to carbon steel's relative ease of sharpening, its edge-holding ability, and the fact that it can be differentially heat-treated–with a very hard edge, for example, and a softer, more flexible spine. Carbon steel can also be used to throw sparks for fire-starting. And for many, the fact that carbon steel will stain over time is a plus. Like a fine wood gunstock that ages and darkens, a blued carbon knife blade wears a story-rich patina.

STUDY UP ON STAINLESS

When chromium is added to a steel alloy and the metal is heat-treated, a protective chromium oxide layer covers the steel surface. This is what makes steel "stainless." Stainless steel blades typically contain between 10.5 percent and 16 percent chromium, but let's be clear: There's no such thing as a truly stainless steel. An alloy that's absolutely impervious to rust would contain so much chromium as to be useless in a knife. The most popular near-stainless steels are 440A, 440B, and 440C, and while it's almost impossible to get them to rust or stain, it's also very difficult to make a very sharp knife from them. What you can do, if you prefer your blade to be sharp and shiny and easy to work with, is upgrade to better stainless steels, such as 154CM, ATS-34, AUS-8, the CPM stainless series, Sandvik 12C27, or VG-10. Or you can buy a Morakniv or Helle knife and bask in the glow of their proprietary, and very fine, stainless steels.

DESIGNERS
WHO CHANGED EVERYTHING

BILL MORAN

Born on a Maryland dairy farm in 1925, Bill Moran learned bladesmithing on his family's coal forge. He sold his first knife when he was 14 years old and was soon pilfering his father's farm tools for their steel. Through the middle part of the 20th century, Moran cut a swath through the bladesmithing world like few others ever had.

Of all his achievements, Moran was perhaps best known for his work in Damascus steel. Sylvester Stallone had Moran build him a knife inlaid with 30 feet of silver wire. King Abdullah II of Jordan visited his tiny shop near Middletown, Maryland, and ordered a combat knife.

Moran died in 2006, but his legacy continues to inform the industry. Indeed, a popular convex blade grind is named for him.

Moran founded and helped create the American Bladesmith Society in 1976, as well as a knife making school on the grounds of Historic Washington State Park in Arkansas. It has now become known as the Bill Moran School of Bladesmithing.

008 CHEMICAL COMPOSITIONS OF BLADE STEELS

A.G. Russell Knives first published its authoritative online steel chart in 1998 and keeps the chart up-to-date with the ever-changing menu of knife steel recipes. (For the complete data, check out agrussell.com/chart.) This chart includes most of the steels found in both production and custom knives, and is a handy tool for

STAINLESS STEELS

STEEL	CARBON (C)	MANGANESE (Mn)	CHROMIUM (Cr)	NICKEL (Ni)	VANADIUM (V)	MOLYBDENUM (Mo)
1.4116	0.45-.050	0.4	14.50–14.80	–	0.1	0.6
154CM	1.05	0.5	14	–	–	4
420HC	0.40–0.50	0.8	12.00–14.00	–	0.18	0.6
440A	0.65–0.75	1	16.00–18.00	–	–	0.75
440B	0.75–0.95	1	16.00–18.00	–	–	0.75
440C	0.95–1.20	1	16.00–18.00	–	–	0.75
8CR13MOV	0.8	0.4	13	0.2	0.1	0.15
9CR13COMOV	0.85	1	13.5	–	0.2	0.2
9CR18MOV	0.95	0.3	16	0.1	–	0.5
ATS-34	1.05	0.4	14	–	–	4
ATS-55	1	0.5	14	–	–	0.6
AUS-8	0.70–0.75	0.5	13.00–14.50	0.49	0.10–0.26	0.10–0.30
AUS-10	0.95–1.10	0.5	13.00–14.50	0.49	0.10–0.27	0.10–0.31
BG-42	1.15	0.5	14.5	–	1.2	4
BOHLER M390	1.9	0.3	20	–	4	1
CPM-154	1.05	0.6	14	–	–	4
CPM-S30V	1.45	–	14	–	4	2
CPM-S35VN	1.4	–	14	–	3	2
CPM-S60V	2.15	0.4	17	–	5.5	0.4
CPM-S90V	2.3	–	14	–	9	1
CTS-40CP	0.90–1.20	1	16.00–18.00	–	–	0.75
ELMAX	1.7	0.3	18	–	3	1
H-1	0.15	2	14.00–16.00	6.00–8.00	–	0.50–1.50
M390	1.9	0.3	20	–	4	1
SANDVIK 12C27	0.6	0.4	13.5	–	–	–
VG-10	0.95–1.05	0.5	14.50–15.50	–	0.10–0.30	0.90–1.20
ZDP-189	3	–	20	–	–	–

CARBON STEELS

STEEL	CARBON (C)	MANGANESE (Mn)	CHROMIUM (Cr)	NICKEL (Ni)	VANADIUM (V)	MOLYBDENUM (Mo)
1095	0.90–1.03	0.30–0.50	–	–	–	–
1095 CRO-VAN	0.95–1.1	0.30–0.50	0.40–0.60	0.25	0.161	0.06
5160	0.56–0.64	0.75–1.00	0.70–0.90	–	–	–
52100	0.98–1.10	0.25–0.45	1.30–1.60	–	–	–
A-2	0.95–1.05	1	4.75–5.50	0.3	0.15–0.50	0.90–1.40
CPM-D2	1.55	–	11.5	–	0.8	0.9
CPM-M4	1.4	0.3	4	–	4	5.25
D-2	1.40–1.60	0.6	11.00–13.00	0.3	1.1	0.70–1.20
DM1	0.95	0.46	0.45	–	0.19	–
M-2	0.95–1.05	0.15–0.40	3.75–4.50	0.3	2.25–2.75	4.75–6.50
O-1	0.85–1.00	1.00–1.40	0.40–0.60	0.3	0.3	–
W-1	0.70–1.50	0.10–0.40	0.15	0.2	0.1	0.1

comparing steels when shopping for a new blade. The percentages expressed of the various elements are based on percentage by weight.

TUNGSTEN (W)	COBALT (Co)	TYPICAL HRC HARDNESS
–	–	55–57
–	–	58–62
–	–	56–58
–	–	55–57
–	–	57–59
–	–	57–59
–	–	58–59
–	1	58–60
–	–	58–60
–	–	59–61
–	0.4	59–61
–	–	57–59
–	–	58–60
–	–	59–61
0.6	–	60–62
–	–	59–61
–	–	59–61
–	–	59–61
–	–	58–60
–	–	56–58
–	–	59–60
–	–	58–62
–	–	••
0.6	–	60–62
–	–	57–59
	1.30-1.50	59–61
–	–	64–66

TUNGSTEN (W)	COBALT (Co)	TYPICAL HRC HARDNESS
–	–	56–58
–	–	56–58
–	–	57–59
–	–	59–61
–	–	59–61
–	–	57–59
5.5	–	59–61
–	–	57–61
–	–	58–59
5.00–6.75	–	61–63
0.5	–	53–54
0.5	–	60–62

009 THE ELEMENTS OF AN ALLOY

Steel makers choose among a wide variety of elements to create different steel recipes. Here's what each material contributes to the final product.

6 C carbon

CARBON Turns iron into steel. High-carbon steel results when 0.5 percent or more carbon (by weight) is present. Iron can only absorb about 0.8 percent carbon. Adding more just increases the hardness.

25 Mn manganese

MANGANESE Increases toughness and ability to be hardened.

24 Cr chromium

CHROMIUM Produces hardness and improved edge-holding ability when combined with other alloying materials. Large amounts result in rust-resistant blades; it takes more than 12.5 percent to produce high-carbon stainless steels.

28 Ni nickel

NICKEL Adds strength and toughness.

23 V vanadium

VANADIUM Helps to produce fine grain during heat treating.

42 Mo molybdenum

MOLYBDENUM Increases hardness in tool steel.

74 W tungsten

TUNGSTEN Utilized in small quantities in several handmade knife steels; helps produce a fine, dense grain structure.

27 Co cobalt

COBALT Increases strength and hardness, and permits quenching in higher temperatures. Intensifies the individual effects of other elements in more complex steels.

010 THE ART AND SCIENCE OF HEAT TREATMENT

Beyond the chemical composition of knife steel lies the complex science of heat-treating steel. The various steps and processes change the chemical and physical properties of knife steel in specific ways. Hardening steel also makes it more brittle, so steel makers have developed a number of ways to mitigate frangible steel.

ANNEALING In this process, the metal is heated to a specific desired temperature, then cooled at a prescribed rate. The process softens the metal and allows atoms to migrate to more stable positions in the metal matrix.

QUENCHING The metal is heated above its critical temperature, then cooled quickly in water, oil, or other liquid. Quenching locks atoms in place in the metal matrix.

TEMPERING This secondary process moderates, or tempers, the metal's hardness by heating it to a temperature below its critical point. Higher temperatures create softer, tougher metals while lower temperatures yield a harder, more brittle material. A skilled smith can forge tool steel to a differential heat treatment so that the edge and point are considerably harder than the spine, but the blade remains very strong. It's possible to accentuate the temper line where the hardness diverges, creating a visual stripe called a *hamon*.

011 TAKE A POWDER

Many new high-tech steels are made of powdered, or pelletized, steel. First the alloy is formulated, then it's melted. This molten metal is processed through a high-pressure air or gas cannon, which atomizes the metal into a fine spray of mistlike droplets. These harden into tiny, perfectly round powder pellets, with very few impurities. The millions of granules of evenly distributed carbides allow for hair-splitting edge grinds and no weak spots in the blade. Many of these steels, such as CPM 154, ZDP189, M390, and Elmax, pretty much do it all, and knife buffs call these "super steels." They're corrosion-resistant, hard, and tough. Naturally, this level of innovation doesn't come cheap.

012 UNDERSTAND THE ROCKWELL SCALE

The hardness of knife steel is measured on the Rockwell "C" Scale, also referred to as HRC. To determine a steel's hardness, a tiny diamond is pressed into the steel as far as it will go, and the depth is measured precisely. The steel is then assigned an HRC number that reflects the depth, and suggests the strength of the blade steel. Knives with lower Rockwell ratings will sharpen more easily, while harder steels will hold an edge better. The best knife steels are hardened to the high 50s or low 60s. But Rockwell hardness only suggests a blade's overall characteristics, since the chemical composition of the alloy can include elements that lend strength, toughness, and wearability as well.

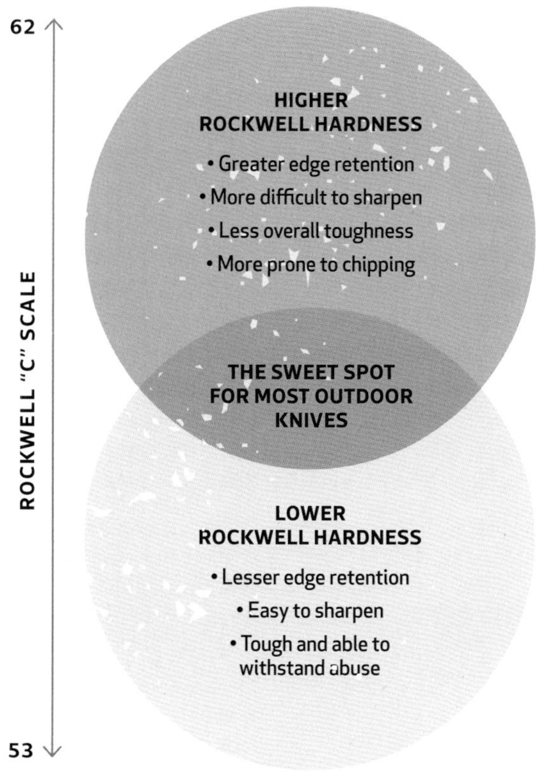

DESIGNERS WHO CHANGED EVERYTHING

A.G. RUSSELL

When A.G. Russell was 9 years old, his great-grandfather helped him make his first knife–a blade, he later described, "that only a mother would be proud of." Long story short: He got better.

Born in Eudora, Arkansas, in 1933, Russell is as responsible as any one person for the custom knife boom that began in the late 1960s and continues to this day, and for the subsequent renaissance of the American cutlery industry.

He started off selling Arkansas whetstones through small advertisements placed in gun magazines. He later added pocket knives to his offerings, and in 1964 he founded A.G. Russell Knives, which is now the country's oldest mail-order knife business. What started out as a company run from his kitchen table in southeastern Arkansas grew into an outbuilding on Russell's farm and morphed over the years into a sprawling complex that is as much a tourist destination for knife nuts as a primary force in the international cutlery business.

He also founded the oldest knife collector's club and the oldest aftermarket knife business. He started two magazines, *Knife World* and *The American Blade*, the latter of which evolved into the voice of the knife-making and knife-collecting worlds: *BLADE*.

His wife, Goldie, is a knife expert in her own right, and the couple oversees a staff of 40 employees devoted to promoting the craft of the cutler. Russell still designs custom knives, blades that just about anyone would be proud of.

013 OUR GO-TO STEELS

CARBON STEELS

Now that you know enough about knife steels to make your own informed decisions, we'll let you in on our favorites. These are the *Field & Stream* staff's top carbon steel choices–and a sweet blade made from each.

1095 A very popular, simple alloy, 1095 is used in many inexpensive knives, but furnishes the blades of some very costly knives, too. It's easy to sharpen and takes a keen edge. Over time, 1095 blues with use, acquiring a pleasing character.

A2 An old standby tool steel that shines if you care for it correctly. It's super tough, though easier to sharpen than some other tool steels.

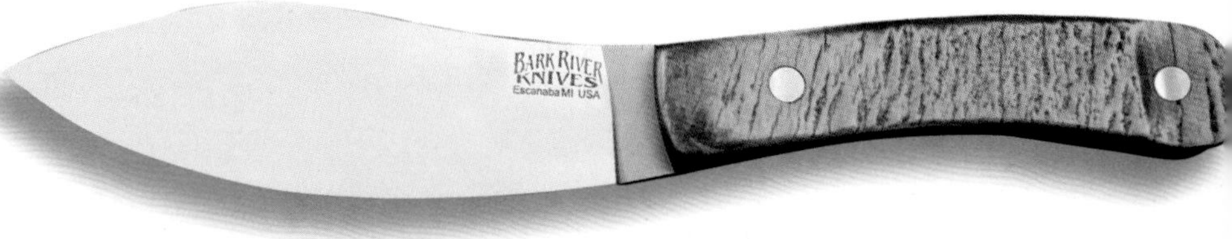

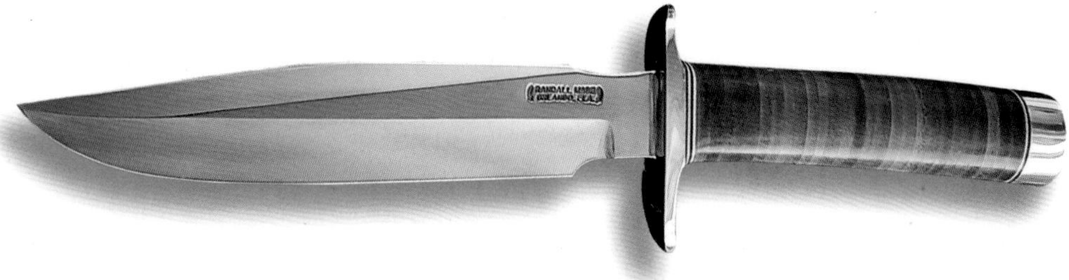

O-1 This steel is favored by the famed knifemaker Bo Randall. With a carbon content nearing 1 percent, it's a hard steel with great edge retention, but is less desirable on large blades due to its brittleness.

D2 Made with almost enough chromium to be considered stainless, D2 is rust-resistant (but will stain), very tough, takes a first-class edge, and holds that edge nearly forever. It's an awesome knife steel, but takes care and skill to sharpen properly.

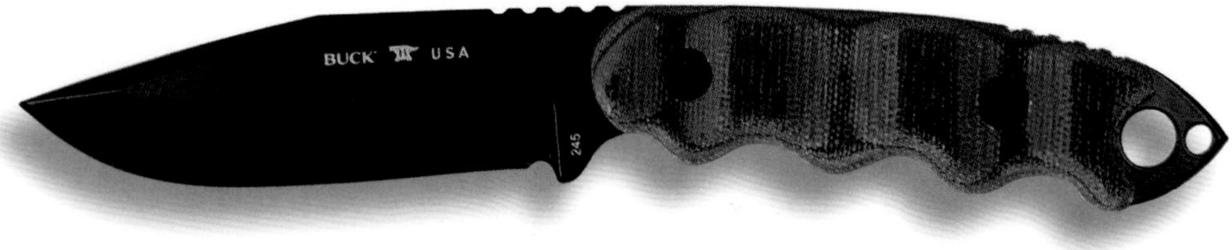

5160 A simple carbon steel with a smidge of chromium for strength, it was considered by the great smith Bill Moran to be the best of the knife steels.

STAINLESS STEELS

There's no shortage of high-quality stainless steel available. Here are some of the *Field & Stream* editors' top choices in this category, with blades to match.

A H-1 With 1 percent nitrogen in the mix, this miracle alloy will cut shrimp, clean your catch, and resist rust no matter how long it bangs around in your saltwater tackle box. It has great edge-holding ability and is perfect for marine environments.

B AUS-8 Japanese steel similar to 420 stainless, with vanadium in the alloy for wear resistance. Not terribly expensive and a lot of bang for the buck.

C 8CR13MOV China-produced steel similar to AUS-8 with slightly more carbon in the alloy, 8Cr13MoV is easy to sharpen and has decent edge retention. It's a great midrange steel when heat treated properly.

D SANDVIK 12C27 This very popular Swedish steel is a definite upgrade over the 440 series. Manganese in the alloy makes it easy to sharpen and great at holding an edge. It's a low-cost choice with high-performance characteristics.

E 154CM A hard American crucible steel with 1.05 percent carbon content and added molybdenum, 154CM holds an edge very well. Often used in high-end custom knives and by top-shelf manufacturers, it has only the slightest potential to rust.

F VG-10 A Japanese steel with better corrosion resistance than 154CM and ATS-34, VG-10 is fairly hard, tough, and relatively easy to sharpen.

G ELMAX The Swedish firm Uddeholm developed this powder steel that's very high in both carbon and chromium, and combines extreme corrosion resistance with high wear resistance. It won't rust, keeps its edge, and is hardened to HRC 60–61. Pretty close to perfect.

H CPM S30V Very popular for upper-end knives, CPM S30V's carbon content of 1.45 percent makes for a tough knife with great wear resistance. The "V" denotes vanadium carbides that boost the steel's hardness. A great choice for all-around performance.

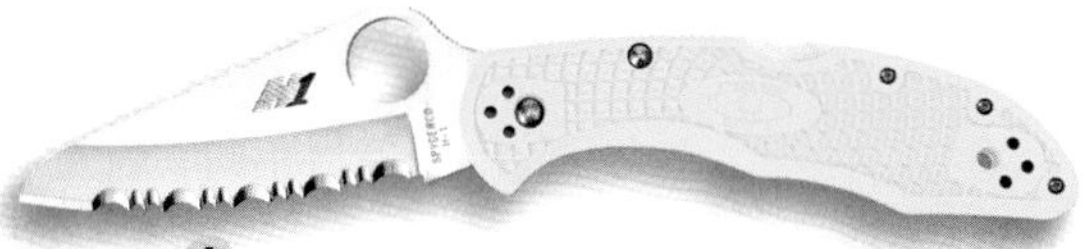
A

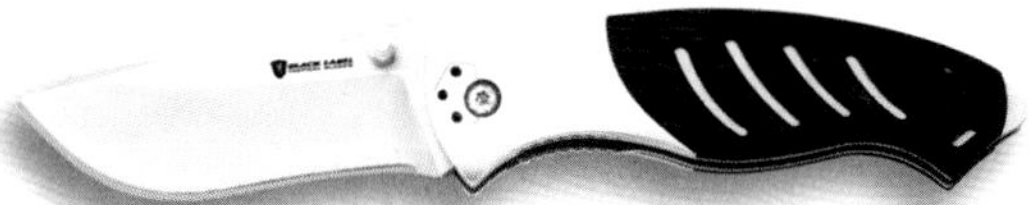
E

B

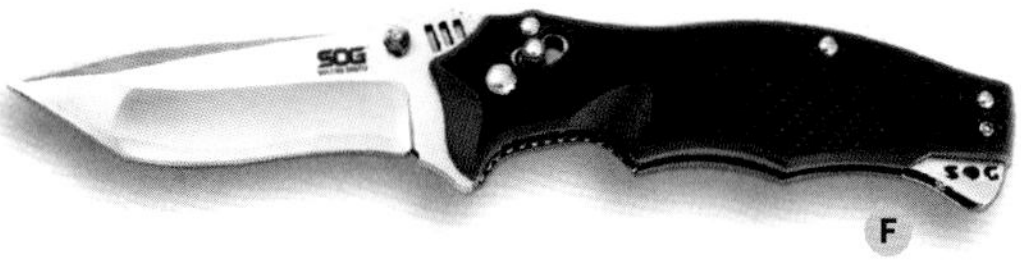

F

C

G

D

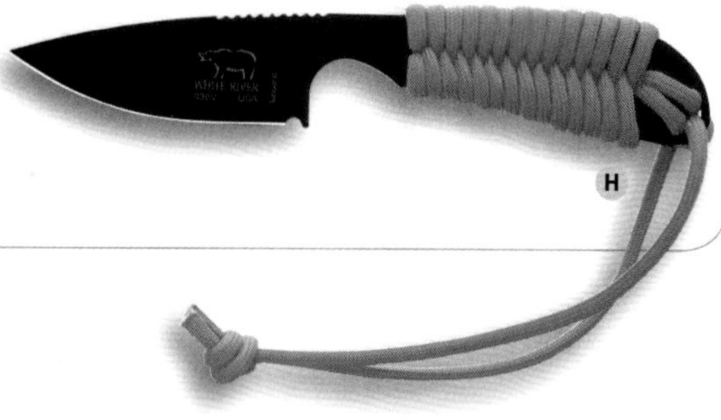
H

014 THE ALLURE OF DAMASCUS STEEL

The best Damascus steel blades, legends held, were quenched in dragon's blood. Or donkey piss. Or the urine of red-headed boys. Or they were cooled by plunging into the body of a muscular slave to transfer the strength of toil to the steel. The myth and lore around Damascus steel is rich. It's said a sword of Damascus would split a falling hair, yet be tough enough to decapitate a mail-clad opponent.

THE BEAUTY Even today, Damascus steel blades stop people in their tracks, stunned by the beauty and mystery held captive in the artistic metal. Comprising hundreds, and often thousands, of layers of forged steel, a Damascus blade shimmers with whorls and patterns. While increasing amounts of cheap, commercially produced Damascus steels are finding their way into so-so knives, most Damascus blades are hand-forged, by a single smith, an expression of individualism.

THE TRUTH Let's set the record straight: Today, hardly anyone makes true Damascus steel; it was originally made in part from ingots of wootz steel, an amalgamation of both low- and high-carbon steels melted together, which originated in Persia and Sri Lanka in the 6th century B.C. and was widely exported. Damascus steel was so strong and so sharp that it gave rise to great dynasties and greater legends–many to do with bodily fluids.

THE NAME The weapons center of Damascus gave the steel its name, but some historians say it comes from the damask textile it resembles, also famed in Damascus. The original forging methods were lost to history, along with the ancient steels whose chemical properties led to the famed metal's strength.

THE REVIVAL Today's craze over Damascus steel began in the 1970s, when knifemaker Bill Moran developed a process that nearly duplicated the steel's legendary aesthetics. Modern Damascus is pattern-welded: A billet of steel is hammered, folded over on itself, heated, hammered, stretched, then heated and folded again and again. Most Damascus steels have hundreds of layers of material, and mystery and lore seem to reside again in today's Damascus steel 2.0.

MULTIBAR TWISTED "W" The "W" pattern is formed by turning the forged billet on its side and hammering from the top. This pattern uses two bars of "W" steel, twisted in opposite directions and forged.

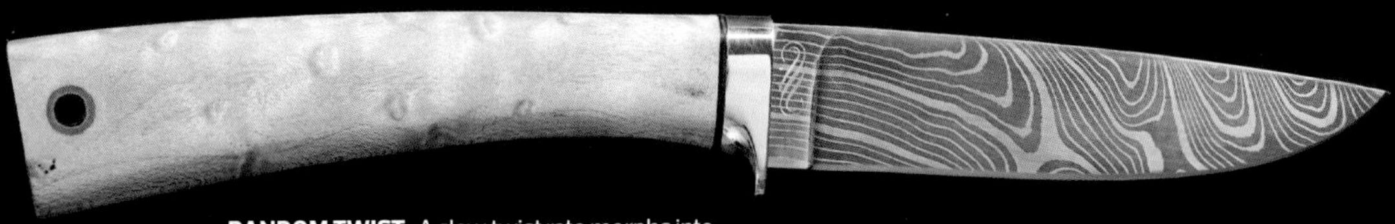

RANDOM TWIST A slow twist rate morphs into a higher twist rate towards the blade tip.

RAINDROP OR POOL-AND-EYE Drilling or punching the billet with multiple shallow divots, then forging and drawing out the metal, creates a pattern like raindrops on water.

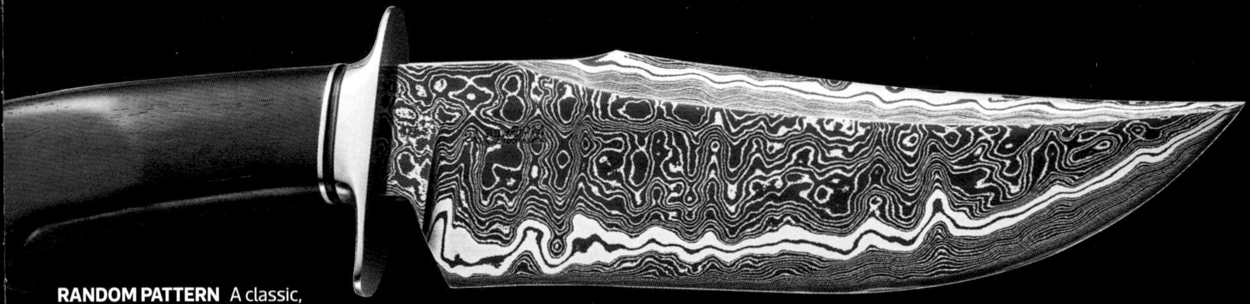

RANDOM PATTERN A classic, rippling pattern. This one was created with three layers of san mai to add a lightning pattern along the edge and spine.

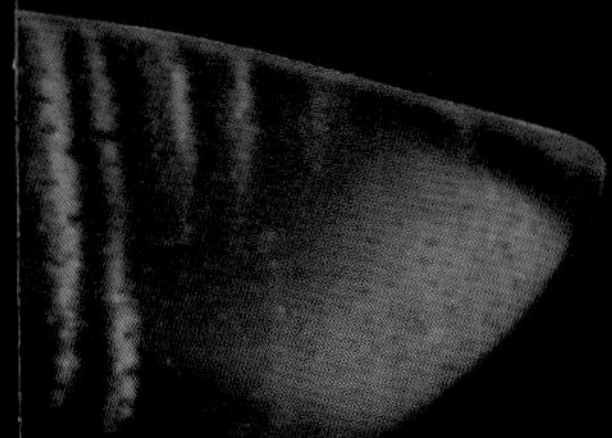

LADDER With replicating bands from tip to handle, the ladder pattern was named after the Biblical Jacob's ladder.

GEOMETRIC MOSAIC Replicating patterns are created by the end grain of the steel billets.

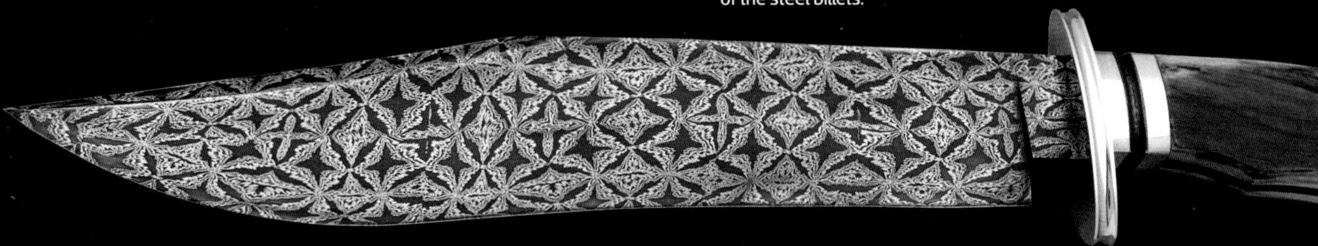

BLADE PROFILES

The shape of a blade in profile can elicit strong emotions. There's something simply classic and familiar about the clip point of a Bowie-style knife. A tanto- or hawkbill-style blade can evoke dark alleys and danger. For many, a knife purchase is based primarily on its blade profile. How a knife performs varies dramatically depending on its profile, and it's a world of tradeoffs. When it comes to the shapes of things that cut, there's far more to the designs than mere aesthetics.

PROFILE	CHARACTERISTICS	BEST FOR	PROS	CONS
A STRAIGHT BACK	A straight spine with an upward curving edge that rises to the spine to form a semi-sharp point.	Bushcrafting; Kitchen tasks; Learning sharpening techniques.	Very strong; Easily batoned through wood; Easy to apply force to spine with fingers or palm.	Not ideal for piercing tasks; Not enough belly for skinning.
B DROP POINT	A favorite of hunters, the drop point features a slight downward curve to the spine to form a lowered, or "dropped," point.	Field dressing and skinning; Everyday carry (EDC).	Strong point retains a bit of belly for skinning; Best for gutting animals, as the point angles away from organs.	With a tip less sharp than those of other profiles, it's not a great piercing blade.
C TRAILING POINT	This blade's spine curves upward, and a trailing point provides a long, curved edge for slicing.	Skinning and caping animals; Filleting fish.	Very sharp point; Lots of belly; Design gives lightweight knives additional length to the cutting edge.	Weak point; Difficult to get in and out of a sheath.
D CLIP POINT	The classic Bowie knife profile. A straight spine drops in a slight angle or concave curve to meet the tip, as if the spine were clipped off.	Skinning and caping animals; Filleting fish.	Very controllable sharp point; Decent belly; Excels at piercing.	If the clip begins too far from the tip, the point of the blade can be weak.

PROFILE	CHARACTERISTICS	BEST FOR	PROS	CONS
E SPEAR POINT	A symmetrical profile with a spine that forms the centerline of the blade. Can be sharpened on one or both sides.	Piercing and thrusting; Throwing knives.	Very sharp tip; Can have a double cutting surface.	Not useful for non-fighting tasks.
F SPEY POINT	A defined, sudden downward curve to the spine that meets a curving, upswept edge. Commonly found on trapper-style pocketknives.	Traditionally used for castrating farm animals.	Easily sharpened; Safe to use when a sharp point isn't needed.	That lack of a sharp point limits piercing ability; Often a short blade.
G LEAF	This hybrid between a drop point and a spear point features a less aggressive downward slope to the spine with a more acute point.	Fine cutting that requires a sharp point; EDC; Self-defense.	Easy to carry, as most leaf point blades are short.	Thin point can be weaker than that of other profiles.
H SHEEPSFOOT	A straight spine curves downward to meet a completely straight edge, with no sharp piercing tip.	Rescue work; Use on inflatable boats; Trimming hooves of small livestock.	Blunt tip can be very thick and strong; Very controllable edge; Easy to sharpen.	With no sharp tip, not useful for piercing tasks.
I WHARNCLIFFE	Similar to a sheepsfoot, with a downward curve or angle to the spine that starts closer to the handle of the knife.	Rescue work; Self-defense; Utility tasks.	Sharp piercing tip; Strong, robust blade often built with thick blade stock.	No belly for skinning tasks.
J HAWKBILL	Shaped like a claw or talon—or a hawk's bill—the hawkbill profile has a sharply concave spine and cutting edge that meet at a downward point.	Utility work, such as cutting carpet and linoleum; Self-defense.	Cutting webbing, heavy cordage and lines; Sharp, inwardly curved tip is great for making long cuts.	No piercing ability; Little utility for hunting and fishing.
K TANTO	Thick, with a straight edge that takes a sudden, upward, uncurved angle near the blade tip to meet the spine at a straight or slightly convex angle.	Self-defense; EDC; General utility tasks.	Extremely strong and sharp tip; Robust blade.	Tricky to sharpen; No belly for skinning.

BLADE GRINDS

When it comes to a knife's performance, a blade's grind is akin to a car's engine: Do you want hard-working, boat-towing torque? Or some real zippy, tire-squealing horsepower? The grind is the shape of the blade when viewed in cross section. Is it thick or thin? Does it taper evenly from the spine to the edge, or does it have a convex or concave shape? There's a world of difference between how a hollow-ground blade moves through a hunk of meat and a compound bevel grind does. Some grinds are sharp, some are strong, and some attempt to straddle the line between durability and a wicked slice.

HOLLOW

PROFILE A concave section is ground into the blade between the spine and edge. In cross section it looks as if metal has been scooped from the blade.

BEST FOR Dressing and skinning game; EDC.

PROS Easy to sharpen; Great for slicing; Combines a thin, sharp edge with a thick, sturdy spine.

CONS The edge can dull, chip, or roll more easily than with other grinds; The hollow can create suction when slicing thick materials.

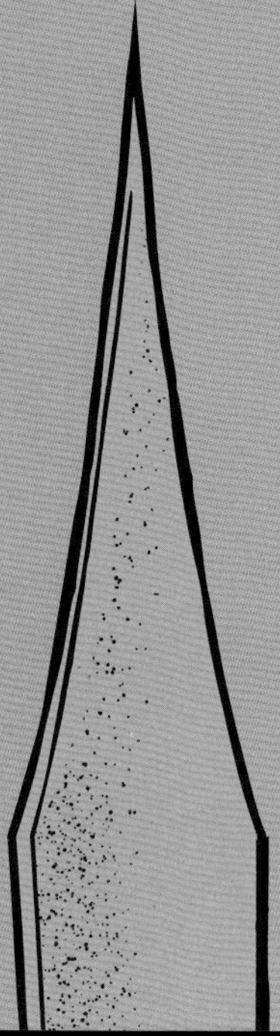

FULL FLAT

PROFILE An even taper from bevel and spine to edge. A full grind's linear taper allows it to pass through material with little resistance.

BEST FOR Dressing and skinning game; Kitchen tasks; Filleting; EDC

PROS Very sharp and easy to resharpen; A great all-around knife grind.

CONS Thin material at the edge can cause a knife to dull quickly.

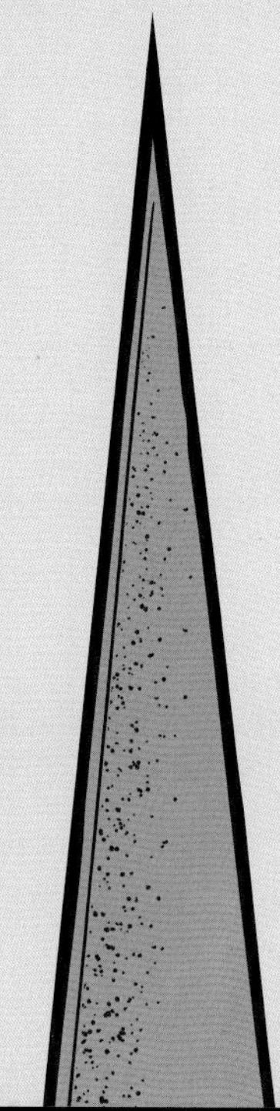

HIGH FLAT

PROFILE Blade retains its thickness to the midpoint of the blade, where the bevel taper begins.

BEST FOR Dressing and skinning game; EDC.; Whittling.

PROS A bit stronger than a full flat grind, but still sharp and easy to retouch.

CONS Not a great chopper.

SCANDINAVIAN

PROFILE Bevel grind begins at or below the midpoint of the blade.

BEST FOR EDC; Camping; Bushcraft.

PROS The strongest of the flat grinds; Easy to sharpen; Better for chopping than full or high flat grinds.

CONS Cutting ability is somewhat sacrificed for added strength.

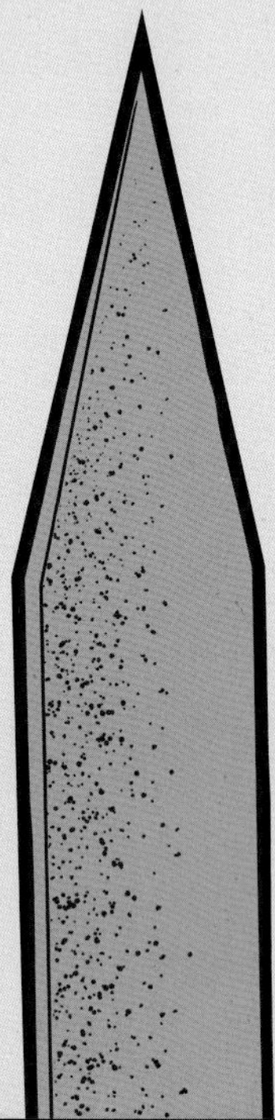

WHAT'S A BEVEL?

In knife geometry, "bevel" refers to the slope and angle of the flat surface of the blade, and many knives have more than one. The primary bevel is the initial slope between the spine and the edge. On most knives, the primary bevel meets an edge bevel at the blade's sharpened edge.

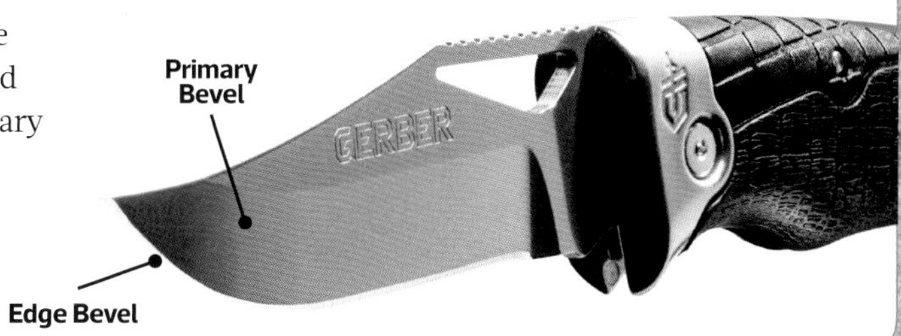

CHISEL

PROFILE Ground only on one side, resembling a chisel. Not common on outdoor knives. but found on Japanese cooking and whittling blades and some machetes.

BEST FOR Rough tasks such as brush clearing and bushcrafting; Slicing.

PROS Strong and fairly easy to sharpen; Very sharp depending on grind angle.

CONS Pulls to one side when slicing.

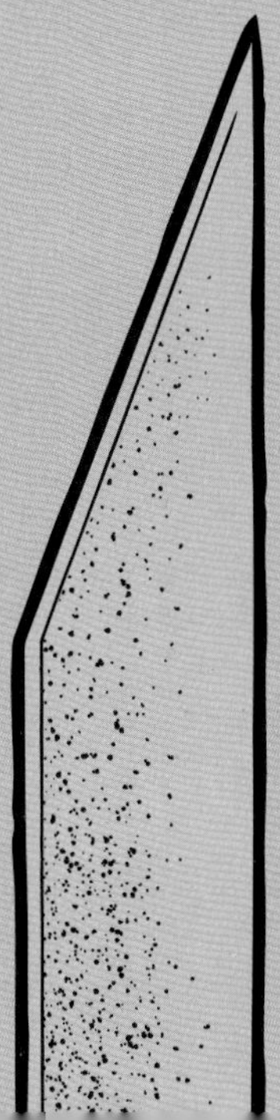

CONVEX

PROFILE A curved, round taper all the way to the edge; almost the opposite of a hollow grind. Found commonly on axes and hatchets.

BEST FOR Chopping and splitting.

PROS Strength due to the amount of steel carried behind the blade edge; Holds its edge well.

CONS Can be tricky to sharpen.

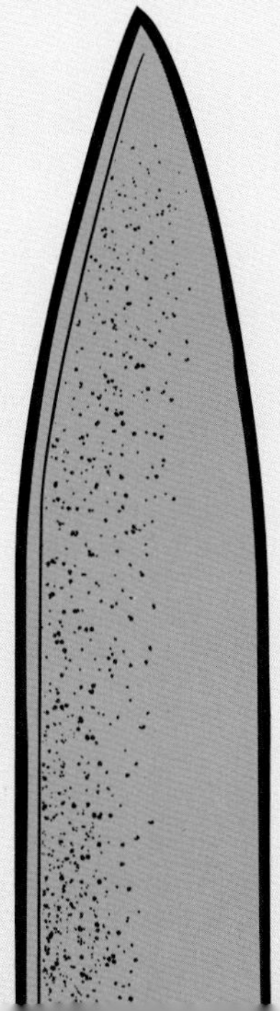

COMPOUND

PROFILE Combines at least two different grinds; includes a back bevel behind the edge bevel and thins toward the cutting edge at a less acute angle while retaining strength from additional steel in the blade.

BEST FOR EDC; General cutting chores.

PROS Less prone to rolling and chipping than thinner grinds; A stronger overall blade.

CONS Sacrifices sharpness for strength.

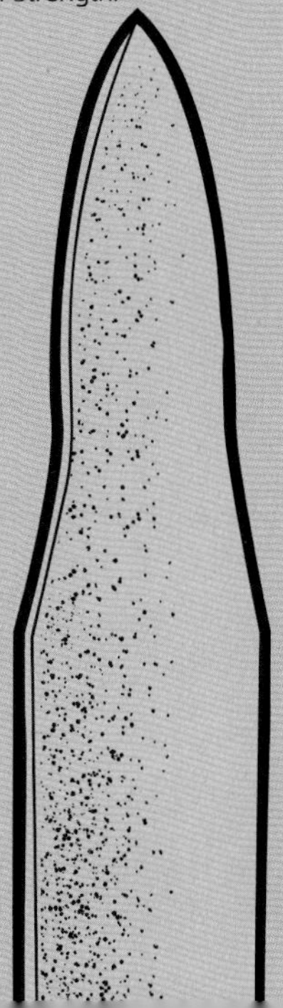

ASYMMETRICAL

PROFILE Each side of the blade carries a different bevel angle, e.g., flat on one side, convex on the other.

BEST FOR Tactical use.

PROS High durability; Easy sharpening; Can combine attributes of each component grind to balance sharpness and durability.

CONS Not as sharp as hollow or flat grinds.

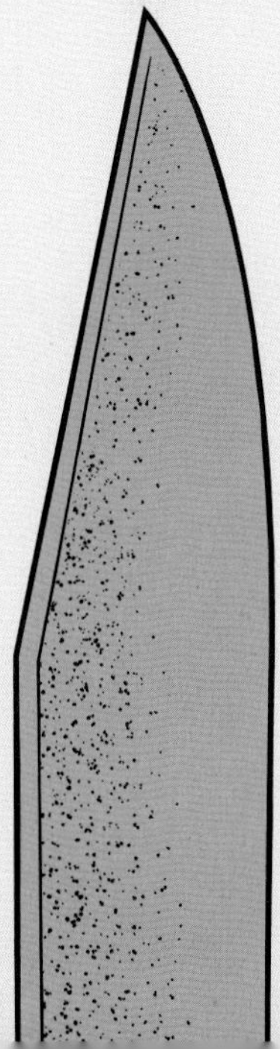

HANDLE MATERIALS

If a knife is destined to ride in a pocket and do little more than open envelopes and slice apples, it doesn't really matter what its handle is made of. Otherwise, a knife's intended purpose plays a large role in determining the proper handle material. Will it get wet, slick, and slimed with animal goo? Will it be pounded and batoned? Will you use it in the snow? Or near corrosive chemicals? Handle materials can be broadly divided into two categories—natural materials and synthetic materials. Generally speaking, natural materials such as wood and bone can be visually appealing and more pleasing to handle but require some care. Synthetic materials such G10 and micarta are known for extreme toughness and ability to withstand abuse but might not have the allure of something like fossilized bone. The good news? There are lots of handle choices. Be sure to make the right one.

A WOOD A classic handle material, handsome and warm to the touch. Maple is tough and resists cracking, and the spalted maples, with wavy black lines, are striking. Desert ironwood is hard, stable, and gorgeous. Tropical hardwoods, such as rosewood and cocobolo, are naturally oily and will stand up to years of wet use.

B LEATHER Often built from stacked leather washers, leather handles will stain and scratch, but such markings are just scars with stories. Treated with clear shoe polish once a year, they'll last for decades.

C STAG Often made from the antlers of sambar deer (found in India), which have a dense, hard core unlike elk or deer antlers. Stag features a dark, tough, knotty "bark" that's prized by knifemakers.

D BONE Perhaps the oldest handle material, contemporary versions range from the low-end (cow and sheep) to the exotic (elephant and giraffe). Bone is a classic material for folding pocket knives, especially when jigged, but it can be slick and porous, and temperature extremes can lead to cracking.

E MAMMOTH The fossilized teeth of the extinct beasts are stabilized with injected resin and polished for a stunning handle material. Over millennia, mammoth teeth absorb minerals from the soil, giving them a wide range of kaleidoscopic colors.

F ALUMINUM Light, tough, and less expensive than other metals, aluminum can be textured to provide a pretty good grip, and anodized to any color. However, it can be cold and unforgiving in the hand in sub-freezing conditions.

G MICARTA Made by soaking fabrics (canvas, paper, and others) in a resin, then forming them under great heat and pressure. It's very light, very tough, and very durable— and depending what it's made of, it can be very pretty. Of course, it costs more than many other synthetics.

H TITANIUM Famously light and durable, titanium is an expensive metal, but it rarely corrodes, is warmer in the hand than other metals, and can be textured for a sure grip. Its springy nature makes it a favored metal for frame-lock folding knives.

I G10 Formed of fiberglass cloth soaked in epoxy and baked under heat and pressure, there's not a tougher handle material. It will not corrode, and it can be easily shaped, textured, and colored. On the downside, it can look and feel like plastic, but it's hard to beat for a hard-use knife.

J CARBON FIBER Durable, lightweight, and impervious to rust and corrosion, these handles are made by setting individual carbon fibers in a dense resin matrix. The embedded fibers reflect light, making carbon fiber a luxurious, striking material. But it can crack with high impact and is slicker than other synthetics.

K NYLON Fiberglass-reinforced nylon (FRN), such as Zytel by DuPont, is inexpensive, durable, and easily molded and shaped, so it's a common handle material on lower-end knives. FRN might not be the most handsome option, but it will last practically forever.

F G H I J K

SERRATIONS

While a plain edge offers a continuous, unbroken cutting edge, a serrated blade has tiny saw-like teeth ground into the edge bevel. These points allow for greater penetration than a plain edge, while protecting the sharpened scalloped surfaces between them. Together, the points and scallops provide a constantly changing cutting angle as the serrations move through the material being cut.

In general, serrated knives excel at cutting fibrous materials, such as polypropylene rope and dense vegetation, and slick stuff like pallet straps. Used with a sawing motion, they'll cut through branches and twigs. However, they're not great at slicing because of the tearing action of the serrations, and they'll make a mess of block cheese or a venison backstrap.

THE GREAT DEBATE Few aspects of knife design spark more debate than the utility of serrated edges. People either love them or hate them. On the love side, serrated knives can rip through tough material like crazy. And a dull serrated blade can cut better than a dull plain edge. But haters say that a serrated blade is a crutch for folks who don't want to learn how to properly sharpen a knife, and that they come up short for fine slicing duties. The good news is no one ever said you can have only one knife.

HOW SERRATION WORKS It's all about geometry and physics. At the start of a cutting move, more pressure can be applied to the points of a serrated blade than can be to a plain edge, so the knife bites more deeply into the material. That really helps when cutting hard materials such as plastic or even when biting into a tomato skin. Then, as the blade is moved, the material is forced into the hooks of each scalloped serration–which is why serrations slice fibrous cord and plants so well. These hollowed-out serrations are typically ground at a lower edge angle than what's found on a typical blade, making them razor sharp.

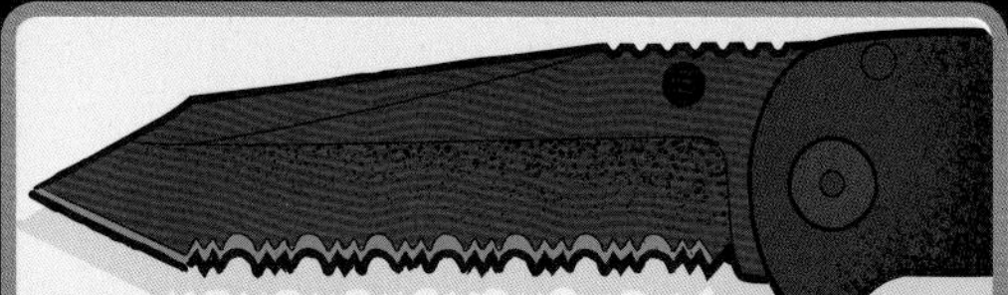

Fully serrated blade

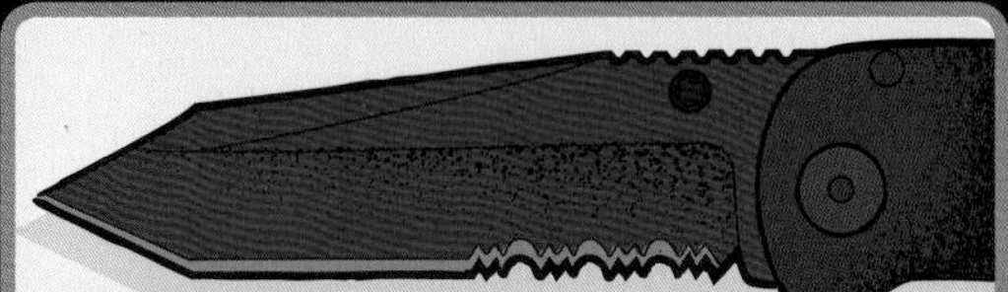

Partially serrated blade

DESIGN VARIATIONS

There is no standard serration grind, and serration design differs from one knifemaker to the next. Some designs are more "spiky" than others and have sharper teeth, though most are ground into only one side of the blade edge, making for easier sharpening.

The best-known serration design is Spyderco's two-step serration, which features a repeated pattern of one large scallop followed by two small scallops.

Designed by Oregon professional sharpener Tom Veff, Veff Serrations are cut on a 50-degree angle and help feed material into the teeth as you pull the knife through. They are easier to sharpen than a traditional serration, but they tend to work best on a pull stroke only. Veff Serrations are available on CRKT knives and through Veff's custom shop.

Cold Steel incorporates an unusual pattern it calls "grip n' rip." Micro serrations are ground into the teeth, resulting in a smoother pattern that's less likely to stick or hang up.

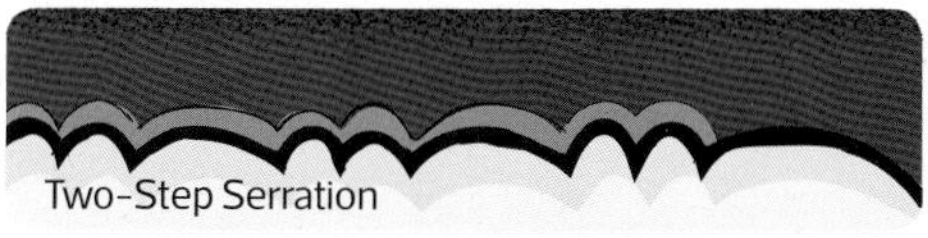
Two-Step Serration

Veff Serration

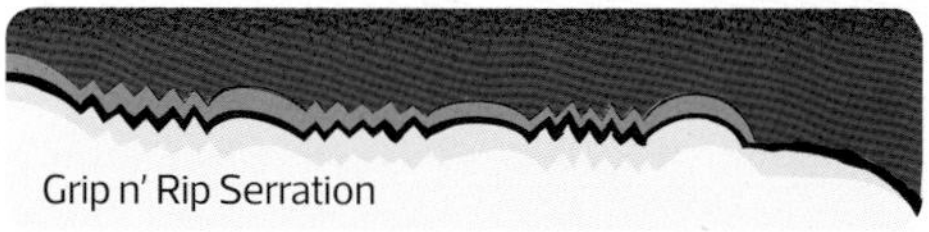
Grip n' Rip Serration

DESIGNERS

WHO CHANGED EVERYTHING

SAL GLESSER

In the late 1970s, Sal Glesser, his wife, and their infant daughter lived in a converted bread delivery truck and traveled from one county fair to the next in order to hawk Ginsu knives. In 1978, Sal developed a knife-sharpening device dubbed the Tri-Angle Sharpmaker. People went crazy for it, and that's when Glesser knew he was onto something.

In 1980, he designed a knife he called the Worker, incorporating a few features that he'd never seen built into a folder before: a pocket clip, and an oversized round hole near the blade's spine for one-handed opening with the thumb. Glesser also studied the serrations of his old Ginsu knives under a microscope, and developed a two-step serration design and a sharpener to go along with it. The pocket clip, thumb hole, and unique serration are now components of one of the world's most beloved knife companies: Spyderco.

Spyderco was the first company to make use of powdered steel–Crucible's S60V–in a production knife; the first company to build a folding knife with a blade of H1 steel, a type that won't rust in saltwater; and one of the first companies to use Maxima steel, which is so hard that it's also used to make the rollers that are employed in rolling out hot steel at a foundry. Today, Spyderco sells $10 million in knives every year, and their blades are favorites among first responders, members of the military, everyday carriers, and outdoors enthusiasts alike.

SHEATHS

Purchasing a new knife initiates a round of soul searching that goes well beyond figuring out how you'll hide your umpteenth blade from your significant other. How will you carry it in the woods? How will you store it when not in use? What kind of sheath will keep you from fumbling for the blade in the dark? Could the sheath hang up on a tree stand ladder? Will it attach to your saddle? Boot? Neck? MOLLE-equipped tactical duck-hunting pack?

Turns out there's more to a knife sheath than meets the steel. Not every sheath will—or should—have all of these elements, but these aspects of sheath design each makes a difference in the field.

RIDING HIGH How will the knife ride on your belt? A traditional tunnel loop works fine, but can snag on brush. Horizontal carry options, where short knives ride parallel to the belt, are becoming popular.

WRAP A STRAP A keeper strap that folds over the handle and snaps or attaches by Velcro or other means will help keep a knife from slipping out of the sheath—but only if a branch or your rifle sling doesn't unsnap it. Make sure the snap is strong and crisp, or opt for a leather sheath that more completely covers the handle.

SPARE CARGO Some sheaths have a pouch to hold a sharpening stone or other tool. It might be a convenient add-on, but it adds bulk.

MOLLE WHO? A military attachment system for all kinds of gear, MOLLE is an acronym for Modular Lightweight Load-Carrying Equipment, and it shows up in many outdoor products these days. It enables pouches, sheaths, and tactical gear to be attached to any item equipped with a matching set of nylon straps called PALS, or Pouch Attachment Ladder System. A mouthful, but dang handy.

SHEATH MATERIALS

You'll find a number of options. Here are some of the most common.

LEATHER A good leather sheath is durable; classic in appearance; holds a knife with a warm, close embrace; and will last for generations. A poor leather sheath–and they are legion–does none of these things. Avoid metal rivets unless they are positioned well away from the knife's edge. Welted sheaths have a strip of leather–the welt–that protects the stitching from the cutting edge and also provides stiffness. Leather sheaths can hold moisture and may contain tanning chemicals unfriendly to metal blades, so avoid using them for long-term knife storage.

NYLON Nylon is a common sheath material because it's inexpensive. There's nothing wrong with a nylon pouch for a multitool or folding knife, but it's a bit flimsy, wets out like cotton, and will grow mildew in a jiffy.

KYDEX This molded thermoplastic is impervious to water, strong as an I-beam, and won't stretch, shrink, or stink. That's a lot of positive traits for one sheath material, but if there's a knock on Kydex it's that raking a twig across it will scatter every critter within earshot. Poorly made Kydex sheaths allow a knife to rattle around inside, but a well-made version fits perfectly snug.

DESIGNERS
WHO CHANGED EVERYTHING

CHARLES ALLEN

According to *Field & Stream*'s longtime knife guru, David E. Petzal, Texas bladesmith Charles Allen has taken knife making to another level. Here's Petzal's take on this one-man revolution:

"Since knives have been around for 1.4 million years, we've had a fair amount of time to work on them. Despite that, there's not much that's radically new, though the knives produced by Charles Allen's DiamondBlade Knives are a step forward.

"In 2006, Allen, an Alaska guide, former Texas game biologist, and founder of Knives of Alaska, adapted for blade forging a method of welding that was first developed for joining submarine hull sections. He starts with a strip of D2 steel and subjects what will be the cutting edge to immense pressure and heat in a process called friction forging. In forging, the smaller you make the steel molecules, and the better aligned they are, the better the edge. Conventional forging operates at the molecular level. Friction forging works at the atomic level, producing an edge with a Rockwell hardness of HRC 65–69. For the sake of comparison, an edge with an HRC of 62 is considered very hard.

"Normally, if you harden a knife to HRC 65–69, it will be so brittle that it's unusable. However, DiamondBlade knives are, in effect, differentially heat-treated. The spines are HRC 38–42 (spring steel is HRC 31–52), and the blades are so strong that I once watched Allen lock one in a vise, put a pipe over the tang for leverage, and bend it to 90 degrees. Then he bent it back again. There was a slight jog in the blade where it had bent, but otherwise it was perfectly usable."

KNIFE TYPES

→ IN THIS SECTION →

MAKING MEAT:

8 ESSENTIAL BLADES FOR GAME CARE

WHAT TO BRING TO A KNIFE FIGHT

BULLS-EYE:

LEARN HOW TO THROW A KNIFE

BOWIE KNIFE:

THE 200-YEAR EVOLUTION OF AN AMERICAN ICON

MIGHTY MINIS:

AN IN-DEPTH LOOK AT MOUSE KNIVES

OVERCOME IT ALL WITH A **BUSHCRAFT KNIFE**

015 POCKET KNIVES

A Swiss Army Knife is a pocket knife, as is a tanto-bladed tactical folder. But the traditional pocket knife is something altogether different. It lacks a clip, is small enough to be slipped into a pocket, and is typically built with a traditional non-locking slipjoint that uses a backspring to hold the blade (or blades) opened or closed. Firms such as W.R. Case Cutlery Company, Buck Knives, and Schrade Cutlery Company–which produces Old Timer and Uncle Henry knives–have created hundreds of different classic pocket knife models. Here are five.

STOCK A STOCKMAN The three-bladed Stockman knife has been around for so long that no one really knows when it was designed. It's typically equipped with clip point, spey, and sheepsfoot blades (the latter of which was traditionally used to trim a sheep's hooves). There are hundreds of Stockman models around; W.R. Case currently makes more than 75.

TEST OUT A TRAPPER Another American icon with obscure beginnings, the Trapper was certainly common by the 1920s. It sports a pair of blades of equal length—a clip point and a spey—that make it useful for skinning small animals.

CARRY A CANOE Named for the shape of its handle, this knife carries a hefty spear-point blade and a smaller penknife blade. Sometimes called a "butterbean," the canoe's rounded shape enables it to be slipped in and out of pockets with ease, and affords a pleasing grip.

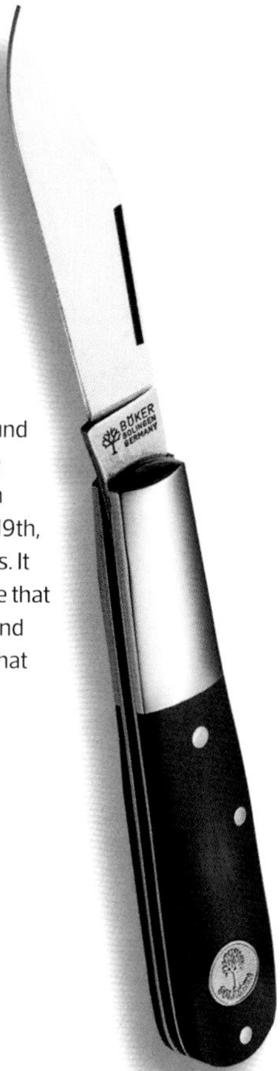

BONE UP WITH A BARLOW Invented in Sheffield, England, around 1670, this knife became a mainstay of American childhoods of the 18th, 19th, and early 20th centuries. It has a tear-shape handle that can be gripped tightly, and a strong metal bolster that stands up to hard use.

TRY A TEXAS TOOTHPICK These long, slender knives, most of which feature metal bolsters fore and aft, appeared on the scene sometime before 1940. Two-bladed Texas Toothpicks aren't unknown, but most have a single blade that fits into a sinuous handle for a handsome, versatile tool. Collectors also call this model a "tickler" or "switch."

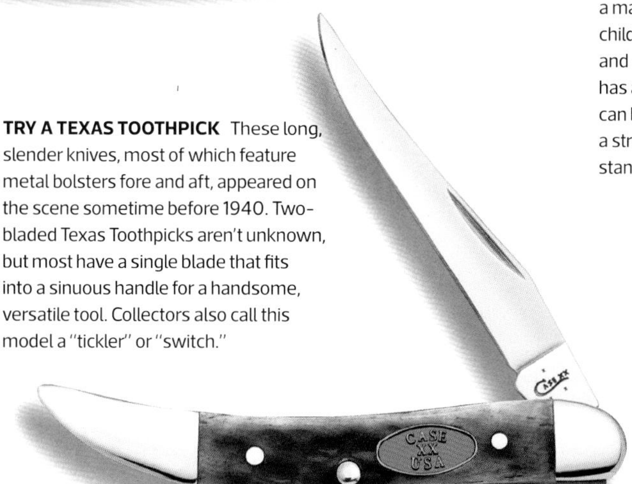

THE KNIFE I CARRY

DAVID E. PETZAL, RIFLES EDITOR

On most days of the year, in a belt sheath on my girlish waist, is a Victorinox Pioneer Alox Silver, a metal-handled version of the old Boy Scout Folding Knife. I have an unnatural fondness for it because the screwdriver/cap lifter blade is perfect for prying staples out of target backers, which I do just about every day of the week. That, and the knife blade, are about all I ever use. But they are enough.

016 GAME PROCESSING TOOLS

Dressing and caring for game involves many different cutting actions, ranging from precision to power to prying. A sharp point is a plus when initiating cuts through a hide, and not so handy when chopping through joints. A solid drop-point knife with a $3^{1}/_{2}$- to 5-inch blade can do it all, but there are specialized game care knives that will handle specific chores with much greater ease.

KEY

- BIG GAME
- SMALL GAME
- BIRD
- FISH

FIELD DRESSING KNIFE The drop point blade of a field dressing knife is perfect for the initial cuts involved with gutting big game, as well as the primary cuts on the insides of the legs when skinning. Finger choils and indents keep you mindful of the knife's orientation when your hand is deep inside a chest cavity. Jimping on the spine helps with grip and finesse when the knife is covered in blood and fat.

SKINNING KNIFE Removing the hide from an animal is easiest with a dedicated skinning blade that has a deep belly for long, slicing cuts. Wider blades give a knife more belly, but smaller skinning blades can be handy for working deep under the hide to separate the skin from tough fascia. Blade steels of Rockwell 56 HRC and higher will hold their edge longer for skinning chores.

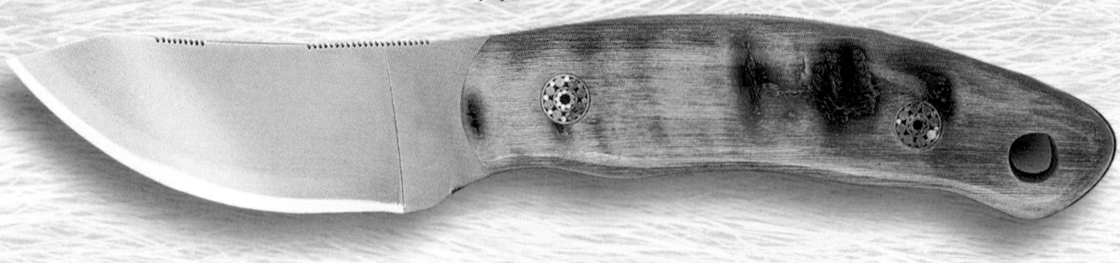

CAPING KNIFE For the close, delicate work of removing the hide from an animal's skull and feet, a caping knife has a short, narrow, pointed blade that lends the precision needed to cut around eyes, lips, and foot joints. Caping knives are also useful for dressing birds and skinning small game such as squirrels and rabbits.

BONING KNIFE This narrow blade is at least five inches in length, with a sharp piercing tip. A gently upswept trailing point helps you feel around joints. Boning knives vary in flexibility. More give is better for thinner cuts and working around bone, but dense meats such as wild hog and larger game animals require more backbone.

BIRD AND TROUT KNIFE This knife has a slim profile and a sharp point. Slightly flexible blades are great for working around the ribs and spine of fish, and for removing breast fillets from ducks and geese. Many models are made of a single piece of steel for easy cleaning.

FILLET KNIFE With a sharp point to pierce tough fish skin, and a long, slender blade, a fillet knife will flex around fish spines and ribs to remove every smidgen of meat. Many fillet knives are inexpensive and can be casually tossed into tackle boxes, but choose a knife with a grippy handle and a solid finger guard to keep your hand from slipping.

CLEAVER Blunt and heavy, a meat cleaver whacks through wing joints and bones, and helps separate large cuts of meat. Given a cleaver's heft, look for a balanced blade you can handle safely.

GAME SHEARS While not a knife, specialized game shears handle many tasks better. Look for a pair that disassembles for easy cleaning. A deep wing notch makes it easier to cut through the wings of everything from doves to geese, and makes short work of removing the feet of smaller, squirrel-size animals.

017 SWAP IT OUT

There's nothing especially elegant about replaceable-blade knives, and their handles are designed for grip rather than aesthetics, but this style of knife has exploded in recent years, and its fans are legion. Most come with multiple stainless steel blades sharp enough for corneal surgery. More knifemakers are jumping into the game, and the knives are becoming increasingly specialized, with smaller caping knives now joining the growing list of technique-specific designs.

018 WHAT IS A BUSHCRAFT BLADE?

If you were dropped into the deep, scary woods to survive for a week or more, what one knife would you want to have with you? Keep in mind it would need to be able to slash tree boughs for shelter, pound stakes, carve delicate triggers for animal snares, spark fire, and withstand punishment as you baton it to split wood. What you'd want is called a bushcraft knife.

A FACILITATOR It's a survival knife of sorts, but the point of a bushcraft knife is not to enable you to live another day. It's to help make your time in the wild a period of primal ease, providing enough comfort to revel in your woodsmanship. This is why the best bushcraft knives are built to take a beating, and are still nimble enough for tasks such as carving a spoon. They possess shaving-sharp edges that can be spiffed up without a fancy sharpener. What a bushcraft knife is not—no matter what the salesman at the military surplus store tells you—is one with a hollow handle for storing fishhooks, and a compass embedded in the handle. Sorry, Rambo.

NORSE ROOTS Many bushcraft knives are modeled after the tough, unadorned, supremely functional knives of the Scandinavian countries. Of those, the foremost maker is Sweden's Morakniv. The Morakniv Companion can be had for less than $20 and has seen the spleens of more small creatures and fed the flames of more life-giving fires than nearly any other blade.

TOTAL PACKAGE The Morakniv Garberg is a heavier, beefier, more expensive version of the Companion, and it possesses just about every feature you could want in a bushcraft knife, including:

SHORT LENGTH Many bushcraft knives have long 5- and 6-inch blades, but this stout 4.3-inch-long, 3.2-millimeter-thick drop point nicely straddles the functionality line, equally adept at fine carving work and tough cutting and wood-splitting chores.

FINE STEEL To produce sparks from flint, you need high-carbon steel. But stainless steel works well with ferrocerium and "metal matches," as long as the spine isn't rounded. With its 90-degree spine edge, the Sandvik stainless steel turns night into day when raked down a ferro rod.

TOUGH CONSTRUCTION A full tang with an exposed pommel aids in pounding stakes. Hard-use bushcraft knife handles must be able to take a beating, and should lack excessive texture or hard angles that could cause hand fatigue.

GRIND A Scandinavian grind is ideal for a bushcraft knife. It retains plenty of spine steel for strength, and is easily sharpened to a wicked edge. It's great for carving and whittling, and is easily controlled for making thin feathersticks.

SHARP POINT A sharp tip is essential for awling fireboard divots and holes in wood.

THE KNIFE I CARRY

BILL HEAVEY, EDITOR-AT-LARGE

I love my Fällkniven F1. It's the official survival knife of Swedish Air Force pilots, which should tell you something. The blade measures 3.8 inches, the knife is 8.3 inches, and weighs just 6 ounces. It's a model of restraint and simplicity, a drop point with a full convex grind. It seems too small at first, until you look at the 4.5 mm spine and realize you could beat on it with a baseball bat. It's easy to sharpen and keeps an edge. The Zytel sheath rattles—a band of electrical tape around the handle could help, but it hasn't bothered me much. One reviewer on Amazon called this a "Goldilocks" knife—just the right balance and feel. No one knife is right for everyone. This one is right for me.

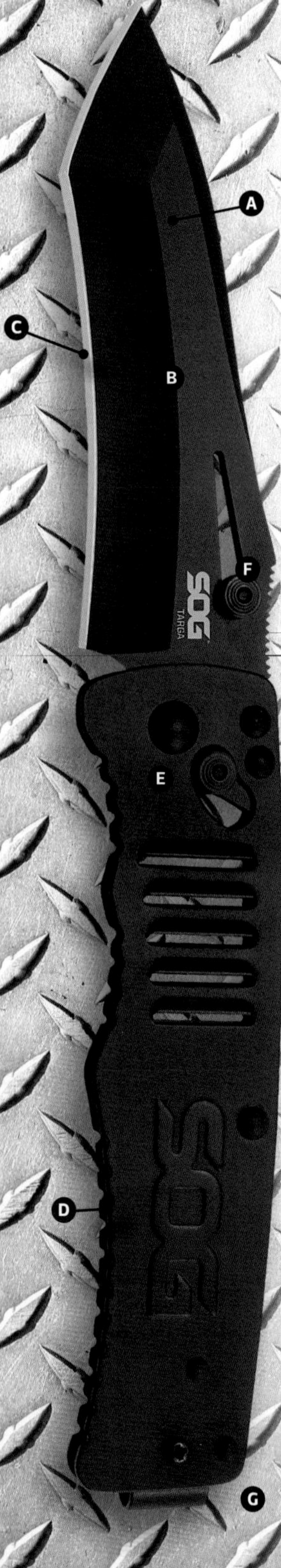

019 LET'S GET TACTICAL

There may be some debate about what exactly constitutes a "tactical" knife, but you can't argue the growing popularity of knives that are designed with military, rescue, and self-defense features. While not specifically intended for combat or fighting, tactical knives often include features desired by first responders, and they're used by many military personnel as backup weapons. There are fixed-blade tactical knives, but most consider a folder's ease of carry and quick deployment better suited for these purposes.

For an early example, look to the Schrade M2 switchblade, issued to U.S. paratroopers during World War II. There were numerous versions, but the most common was an automatic opener with a clip-point blade just over 3 inches long, and a metal bail. Paratroopers carried the knife in a breast pocket, where it was easy to reach if they became entangled on a jump and needed to cut the parachute's lines to get free.

Few tactical folders sold today will be deployed in such a life-or-death situation, but this increasingly popular modern breed of hard-use knife still has plenty of applications for self defense, rescue operations, and everyday carry.

TACTICAL KNIFE FEATURES

What makes a tactical blade so greatly appealing and useful? Let's have a look at the most well-known and important features of the popular tanto knife, such as this particular model that was created by SOG knives. This all-American knife was inspired by the artistry of Japanese swordsmiths. It's been widely considered a great all-around tactical choice.

A THICK BLADE While blade grinds vary, a tanto carries the blade's full thickness close to the tip for strength, and still offers a sharp, piercing point.

B BLACKED-OUT DESIGN Many tactical knife users prefer non-glare finishes on the steel.

C HARD STEEL Durability and edge retention are favored over ease of sharpening.

D NONSLIP GRIP Strong, man-made materials, such as metal, G10, and micarta, stand up to torque and impact better than wood, bone, and other natural materials.

E TIGHT LOCK A heavy-duty blade locking mechanism, such as SOG's Arc Lock, is required of a tactical folding knife.

F FAST OPENING Many tactical knives have assisted-open or automatic-open actions for swift, easy deployment in challenging circumstances.

G CONCEALABLE CARRY Self-defense knives, in particular, feature pocket clips that allow inconspicuous, deep-pocket carry.

020 THREE GREAT TACTICAL KNIVES

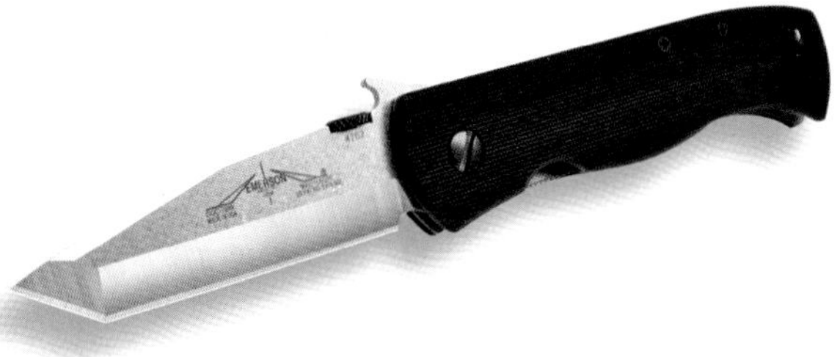

EMERSON CQC-7BW The CQC-7 stands as one of the progenitors of the modern tactical knife. CQC stands for "close quarters combat," and the knife's modified sharp tanto point and chisel-ground blade helped set the category standard. This version incorporates Emerson's famed "wave" feature for lightning-fast deployment out of a pocket.

CRKT M16 SERIES With its Kit Carson-designed flipper, this affordable tactical knife is one of the most popular on the market. It features a huge array of design options, including serrations, a tanto blade, and dual-hilt blade guards.

TOPS/BUCK CSAR-T For many tactical knife users, "rugged and tough" tops "bells and whistles." The 154CM modified tanto blade on the Combat Search & Rescue Tool cuts, pries, digs, and chops, and the grooved G10 handle won't slip in sweaty hands. There's a hex driver in the handle, but that's about the only snazzy design feature other than brute strength.

DESIGNERS
WHO CHANGED EVERYTHING

KEN ONION

Born on a 213-acre West Virginia farm, Ken Onion was raised in an environment where it was perfectly natural to see a 3-year-old kid whittling on a front porch. While he was stationed in Hawaii with the U.S. Marine Corps, he came across a copy of *Knives Illustrated* magazine, and proceeded to devote himself to knife making with a passion that would transform the industry.

In 1996, while recovering from back surgery, Onion decided to design a knife that was easier to open than even the slickest folder, but would still not be considered a switchblade. He pored over plenty of legal definitions, modeled a few ideas, and at last came up with the assisted opener. Unlike a switchblade, in which the knife blade is under constant spring pressure, Onion's design employs spring pressure only when a button is pushed to engage the opening mechanism.

Onion shopped his SpeedSafe system around until he found a taker in Kershaw, for whom he designed until 2010. His increasing fame brought about custom knife commissions from the likes of Kid Rock and Steven Tyler. In 2008, at the age of 45, Onion became the youngest member of the *BLADE* magazine Hall of Fame.

He still lives in Hawaii—where he is a passionate bluewater angler—and still designs both custom knives and knives for top-shelf brands such as CRKT and Chef Works.

021 PICK A FIGHTING KNIFE

Designed to kill, and for various related tasks–cutting concertina wire, prying open doors, affixing to a rifle as a bayonet–large, robust fighting knives are a soldier's last resort. Whether we're talking about the M1917 trench knife of World War I, the KA-BAR USMC Fighting and Utility Knife of World War II, the Gerber Mark II fighting knife of Vietnam, or any other blade, there is plenty of allure to the armed services' official knives. While some services issue specific blades, not all fighting units have an official one. Many soldiers purchase additional knives for field use, be they large combat fixed-blade knives or folders. Here are some of the most commonly used knives in the U.S. military. Among them are some of the most capable–and fearsome–edged weapons ever known.

U.S. ARMY
M9 BAYONET
Designed to replace the Vietnam-era M7, the M9 bayonet has a 7-inch nonserrated blade and, depending on the manufacturer, a fuller. The knife was designed by Charles "Mickey" Finn, and was originally built by his company, Qual-A-Tec, as the Phrobis III. A hole near the tip of the blade, when fitted to a tab on the sheath, makes the knife a wire cutter for clearing concertina wire.

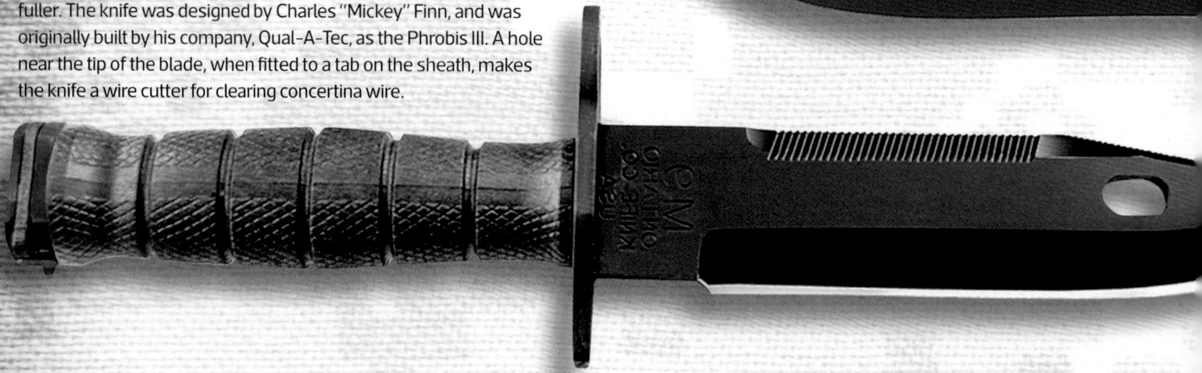

U.S. AIR FORCE
AIRCREW SURVIVAL EGRESS KNIFE
With a 5-inch-long blade of 1095 steel, the ASEK is able to saw through an aircraft's aluminum skin and break out its windows. The handle's insulated material lets it cut through hot wires, and features lashing holes to attach it to a pole as a spear. Originally from Ontario Knife Company, the ASEK is also made by Gerber Legendary Blades.

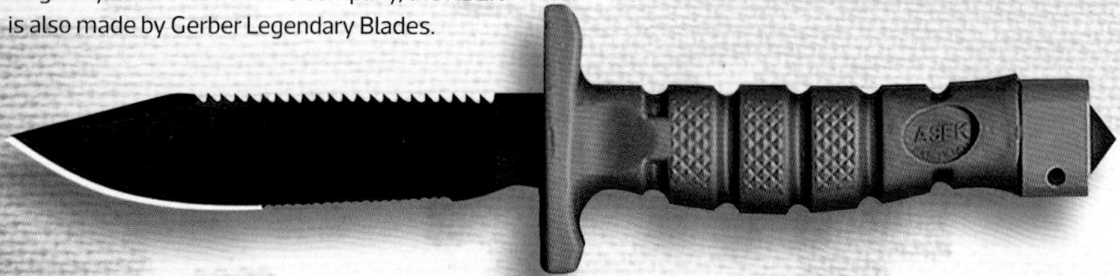

U.S. NAVY
ONTARIO MARK III

The standard-issue knife of both the U.S. Navy and Navy SEALs, the Mark III is designed for use in marine environments. It carries a 6 ½-inch blade of 440A stainless steel with a black oxide finish, a clip point, a saw-toothed spine, and a molded, high-impact handle with stippling for added grip.

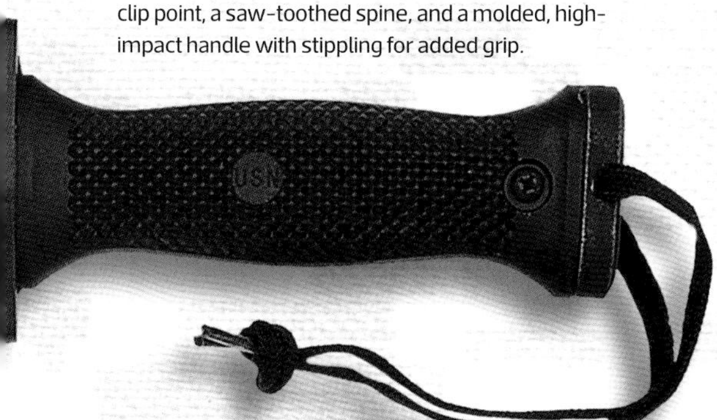

U.S. MARINE CORPS
OKC-3S BAYONET

Thinner and lighter than the M9, the OKC-3S has an 8-inch blade of 1095 steel, with a non-reflective finish, a clip point, sharpened false edge, and nearly 2 inches of serrations. The handle helps prevent hand fatigue and blisters. The sheath is made of a polyester elastomer material, and carries a sharpening rod.

U.S. COAST GUARD
USCG RESCUE & SURVIVAL KNIFE

Benchmade's USCG Rescue & Survival Knife was designed for boat crews with a blunt-tip blade of corrosion-resistant N680 steel, an integrated web and strap cutter, and both straight and serrated edges.

BLADES THAT MATTERED

KA-BAR USMC UTILITY KNIFE

In December of 1942, in the early months of World War II, KA-BAR began working with the Marine Quartermaster Department on a fighting and utility knife design that was destined to become one of the most recognizable knives in cutlery history. In 1943, the U.S. Marine Corps issued a knife to its fun-loving members. It was made by Camillus Cutlery Co. and stamped with its KA-BAR trademark. Its equipment number was 1219C2. The knife had a 7-inch Bowie-type blade with fuller, a leather-washer handle, and a steel butt cap. It was one of the most successful pieces of military equipment ever. The Navy had its own variant called the MK-2, and envious soldiers tried to steal both. Ultimately, the USMC KA-BAR was adopted by the Marines, Army, Navy, Coast Guard, and underwater demolition teams. In later years it was unofficially reactivated in the Korean, Vietnam, Desert Storm, and Iraqi conflicts. It is still carried by soldiers deployed in deserts, tundra, rainforests, and urban regions.

022 KNOW YOUR THROWING KNIVES

Maybe you can squat 600 pounds or throw a baseball 100 miles per hour, but do you have the awe-inspiring talent needed to hurl a knife and hit a target at 30 feet? Knife throwing is a part of American myth and legend–a staple of Westerns, war movies, and old circus acts alike. But there's nothing mystical about throwing a knife. The masters can accurately gauge distance and the number of revolutions a blade makes on its way to a target.

Throwing knives are built to withstand the abuse they incur while you're learning how to throw them. There are three types: handle-heavy, blade-heavy, and balanced. Beginners do best with a blade-heavy knife thrown by the handle. Buy a set of three matched knives–avoid lightweight blades, which tend to wobble in the air–and learn to throw (and stick) them with lots of practice.

023 GO PRO

Think you're a good knife thrower? You can show off your skills at a knife-throwing contest sanctioned by the International Knife Throwers Hall of Fame. Based in Austin, Texas, the organization schedules knife and tomahawk hurling tournaments around the country, with contests such as Speed Throw, Texas Three Step Fast Draw, and Fast Draw Long Distance Hawk.

024 MEET THE WORLD'S GREATEST KNIFE THROWERS

All those movie scenes of knife throwers sticking wicked blades a half-inch from an assistant lashed to a spinning target aren't just Hollywood magic. The skill is real. Here are three of the best-known blade chuckers of all time.

CHE CHE WHITE CLOUD A mixed Seneca and Onondaga from New York, Kenneth Lawrence Pierce, aka Che Che White Cloud, has knife throwing in his blood–his father, Lawrence (Chief White Cloud), threw in the Buffalo Bill Wild West Show. Fanning knives in his hand like cards, White Cloud throws knives less than a second apart. In 2004, he was named "Outstanding Knife Thrower of the 20th Century" by the International Knife Throwers Hall of Fame.

PAUL LACROSS Growing up in Vermont, Paul LaCross learned to throw knives while on long Boy Scout hikes. He performed at rodeos and fairs, on stage, and on *The Tonight Show*. In his Wheel of Death routine, an assistant was tied to a wooden wheel that spun two revolutions per second as LaCross outlined her body with knives.

DAVID ADAMOVICH Known as The Great Throwdini, David Adamovich is a retired exercise physiology professor and minister who has set or broken 38 world records. Among them is: "Most Knives Thrown Around a Human Target in 1 Minute"(144 to be exact). He's also been known to extinguish a cigarette in an assistant's mouth with a 14-inch knife.

025 ETHNIC KNIFE DESIGNS

Traditional knives from around the world have lent their shapes, construction, and design to even the most modern knives. Some, such as the ulu and puukko, are virtually unchanged. Others, like the Pesh-Kabz, are reflected in modern iterations inspired by knife blades of centuries ago.

BALISONG Also called the "butterfly knife," the balisong is a traditional folding knife from the Philippines, and there's nothing else in the world like it. When closed, the blade is hidden inside grooves in the two handles. To open, the handles are flipped around a tang like the wings of a butterfly. Flipping a balisong can be a mesmerizing action, which helps explain why it's a Hollywood favorite for action flicks. The fact that balisongs are regulated—and in some places outlawed—only adds to their pop culture allure.

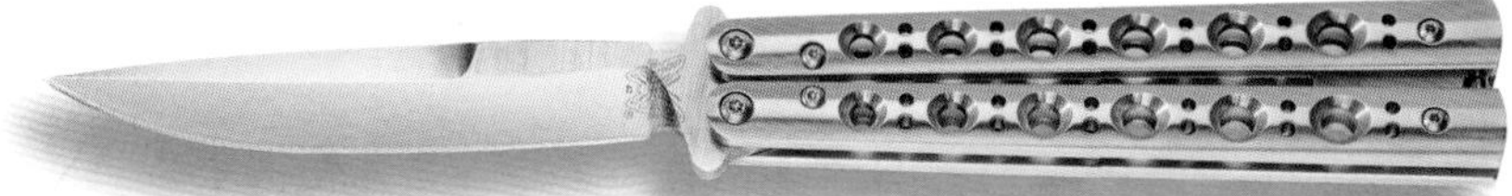

ULU A distinctive knife of the Arctic's First Nations, the half-moon-shaped ulu is a terrific chopper, scraper, flesher, and skinner. The handle rides directly above the cutting edge, which allows the user to place plenty of force behind the blade. The curved blade can be used with a rocking motion, which makes it a great kitchen chopper. Traditionally, handles were made of caribou antler and muskox horn, with a slate blade. Smaller ulus could be used for cutting sinew and carving bone. Larger blades were used to process caribou, seals, and whales. Most ulus available commercially are cheap tourist souvenirs, but Knives of Alaska makes an ulu worthy of its heritage.

KUKRI A traditional Nepalese knife, the kukri was used extensively by the Royal Gurkha Rifles of the British Army and is commonly called a Gurkha knife. The sickle-shape, inwardly curved blade makes for a wicked chopper, one reason it was utilized as a fighting knife. The most traditional kukri knives have a small notch at the base of the blade. Legend holds that it enabled blood to drip more cleanly from the knife. Today, kukri-style blades are found on everything from full machete-size knives to pocket folders.

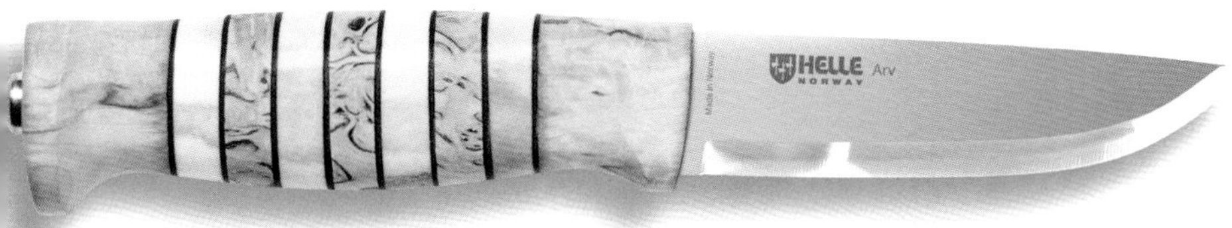

PUUKKO The traditional Scandinavian knife evolved over centuries of hard use by nomadic peoples: The unadorned lines of the blade allow for slicing, skinning, and penetration. The full, sculpted handle is easy to grip with heavy gloves, and the flat pommel is easily pushed into dense, tough material. Most puukkos have a laminate blade, in which a core of high-carbon steel is sandwiched between two layers of stainless steel.

STILETTO Originally thin-bladed Italian daggers of the 15th century, stilettos became a favorite of knights, strong enough to pierce mail, agile enough to find its way between plate armor, and thin enough to slip through the eye slits of an enemy's helmet. It's no surprise the stiletto became a weapon of troops in both WWI and WWII, and criminals everywhere.

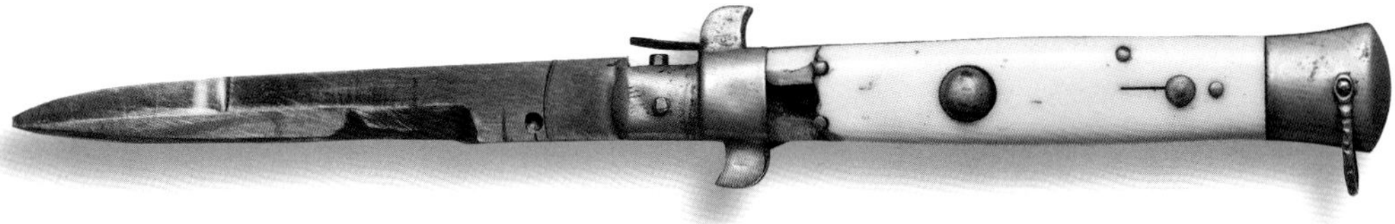

PESH-KABZ So-called "Persian" style knives abound, and perhaps the most traditional ancestor is the Pesh-Kabz knife, a mail-armor-piercing blade from Iran. The upswept blade with a reinforced tip was often forged with a T-shape in cross section for added strength, and was wide enough for both thrusting and slashing.

SCOTTISH DIRK A thrusting dagger, the Scottish or Highland dirk was popular in the 18th century, and is still a ceremonial knife of Scottish Highland regiments. It is related to the naval dirk, frequently used by low-ranking sailors and officers who fought hand-to-hand as they boarded sailing vessels.

KARAMBIT Legend holds that the karambit's narrow sweeping tip was modeled after a tiger's claw. Originally an agricultural tool in Indonesia, it was used to gather rice and roots, and was used as a fighting tool for centuries. Some say the blade was smeared with poison before a fight. The current fighting knife revival has seen the distinctive profile on many commercial knives.

026 TRAP A MOUSE KNIFE

It was a natural evolution: As folding knives became more technical and specialized, it only made sense that knifemakers would begin stuffing all those goodies into smaller and smaller packages. Thus was born the mouse knife, one of the newest categories of cutlery, built like a baby rhino. Also called "runts," mouse knives punch far above their weight. Most have 2- to 3-inch blades built from stout steel stock, with similarly beefy frames and all the high-tech design a maker can cram into it. Some are destined for everyday carry; others are built with the big-brother DNA of tactical folders or hunting-specific blade shapes. The best are suited for hard use, and nearly all are worthy of a look.

A TINY EDC The beefy blades and grinds of mouse knives are suited to tasks far more demanding than opening mail. They're made for slicing through pallet straps, carpet, webbing, and the occasional whitetail sternum. It's tempting to think of an EDC mouse as a box cutter on steroids, but many have features and materials found on top-shelf full-size knives, such as technical locking mechanisms.

B FIGHTING FOLDERS Mouse knives are small enough for deeply concealed carry and light enough to wear around the neck. As such, some self-defense experts tout a mouse knife as the perfect backup blade. Short blades have limited piercing ability and can bind in the fabric of a heavily clothed attacker, but the small size enables it to be gripped tightly and not easily dislodged from your hand. And their size aids in strong pressure cuts when a thumb is placed on top of the blade.

C TEACUP TACTICAL As backup utility, rescue, and tactical blades, mouse knives excel. They come in blade shapes as varied as tanto, sheepsfoot, and recurve, with added features like glass breakers and seat belt cutters. Since grip area is reduced with short handles, look for knives with finger grooves and plenty of jimping.

D SKIN A LITTLE Short, wide blades can be designed with lots of belly, which makes runts great for skinning.

E WICKED NECKLACE Neck knives are light, tiny, and never far from hand. Given their small size, neck knives frequently feature heavily textured and contoured handles.

BLADES THAT MATTERED

ARKANSAS TOOTHPICK

The Arkansas Toothpick didn't get its name for its diminutive size. In fact, this is a whopper of a blade–a piercing dagger that can be a foot long or more. Legend holds that the blade was devised by James Black, the Arkansas cutler who many claim made the original Bowie knife for James Bowie (see next page). For many years, in fact, the term "Bowie knife" and "Arkansas Toothpick" were used interchangeably, and the knives were so feared that some state legislatures outlawed them.

Eventually, the knife that came to be called the Arkansas Toothpick took on its own shape and form: a double-edged stiletto-styled dagger with double quillons to protect the fighter's hand. Some were balanced for throwing, and there are reports that they could be worn in a holster-like sheath slung across the middle of the back so the knife could be drawn over the shoulder and thrown in a single motion. Many accounts refer to Arkansas Toothpicks as a favorite of Confederate soldiers. But like its kin, the Bowie knife, the beginnings of the Arkansas Toothpick are shrouded in legend and myth.

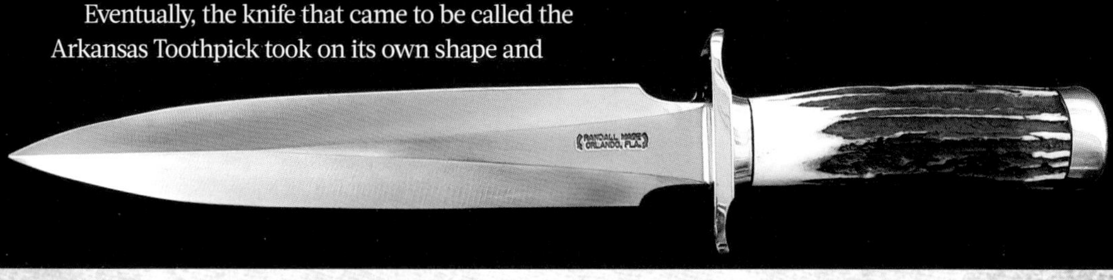

BOWIE KNIVES THEN & NOW

No American knife design carries the heft of history like the famous Bowie (pronounced BOO-ee). The knife's history—more accurately, legend—has shaped American ideals of knives for nearly 200 years. It's been a fixture in hunting camps nationwide; most outdoorsmen recognize the knife instantly. And yet, James Bowie, famed Indian fighter, Alamo martyr, and the knife's namesake, might not even recognize the thing in its current form.

THE SANDBAR FIGHT

The unlikely epic of the Bowie knife began on the Vidalia Sandbar in the Mississippi River, near Natchez, in mid-September 1827. A crowd gathered for a formal duel between Samuel Levi Wells and Dr. Thomas H. Maddox. The offense was an insult to a woman, long forgotten. As was customary, each duelist brought an entourage. Among the group with Wells was a land speculator and Louisiana planter named James Bowie.

Maddox and Wells each fired twice, missed both times, and shook hands. As they left the dueling grounds, however, their companions decided to settle a few old scores. One man fired at Bowie, who drew a large knife and took chase; he was then shot through the chest, clubbed with a pistol, and shot twice more. While he was down, two assailants attacked with sword canes. Bowie slashed one in the gut; the other stabbed him through the hand and body. Still impaled, Bowie grabbed the man's coat and sank his blade heart-deep.

At the end of the "horrid outrage," as one newspaper account billed it, Bowie had suffered seven wounds. He lived another nine years, perishing in the Battle of the Alamo. But from the Sandbar Fight rose his reputation as a knife fighter that grew to mythic proportions, fueled in part by the frontier public's infatuation with his knife.

A LIFE OF ITS OWN

"Nobody knows who made it or what it looked like," says James L. Batson, past president of the American Bladesmith Society and author of *James Bowie and the Sandbar Fight*. Whatever its original shape, within a few years the so-called Bowie knife assumed some more modern characteristics: the coffin-shape handle, heavy crossguard, and sweeping clip blade with partly sharpened top edge.

The knife's first iterations were definitely lethal. According to one account, Bowies were "drinking blood from New Orleans to Dubuque and from Savannah to Brazos." In 1837, the Arkansas Speaker of the House killed a fellow legislator with one on the floor of the Arkansas House of Representatives. That year, Alabama passed a law calling for those who killed with a Bowie knife to "suffer the same as if the killing had been by malice and aforethought." In 1828 Tennessee banned their sale. During the Civil War, many were as large as small swords.

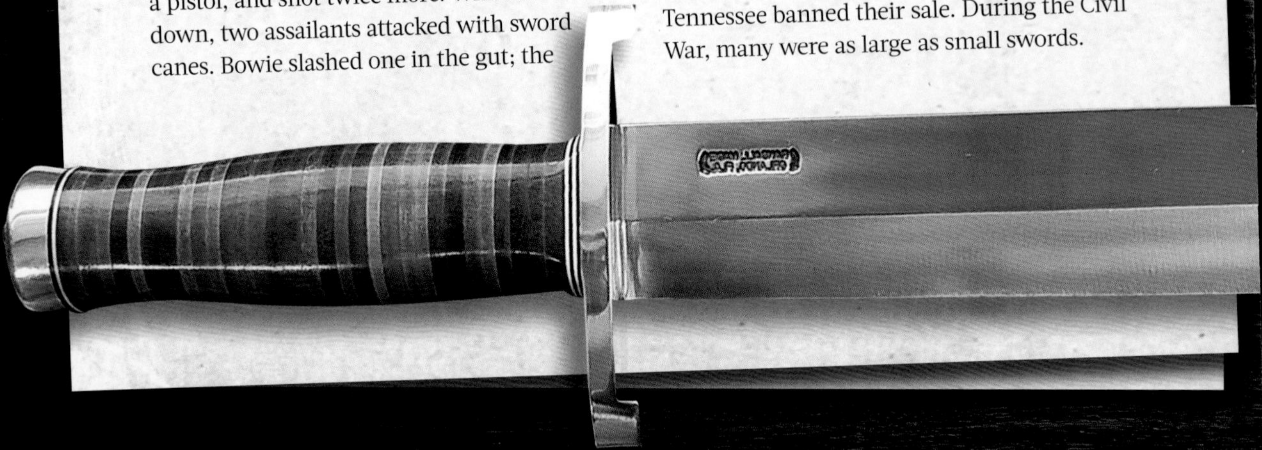

TRUE-BLUE BOWIE

Many serious Bowie knife students, says Mark Zalesky, editor of *Knife World*, look to a somewhat subdued knife as "an early example of the intermediary steps between the blade of the Sandbar Fight and later forms." The Searles/Fowler Bowie has long been displayed at the Alamo. This straight-backed knife (top) sports a checked ebony handle and a tiny cross guard and was given as a gift by Bowie's older brother, Rezin, in the late 1830s, and so it bears the stamp of Bowie family approval.

Other knife historians hold that perhaps the truest Bowie knife still around, with a defensible connection to James Bowie himself, is Bowie No. 1, (bottom) an exquisite work owned by and exhibited at the Historic Arkansas Museum in Little Rock. It's an awesome piece of steel, more than 18 inches long, manufactured with a coffin-shape handle wrapped in silver, and lacking the signature guard that would define the later Bowie aesthetic. By most accounts, the knife was made by James Black, a Washington, Arkansas, blacksmith whom the *Washington Telegraph* blamed in 1841 for "inventing this far famed deadly instrument." Engraved on the knife's escutcheon plate is the phrase "Bowie No. 1." Some historians figure this one was so important that Black or a later engraver marked it as such.

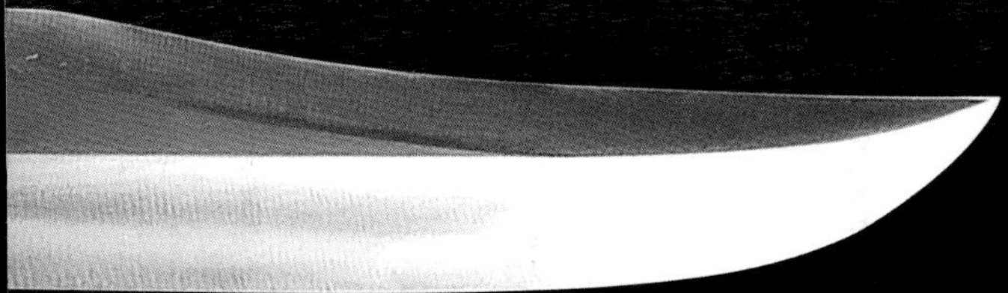

THREE MODERN BOWIES

The Bowie has shown up in a number of modern iterations. Here are three famous examples.

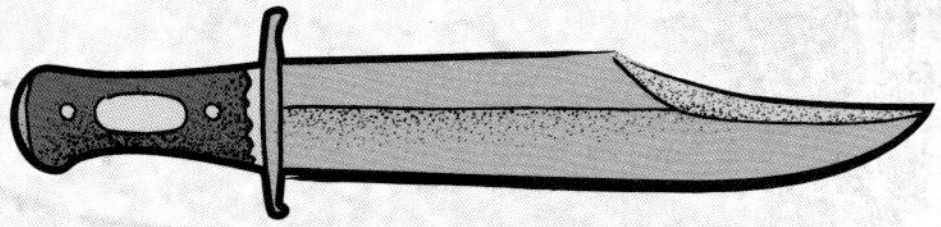

THE IRON MISTRESS In the 1952 movie, *The Iron Mistress*, Alan Ladd plays the knife-wielding Jim Bowie. The star of the show was a 12-inch-long, deeply clipped Bowie knife that sparked a wave of designs and embedded itself into the psyche of a generation.

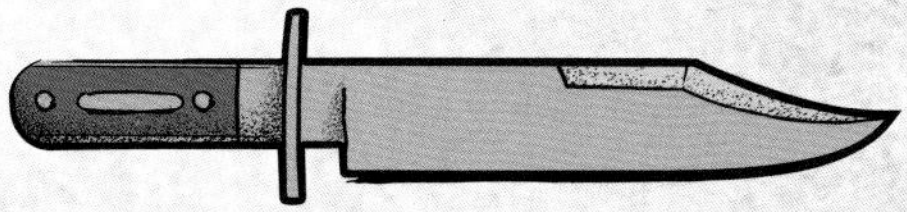

HENRY'S VERSION In the early 1960s, custom knifemakers began making reproductions of the Bowie knives that were produced by Sheffield cutlers during the mid-19th century. D.E. Henry was among the best, light-years ahead of everyone else in his grinding and polishing, fit, finish, and grace of line.

RAMBO The whopper of a Bowie Sylvester Stallone's character carried in the 1982 blockbuster *First Blood* was made by Arkansas bladesmith Jimmy Lile. It sported a 13.8-inch blade with a saw-toothed spine and handle wrapped in fishing line.

MULTI-TOOLS

→ IN THIS SECTION →

WENGER VS. VICTORINOX: THE COMPLICATED HISTORY OF THE SWISS ARMY KNIFE

LEATHERMAN: *FROM A PORTLAND GARAGE TO AN INTERNATIONAL EMPIRE*

VERSATILE ARTIFACT: THE 1,700-YEAR-OLD MULTITOOL

027 JOIN THE SWISS ARMY

It had to be a little embarrassing for the Swiss. The country's military officials wanted a new pocketknife for their soldiers that would be capable of opening canned food and breaking down the Swiss Schmidt-Rubin rifle. But in 1891, no Swiss company was capable of making enough of the knives, so the contract went to a German firm. That was the only year the Swiss Army Knife has been manufactured outside of Switzerland. By the end of 1891, a Swiss surgical toolmaker, Karl Elsener, ramped up production of his own Model 1890 Soldier Knife for the Swiss Army, compete with blade, reamer, can opener, screwdriver, and oak handles.

THE ARMS RACE A few years later, Elsener would rename his company Victoria, in honor of his recently deceased mother. In 1921, when stainless steel was introduced to the line, he combined the name with *inox*, a French term for stainless steel–ergo, Victorinox. In 1893, the forerunner of what would be called the Wenger Company started selling similar knives, and the multitool arms race began. For more than a century, these two separate companies manufactured knives under the Swiss Army Knife name, and the Swiss Army bought an equal number from each. Tens of millions more were sold to civilian consumers. Each used Swedish steel from Sandvik; knife aficionados still debate which was better.

MANY VARIATIONS Together, there have been hundreds of Swiss Army Knife models, with tools such as ski wax scrapers, cleat wrenches for rugby and golf studs. Cigar cutters and orthodontic tools to adjust braces. Hoof cleaners and a pressurized ballpoint pen. Recent models forgo the rifle-stripping tools for Bluetooth controllers and USB flash drives.

028 DRAW THE BATTLE LINES

Victorinox purchased the Wenger Company in 2005 and continued production of the brands for a decade, but one of the knife world's longest-running feuds was settled forever in 2013 when Victorinox discontinued the Wenger line. One possible reason the brand didn't survive? In the wake of the September 11, 2001, terror attacks in New York and Washington, airport stores returned vast numbers of knives to the manufacturer. Swiss Army Knife sales fell 40 percent.

For the time being, every new Swiss Army Knife will be a Victorinox. But there are still hundreds of millions of Wengers out there, and that's reason enough to continue the century-old argument: Who makes–or made–the better Swiss Army Knife? Here are some factors touted by partisans.

NAME CLAIM Victorinox was first to the plate, so by mutual agreement the brand was allowed to use the tagline "Original Swiss Army Knife." Wenger settled for "Genuine Swiss Army Knife."

CONSTRUCTION Although many Wenger fans cry foul, Victorinox knives were typically considered to have better fit and finish.

SCISSORS There are significant differences in the scissors. Victorinox scissors have a separate spring; Wenger scissors are driven by a lever. There are microserrations on the Wenger scissors blade, none on the Victorinox scissors.

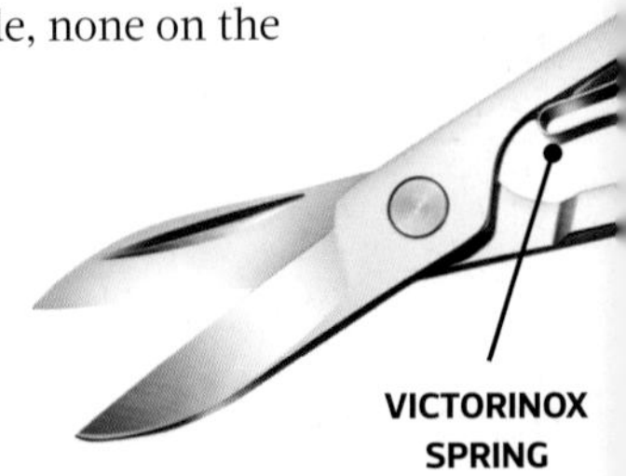

VICTORINOX SPRING

OPTIONS Both brands made knives with a disorienting number of blades and tools, but Wenger was known for sports- and hobby-specific tools, such as a choke tube tool, a chain rivet tool for mountain bikers, and a laser pointer.

029 OWN A CLASSIC

No one can own every Swiss Army Knife ever made, but here are five must-have models.

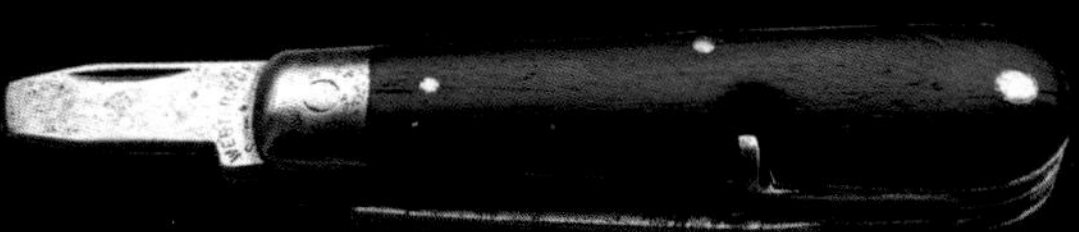

SWISS ARMY SOLDIER KNIFE (1891)
This OG model barely changed over the 60 years it was made (1891–1951), with a blade, screwdriver, reamer, and can opener.

CLASSIC (1935)
Weighing less than an ounce, the Classic has a blade, nail file, key ring, screwdriver, toothpick, tweezers, and scissors.

SWISS CHAMP (1985) In terms of utility, perhaps the best Swiss Army Knife available. It's about as large as you want to carry in a pocket—and perhaps a bit too large for that—but there are lots of aftermarket sheaths available.

WENGER 16999 GIANT (2006)
Maybe "Humongous" would have been a better name for this 9-inch-wide, 2-pound Swiss Army Knife with 87 "implements." In other words, just about every option it ever made.

VICTORINOX SOLDIER (2008) This is the most recent version of the knife issued to members of the Swiss Army. It features a partially serrated, one-handed opening blade that locks with a liner lock; a wicked wood saw; as well as a locking cap lifter and a screwdriver. The injection-molded handle was designed for a better grip in wet conditions.

DESIGNERS
WHO CHANGED EVERYTHING

TIM LEATHERMAN

The idea was to bolt a pair of pliers onto a pocketknife. Tim Leatherman's old Boy Scout knife just wasn't cutting it anymore (forgive the pun). Granted, it had helped him with everything from roadside breakdowns to leaky plumbing in cheap hotels on his 1975 honeymoon through Europe and the Middle East. But Leatherman, who has a degree in mechanical engineering, yearned for more. When he returned home to Portland, Oregon, he set to tinkering in his garage shop. He first made a bunch of cardboard prototypes, then graduated to wood and metal.

It took a while to perfect, but in 1981 Leatherman received a patent for "Mr. Crunch," which he called a "multitool." No one was interested. More refinement followed, along with a slew of rejections from retailers. Leatherman teamed up with his college friend, Steve Berliner, to manufacture and market the product, and in the spring of 1983, Leatherman Tool Group brought out the Pocket Survival Tool, or PST. A legend, an empire, and a new category of cutlery was born. In 1984, Leatherman made 30,000 tools. By 1993, more than a million PSTs alone had been sold. Each came with a 25-year, no-questions-asked guarantee.

Belts had never seen anything like a Leatherman, and before long, a chocolate-color sheath on a pair of blue jeans became the mark of someone who could get things done. More blades, tools, plier configurations, wrenches, and widgets followed. The Leatherman Tool Company remains a leader, but the multitool universe is filled with strong companies making wondrous devices.

030 CHOOSE THE RIGHT TOOL

There is no shortage of multitools on the market and no end in sight of new models being developed and manufactured. Sorting through the choices can be overwhelming, so here are some things to consider when shopping.

CARRY IT YOUR WAY There are three options: keychain, pocket, and belt pouch. Any multitool small enough to fit on a keychain is probably too small to get you out of much of a jam. There are plenty of pocket-friendly tools out there, but consider a decent EDC folding knife for your pocket and a full-size multitool for your belt.

ADD THE KITCHEN SINK Lots of gimmicky and just plain dumb implements can be shoehorned into multitools, but some options are definitely worth considering. A bit driver and the associated bits might bulk up the package, but they can keep you from having to carry a toolbox altogether.

KEEP COMFY When evaluating a multitool, grasp it firmly and beware of sharp handle angles and protruding tabs and buttons. You'll likely need to bear down hard on this tool sooner or later, so avoid hotspots. New ergonomics, such as curved and offset screwdrivers that center the axis of rotation, are a definite plus.

GO ONE-HANDED Oftentimes, you'll need a multitool when a single hand is all you can spare—holding onto a ladder, crawling on all fours, etc. One-handed pliers and knife deployment are a big plus.

LOCK IT OUT Similarly, if you're in need of a multitool, it's probably not a good time for a fresh wound. Locking blades are a must.

YOU DO YOU There's a good chance that someone sells a multitool tailored to your specific needs. Special-purpose tools are made for everything from servicing firearms in the field to handling rescue tasks (thanks to strap cutters and window breakers) to fixing various gadgets such as bicycle chains and computer motherboards.

031 KNOW YOUR HISTORY

Not to take anything away from Tim Leatherman's vision, but a multitool is such a handy solution that it's no wonder it had been dreamed up in earlier, less elegant versions. Here's a trio of multitools that never quite made it to the corner hardware store.

SNAIL-EATING TOOL A Roman dude's got to eat, right? In the Fitzwilliam Museum in Cambridge, England, there's a handy hand-tool dating to the third century A.D., found in the Mediterranean region. The tool includes a spoon, fork, pick, knife, and a thin spike, which some researchers believe was used to fish snack-size snails out of their shells.

SHIP-SHAPE TOOL Some 50 years before the introduction of the first Swiss Army Knife, Herman Melville wrote in *Moby Dick* that the carpenter of Captain Ahab's whale-hunting ship, the *Pequod*, carried one of those "highly useful ...Sheffield contrivances... containing not only blades of various sizes, but also screw-drivers, cork-screws, tweezers, awls, pens, rulers, nail-files, countersinkers."

OVER-THE-TOP TOOL This knife was made in Germany around 1880, a few years before the Swiss Army Knife, as a display model for John Holler's New York cutlery shop. It weighed an estimated 10 pounds.

CUSTOM KNIVES

→ IN THIS SECTION →

ONE OF A KIND:

THE ALLURE OF CUSTOM BLADES

INSIDE THE HIGH-DOLLAR WORLD OF ART KNIVES

WORLD TOUR:

THE TEN CAPITALS OF KNIFE MAKING

LEARN HOW TO BECOME A MASTER SMITH

032 GET INTO CUSTOM KNIVES

Sooner or later, the custom knife bug will bite. Few are immune to the charms of a handcrafted knife, with its incredible detail, artistic flair, and the allure of its one-of-a-kind nature. But it's best to step into the custom knife world with eyes wide open. Knife values rise and plummet. Trends are hot, then fade away. And knifemakers with star-power names have waiting lists measured in years–if they take on new customers at all. But few folks who buy a custom knife–or even a hundred–ever regret it. And while custom knives can command thousands of dollars, there are plenty to be had for far less.

REVIEW YOUR CUSTOM OPTIONS In its purist sense, a custom knife is a collaboration between maker and customer to produce a truly unique knife. The two parties agree on every aspect–from steel type to blade profile to handle material–and then, piece-by-piece, it is crafted by hand. No CNC milling, no ultramodern processes.

Of course, adherence to that ideal is practically impossible for many popular knifemakers who simply can't keep up with demand. Enter the "benchmade" category (not to be confused with the manufacturer of the same name), in which makers produce limited numbers of custom-designed knives. These aren't the products of unique collaborations, but they're a great way to land a knife with a trophy name attached–and not have to wait a decade for it to arrive.

ANOTHER OPTION is what some knife nuts call "midtech" knives. Machines and paid apprentices produce the less precision-oriented components of the knife, while the knifemaker fits the parts, polishes the washers, finalizes the grind, and handles the other tasks that require a master's touch. The best midtech knives are very close in quality to benchmade custom blades–and you'll save enough money to feed your hunger for more.

033 TRACK DOWN A CUSTOM BLADE

Want to find a custom knife for yourself? Here are three of the most common ways to get your hands on a great blade.

LOOK FOR A GUILD Choose a local knifemaker who belongs to an organized group, and the odds are good that you'll do business with a reputable, established craftsperson. Search the internet for "knife making guilds" and "knife making associations" in your state.

GET ONLINE Purchasing a used knife in the secondary market saves money and time. Check out sites such as bladeforums.com and usualsuspect.net.

GO TO A SHOW Nothing beats being able to handle a ton of knives in one place. Knife shows put buyers and collectors face-to-face with knifemakers. The biggest and baddest is the fabulous BLADE Show in Atlanta, Georgia. Other don't-miss shows are the Oregon Knife Show in Eugene, Texas's Lone Star Knife Expo, and the East Coast Custom Knife Show in Jersey City, New Jersey.

034 WIN THE LOTTERY

The waiting list for placing an order with the best knifemakers can be years long, so a growing number take part in knife lotteries. Buyers enter a drawing in which the lucky winners get to jump in line for placing a custom order or choose from a knifemaker's offerings at a knife show. Some knifemakers create lotteries from their email lists or lists of social media followers. Winning a knife lottery could be your best bet for landing a prized custom knife.

DESIGNERS
WHO CHANGED EVERYTHING

W.D. "BO" RANDALL

In 1937, W.D. Randall saw a man scraping paint from a boat with an unusual knife. He wound up buying the blade–a handmade knife by W.W. Scagel–and began a lifetime of custom knife making that changed the knife industry. Randall sold knives out of his father-in-law's Orlando, Florida, clothing store, and his reputation grew. When he made a fighting knife for a World War II sailor, word spread, and soon Randall was so well-known that letters addressed to "Knife Man, Orlando, Florida" flooded the shop. Randall is credited with helping kick off a craze for custom knives, and though he passed away in 1989, Randall Made knives are still crafted in his shop, now run by son Gary and grandsons Jason and Michael. Take a number, though. The waiting list for a Randall Made knife is currently five years long.

035 WHY DOES THIS KNIFE COST $1,500?

Near Bristol, Virginia, custom knifemaker Burt Foster builds beautiful, functional, meticulously crafted knives. In this hunting knife, the acid-etched blade shows off each layer of steel, the bolster seems alive with its layers of metal, and the gleaming, sinuous handle looks like it was carved from a lightning bolt. But he insists that there is more to a custom knife than bells and fancy bolsters.

"If you own a knife that belonged to a special person, or you used it in some meaningful way, then it has value because of that story," Foster says. "That's what is unique about a handmade knife. It has a story before you ever use it."

But there's more to a custom blade than a cool story. Here's why such a knife is worth every dollar.

STEEL Foster forges a laminated steel consisting of an inner layer of high-carbon 52100 steel sandwiched between two layers of 410 stainless steel.

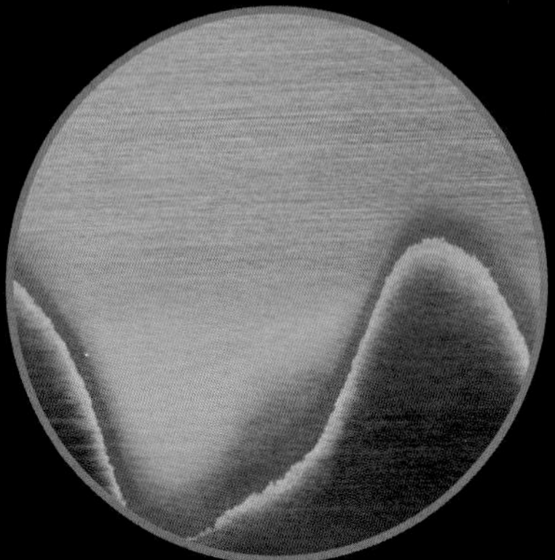

DESIGN Look closely: There's not a straight line on the knife. Foster abhors straight lines and fashions his knives so that all the curves—those between bolster and handle and along the spine, as well as the swells and rolls of the handle—form an organic whole.

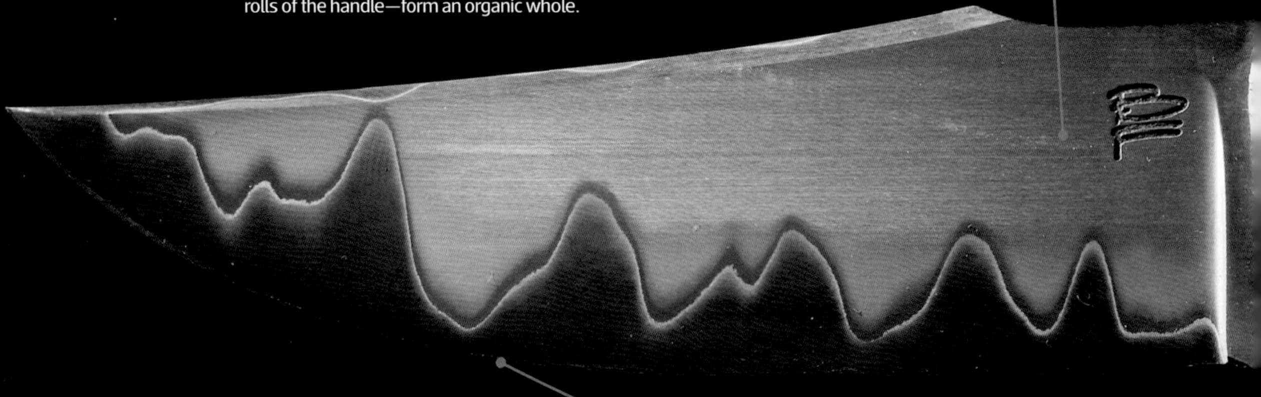

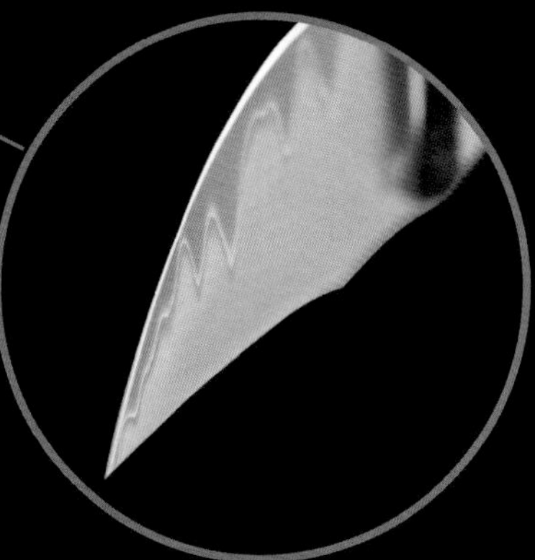

BLADE PROFILE AND GRIND A 4 ⅛-inch clip-point blade with a false edge sports a flat grind to a convex edge bevel for added strength. The ramped blade spine serves as an index for your thumb. "Plus it looks cool," Fosters says. "Nothing wrong with that."

BOLSTER The Damascus-steel bolster is forged of 1084 and 15N20 steels in a mosaic W pattern. Traditional Damascus steel is stacked like a deck of cards. With mosaic Damascus, the end grain of the steel billet is exposed and polished to highlight what Foster calls a "firestorm effect."

HANDLE Foster salvaged wood from an ancient maple tree on the site of the oldest Roman Catholic church in the Bristol, Virginia, area. The black vermiculations are decayed wood called "spalting." Punky and fragile in its original form, it's stabilized with injected acrylic.

TANG A full tapered tang is a critical design feature that adds balance and elegance. Foster doesn't grind the tang to the finished thickness, but forges it so that all three layers of steel remain in proportion.

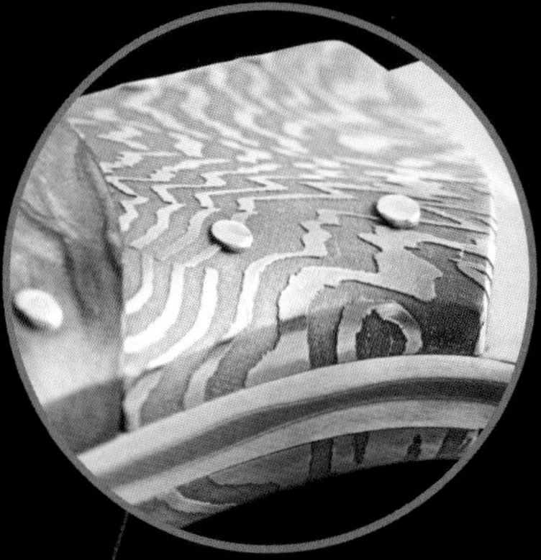

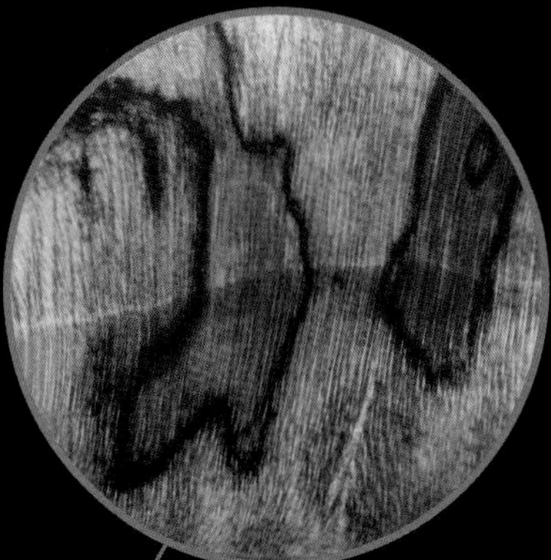

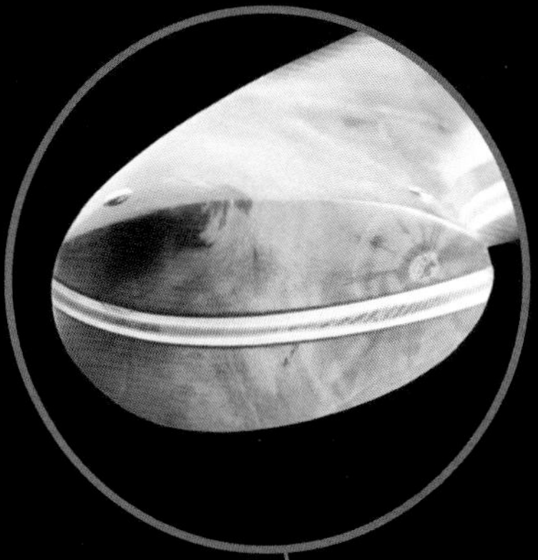

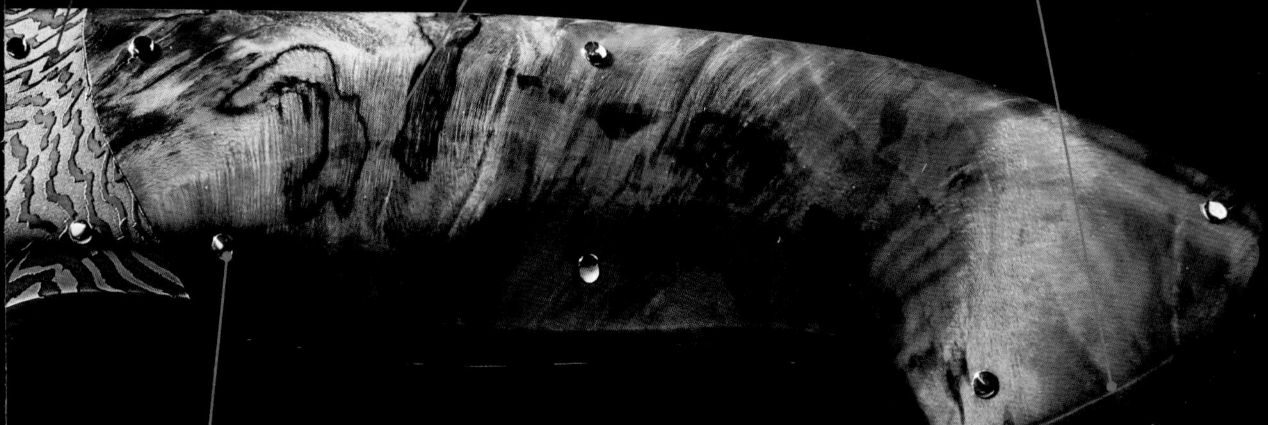

PINS Each of the 10 handmade nickel-silver pins functions as a rivet. They are clipped, ground off, then domed with a hammer and polished.

INTANGIBLES A Burt Foster knife is paired with a beautifully crafted leather sheath, and comes boxed with the reputation of one of America's finest knifemakers. It's hard to put a price on that.

036 BECOME A BLADESMITH

The pinnacle achievement of custom knife making is the Master Smith rating of the American Bladesmith Society. Attaining the rating is a process so rigorous that fewer than 125 knifemakers are currently on the list. To make the cut, smiths must first reach the Journeyman Smith level–no easy feat in itself. Next, under the watchful gaze of a current Master Smith, an applicant has to pass a series of tests that measure their ability to craft a knife that looks and performs among the best in the world. Want to be a Master Smith? Here's what you need to do.

FORGE THE BLADE The smith must first make a large test knife no longer than 10 inches (with an overall maximum length of 15 inches) and no wider than 2 inches. The tang must be a stick or hidden design, and the blade must be forged of at least 300 layers of pattern-welded Damascus steel made by the applicant.

SHOW ITS SHARPNESS To test its geometry and sharpness, the knife must sever a hanging 1-inch-thick sisal or manila rope with one slicing cut.

ENSURE ITS TOUGHNESS Next, the knife has to chop completely through a construction-grade wood 2×4 stud at least twice. Following the test, the Master Smith will inspect the edge for any noticeable damage to the blade. Any nicks, chips, flat spots, rolled edges, or other deformations, including bending, mean failure.

KEEP THE EDGE After those two tests, the applicant must shave hair from his or her arm, using the blade section that was used most in the cutting and chopping tests.

GET BENT The last test determines heat treatment for a soft back and hard edge. First, the blade's edge and point are dulled, then the Master Smith marks a line across the width of the blade approximately 3 inches from the tip. The blade is then inserted in a vise up to the mark and bent by force to a 90-degree angle. The supervising Master Smith will examine the blade. The blade is allowed to crack at the edge on bending, but not beyond approximately one-third the width of the blade. If any part of the blade chips, or any part of the blade or tang breaks off, the applicant fails.

STAND FOR JUDGMENT Once an applicant's test blade survives this series of torture tests, it's on to the big show: The applicant submits a minimum of five completely forged knives to the American Bladesmithing Annual Show and Meeting for judging. At the show, any of the judges can nix the application.

Opposite: Scott McGhee at his Guinea Hog Forge in North Carolina. He is one of less than 120 living Master Smiths. Above: Scott McGhee's massive blade for his Master Smith test. Made of 425 layers of pattern-welded steel and a bird's-eye maple handle, it was bent to 90 degrees and never cracked, split, or chipped.

037 TAKE A WORLD TOUR

Most early knife-making centers sprang up where the right resources came together: running water for mills, ore for metals, hard-working smiths to pound it all together. Today, a handful of knife towns and regions account for some of the finest and most-recognized knife brands in the world.

YANGJIANG, CHINA
Legend holds that 19th century American missionaries returned home with Yangjiang knives, introducing the U.S. to the Chinese city's 1,400-year-old knifemaking tradition. What is certain is that Yangjiang is a modern powerhouse of cutlery, with more than 1,000 factories accounting for 70 percent of China's knife and scissors production.

PORTLAND, OREGON
In the late 1930s, Joseph Gerber sent a few locally made knives to clients of his family's Portland advertising agency. The clients loved them, and in 1939, he launched Gerber Legendary Blades with a first sale to Abercrombie & Fitch. Many designers got their start at Gerber and then went big time on their own, including the founders of Al Mar Knives and Kershaw Knives. Leatherman Tool Group is also in Portland. Oregon is a knife-friendly state, with few laws regulating knives, including switchblades and balisongs. Indeed, that's one reason Benchmade put down roots there in 1990–the company was founded on the balisong.

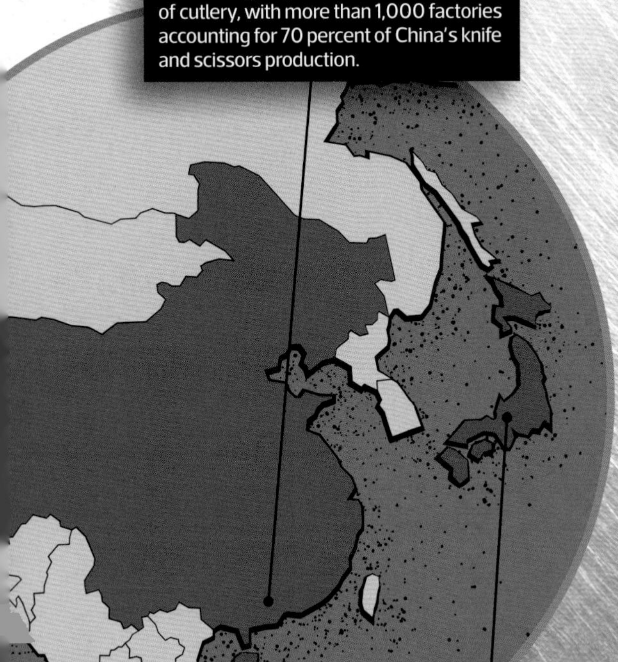

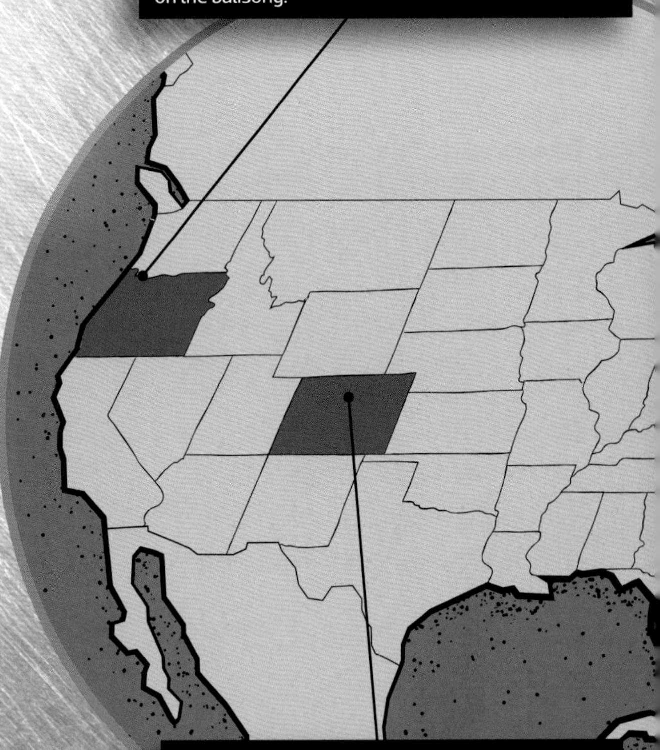

SEKI CITY, JAPAN
In the mid-13th century, a famed swordmaker named Motoshige worked here, spawning a heritage of fine swordmaking that would grow to more than 300 swordsmiths by the Middle Ages. In 1876, however, Japan outlawed the private possession of swords. Many cutlers shifted easily to knives, and Seki City began a second golden era of producing high-quality knives at very attractive prices. Today, in addition to Japanese brands, U.S. companies such as Browning, Cold Steel, Spyderco, Al Mar, and SOG manufacture knives in Seki City.

GOLDEN, COLORADO
It's not the biggest knife town in the world, but Golden is home to one of the most recognizable brands, Spyderco. While the company uses factories around the world, it makes some of its most popular knives in Golden, including the Manix, Military, Native 5, Para 3, and Police models. Blades made here are stamped "Golden, Colorado U.S.A. Earth."

SHEFFIELD, ENGLAND
England's first great knife town, Sheffield had rivers for water power, forests for charcoal, and sandstone for grinding wheels. By 1740, as many as 100 water-driven mills near Sheffield powered forge hammers and rolling mills. Uncountable numbers of Bowie knives were born here. In 1900, the Joseph Rodgers and Sons company alone produced 3 million knives. The dawn of mass manufacturing sacked Sheffield's status as a world knife capital, but its heritage has today spawned a generation of custom cutlers here.

HOLMEDAL, NORWAY
On the Norwegian coast, surrounded by fjords and the open sea, Holmedal is the home of Helle, formed in 1932 by two unemployed brothers who rode their bicycles to Oslo for their initial sales calls. The village still has only 500 inhabitants, but these watermen, sailors, and farmers make some of the finest traditional Scandinavian knives on the planet.

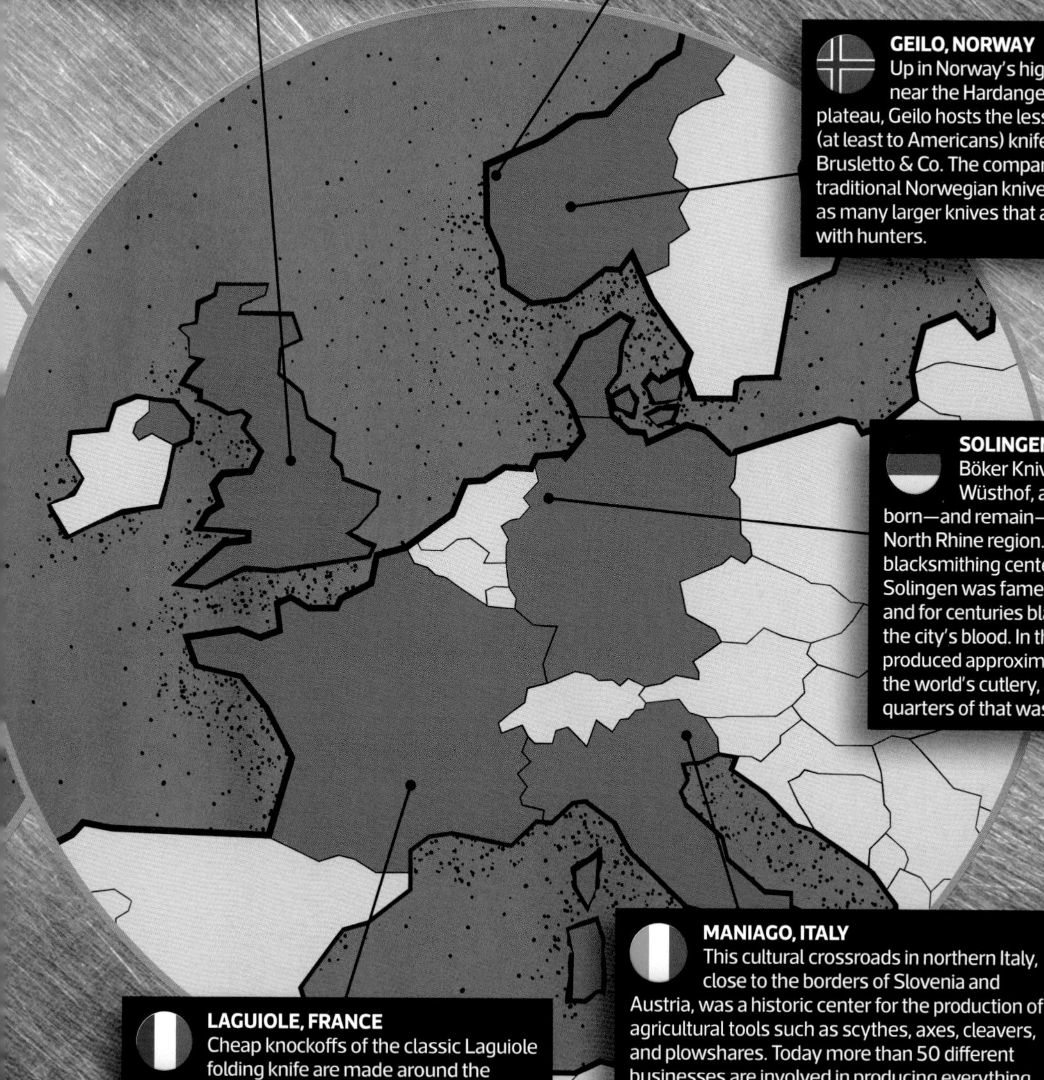

GEILO, NORWAY
Up in Norway's high mountains, near the Hardangervidda plateau, Geilo hosts the lesser-known (at least to Americans) knife maker, Brusletto & Co. The company makes traditional Norwegian knives, as well as many larger knives that are popular with hunters.

SOLINGEN, GERMANY
Böker Knives, J.A. Henckels, Wüsthof, and Puma all were born—and remain—in Solingen, in the North Rhine region. A smelting and blacksmithing center in the Middle Ages, Solingen was famed for its fine swords, and for centuries bladesmithing ran in the city's blood. In the 1960s, Germany produced approximately 60 percent of all the world's cutlery, and nearly three-quarters of that was produced in Solingen.

MANIAGO, ITALY
This cultural crossroads in northern Italy, close to the borders of Slovenia and Austria, was a historic center for the production of agricultural tools such as scythes, axes, cleavers, and plowshares. Today more than 50 different businesses are involved in producing everything from knives to scissors to cheese spreaders. Among the better-known are LionSteel, winner of numerous "knife of the year" honors, and FOX Cutlery.

LAGUIOLE, FRANCE
Cheap knockoffs of the classic Laguiole folding knife are made around the world, but the real deal comes from the knife-making city of Thiers and the nearby village of Laguiole, both in the Aveyron region of France. True Laguiole knives will have the forge name and "Made in France" engraved or stamped on the blade.

038 A CUT ABOVE

An art knife must be sharp, and it must fit to the hand. Otherwise, there are no constraints to fetter the knifemaker, to shackle the engraver, or to stymie the creative collaboration between artists who might work continents apart but pursue their passions at the peak of their powers. Merging the exacting, creative work of the most innovative knifemakers ever known with the finest sporting engravers alive on the planet, today's art knives are a virtual canvas for some of the most accomplished designers and artists working in steel.

UNCOMMON GOODS "The truth is that few people have ever seen a truly high-end art knife," says Paul Shindler, whose Knife Legends is one of the world's most esteemed purveyors of custom, high-end art knives. "In fact, few people even know that these knives exist."

A MULTIDISCIPLINARY WORK OF ART An alchemy of engineering, sculpture, steelmaking and engraving at the highest levels, art knives have begun to attract the attention of serious collectors. In the past 12 years Shindler alone has sold more than 5,000 knives, with a staggering value in the tens of millions of dollars.

The knives on these two pages and the following two, sold by Knife Legends, shows off the vast breadth and depth of possibility. Some of the artists whose work is shown here are members of the Art Knife Invitational (AKI), a group of 25 makers of highly collectible knives who extend an invitation for membership only when a current member drops out. All are reshaping the boundaries of what a knife can be.

SAVAGE BEAUTY

Maker: Salvatore Puddu
Engraver: Valerio Peli

This beauty from Italian Salvatore Puddu actually gives a nod to seminal American knifemaker James A. Schmidt, who died in 2000, with its oversize thumb stud. The materials are top-shelf: a dagger blade of RWL34 stainless steel, a frame of 416 stainless steel, and gold-plated titanium liners with extensive filework on the knife's backspacer and liners. Puddu's blade polish is second to none. Its sheen provides an elegant counterpoint to engraving by Valerio Peli, another highly sought engraver of bespoke shotguns. From the prolific Creative Arts Engraving Studio, in Gardone, Italy, Peli combines Bulino and cut-in engraving styles. Presentation-grade amber inlays in the handle set off the gold highlights beautifully. Approximate value: $14,500.

A BIRD IN HAND

Maker: Charles Bennica
Engraver: Aldo Rizzini

French knifemaker Charles Bennica—a recent inductee into AKI—is known for his proprietary tail lock, in which the tail of the knife moves away from the frame to release the blade. The dendritic bands in the Noreena jasper handle inlays—the gemstone is found only in the Australian outback—speak of the tangled woodlands that are the haunt of woodcock, wonderfully rendered in the Bulino style by veteran bespoke shotgun engraver Aldo Rizzini. Many a shooter will recognize the complexities suggested by the mosaic patterns in the Damascus steel of Claude Shoessler of France. Approximate value: $8,500.

UNDERSTATED ELEGANCE

Maker: Ron Lake
Engraver: Tim George

A preeminent maker of custom art folding knives, Ron Lake of Oregon invented the interframe design and builds many knives with a patented tail-lock release. His work is clean and minimalistic, bearing the mark of 50 years of experience as a machinist and knifemaker. This model pairs those clean lines with classic hammer-and-chisel engraving from Virginian Tim George, who apprenticed with former Colt custom-shop master Ken Hurst. Flush gold inlays play off the sambar stag handle scales. Approximate value: $19,500.

RAPTOR ATTENTION

Maker: Owen Wood
Engraver: Giovanni Steduto

South Africa-born knifemaker Wood forges his own complex mosaic Damascus steels; this blade incorporates three different Damascus layers. Its liners are gold-anodized titanium with a backspacer blued in two separate processes and the 18-caret gold pivot collar wraps a medallion of black-lip pearl. Engraver Giovanni Steduto of Italy's Creative Arts Engraving Studio is known for exquisite, mixed human and animal faces engraved in the Bulino style. A sexy knife with a lush Art Deco aesthetic.
Approximate value: $13,500.

INTEGRAL PIECE

Maker: Dietmar Kressler
Engraver: Manfred Fleisher

In an integral knife, the whole thing is one piece of steel. Making such a knife is logistically complex, as engraving can't be performed on hardened steel. Dietmar Kressler had to machine the knife, then send it to fellow German Manfred Fleisher for ornamentation. Fleisher returned it for fitting with an ironwood handle, and metal finishing and hardening. Fleischer is venerated for his deeply cut, almost sculptural three-dimensional engraving of detailed big-game portraiture; his choice of a sinuous, curvilinear snail on essentially a fighting knife is curious to reflect upon. Approximate value: $12,500.

MAMMOTH ACHIEVEMENT

Maker: Fabrizio Silvestrelli
Engraver: Luca Casari

Silvestrelli's background in painting and sculpture shape this stunning folder. The rounded liners have extensive decorative filing, and the fossil mammoth handle (50,000 to 75,000 years old) is well shaped. Many consider Silvestrelli's hand-rubbed satin finish the best in the world. The engraving bridges many classic cut-in engraving styles in floral, scrollwork and banknote, a signature of Luca Casari, the chief master engraver for Beretta. This is a large knife, more than nine inches long. Approximate value: $8,500.

INTRICATE IRIDESCENCE

Maker: Steve Johnson
Engraver: Gianfranco Pederdsoli

Many consider Steve Johnson the greatest disciple of famed American knifemaker Bob Loveless. The blade of this mini dirk-style thrusting knife features a hand-filed checkered finger groove and spine; a full, tapered tang for strength and balance; and scales of presentation-grade mother of pearl. Italian engraver Gianfranco Pedersoli uses every surface available. Known by gunmakers for a Grotesque style, here his highly ornamental floral style is fern- and featherlike, with a sensual symmetry that seems to hold together the lines of blade and handle. Approximate value: $7,000.

039 KNOW YOUR KNIFE LAWS

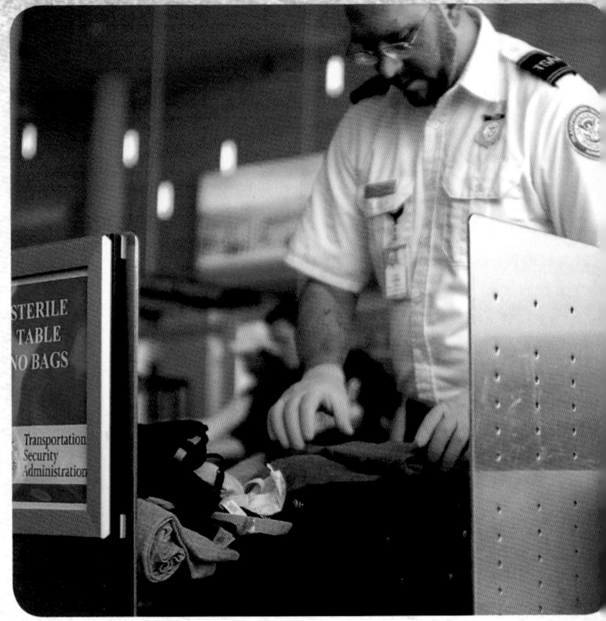

Knife laws regulate both the type of knives you can own, and when and where you can carry a legal knife. Knife laws, however, vary wildly from state to state, and even from one city to the next within a state. That means it's possible to drive from one state that allows automatic knives into another with a, say, Kershaw Launch in your pocket and wind up on the wrong side of the law.

On top of that, knife laws change frequently. For the most up-do-date, state-by-state information, visit the American Knife & Tool Institute website at akti.org. For international information, the Wikipedia "Knife Legislation" page catalogs the laws of 25 nations.

COMMONLY REGULATED KNIVES

Old laws and advances in knife design have created confusion over knives that rely on mechanical devices for full or partial opening. The Switchblade Act of 1958 is the only federal law for these knives; it prohibits the importation and interstate commerce of switchblades. The law was changed in 2009 to keep one-handed opening and assisted-opening knives from being considered switchblades or gravity knives. But what's a switchblade compared to a push-button automatic or a spring-assisted folder?

SWITCHBLADE This is defined as any knife that opens exclusively by the release of a compressed spring. The blade on a switchblade must be inclined to open; it must be held closed by some mechanical means.

ASSISTED-OPENING KNIFE Also called a spring-assisted knife, an assisted-opening knife opens only when the blade is first pushed open slightly by some force, most commonly a flipper tab or push button. The blade on an assisted opener is inclined to stay closed, and must open by nonmechanical means.

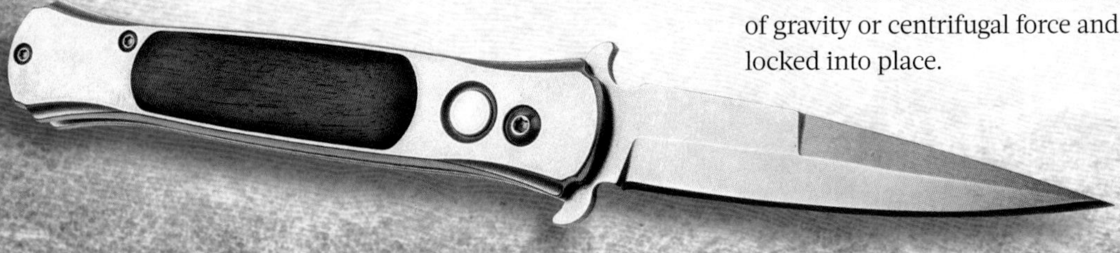

AUTOMATIC KNIFE These are designed with a bias toward closure, meaning that exertion must be applied to the blade by hand, wrist, or arm to assist in opening the knife. But that's the federal law. Some states have no automatic knife restrictions; while others limit blade length on automatics, allow carry only with a license, or ban them altogether.

BALLISTIC KNIFE Prohibited in most states, a ballistic knife is one with a detachable blade propelled by a spring-operated mechanism. These are not throwing knives.

DAGGERS, DIRKS, AND BOWIE KNIVES Some states prohibit these knives or poorly define them. Daggers typically have a straight blade with two cutting edges. California law defines them in a way that includes anything that could be used as a stabbing weapon (including dirks). And there is no agreement on what is and what isn't a Bowie knife.

GRAVITY KNIFE Often described as a knife with a blade that is released from the handle by the force of gravity or centrifugal force and, when opened, is locked into place.

CONCEALED CARRY

Figuring out the particulars of which knives can be carried concealed and where can be extremely vexing. For example, in the District of Columbia it's illegal to carry any knife that is capable of being concealed. Strictly speaking, that could include granddad's hand-me-down mini Stockman. In some states, a folding knife's exposed pocket clip can be grounds for a law enforcement officer to stop and search the person.

THE COLLEGE CONUNDRUM

Regulations on college campuses vary, though some states are very specific. In California, for instance, it's illegal to carry a knife with a blade longer than 2.5 inches on a college campus. In Massachusetts, carrying any knife is illegal on all college campuses. Check local regulations carefully if this is the kind of thing you'll need to know.

THE KNIFE I CARRY

COLIN KEARNS, EDITOR-IN-CHIEF

Years ago, as T. Edward Nickens and I were driving to his hunt camp, he asked me, "Did you bring a knife?" In my rush to pack and leave for the airport, I'd left mine at home. I remember Eddie shrugging it off. We'd figure something out. Two days later I shot my first whitetail buck. After a few photos, Eddie presented me with a Benchmade Griptilian—a knife, I would learn, he'd planned to give me regardless. I don't recall what I said to Eddie, but I hope I was as grateful as I am now. I always grab that knife first, and I used it on my first deer, duck, and pronghorn. It's served me well, and brings me luck and comfort In more ways than one, the knife is a gift.

USE THE KNIFE

GAINING AN EDGE

I hold the knife in my right hand, thumb on the blade spine. My left thumb guides the edge along a blade-sharpening stone at as close to a 20-degree angle as possible. The screech of diamond dust biting steel is like a door creaking open in a slasher film. I haven't broken such a nervous sweat since Mrs. Evans made me read about tarantulas to the entire third-grade class.

"Visualize the matrix," Big D says. His eyes gaze toward a place I cannot yet see.

"Big D" is Donavon Phillips—Nissan factory mechanic, knifemaker, and three-time national BladeSports International cutting champion. We're in his Mississippi shop as a cold rain patters on the tin roof. Phillips knows knives very well: He designs them, makes them, and competes with them in a little-known circuit that draws the world's finest bladesmiths. His slash through 27 water bottles is the official world record. "It's unfortunate that cutting sports intimidate a lot of people," he says. "Most sportsmen grew up hearing their parents say, 'Don't play with knives.'" But Phillips grew up in the Mississippi Delta. "A machete, a knife, and some sticks—when I was 7 years old, those were all the toys I had."

Phillips peers over my shoulder, so close that his shadow blocks the overhead light. I try visualizing the matrix Phillips described to me earlier: A knife edge, he explained, is simply a microscopic saw. The teeth are formed of carbides in the steel, locked in a matrix whose spaces hold other elements—vanadium, chromium, molybdenum—that support the carbides. "To sharpen a knife," he told me, "you bring the opposing planes of the blade together, approaching infinity. They never touch. But, of course, they do." This is another metaphysical puzzler I've been asked to visualize.

With the focus of a brain surgeon, I guide the knife along the five-inch stone once more. My blade has a bit of belly, and Phillips tells me that only a beginner sharpens the blade tip without adjusting the angle for the curve. As I move the belly across the stone, I lift my right elbow to increase the angle. It feels good.

Phillips cranes his neck and spits a stream of Copenhagen into a 55-gallon trash can four feet away. It's a rifle shot. Doesn't arc two inches. Everything about this man speaks of precision. His shadow gives a little dip. "That ain't bad," he says. "Angle's a little sharp, maybe." I feel a drop of sweat glide down my back.

Sharpening a knife is a skill that eludes many hunters, anglers, campers, and other outdoors folk. Knife geeks talk about sharpening in near-spiritual tones, but there's nothing mystical about sharpening a knife. And there's certainly nothing mystical about using one. Skinning, gutting, whittling, filleting—you'll learn about all sorts of skills in the following pages.

KNIFE CARE

→ IN THIS SECTION →

STONE COLD TRUTH:

YOUR GUIDE TO SHARPENING STONES

FACE TIME:

HOW TO SHAVE WITH A KNIFE.

(REALLY.)

TOOTH BY TOOTH:

HOW TO SHARPEN SERRATED BLADES

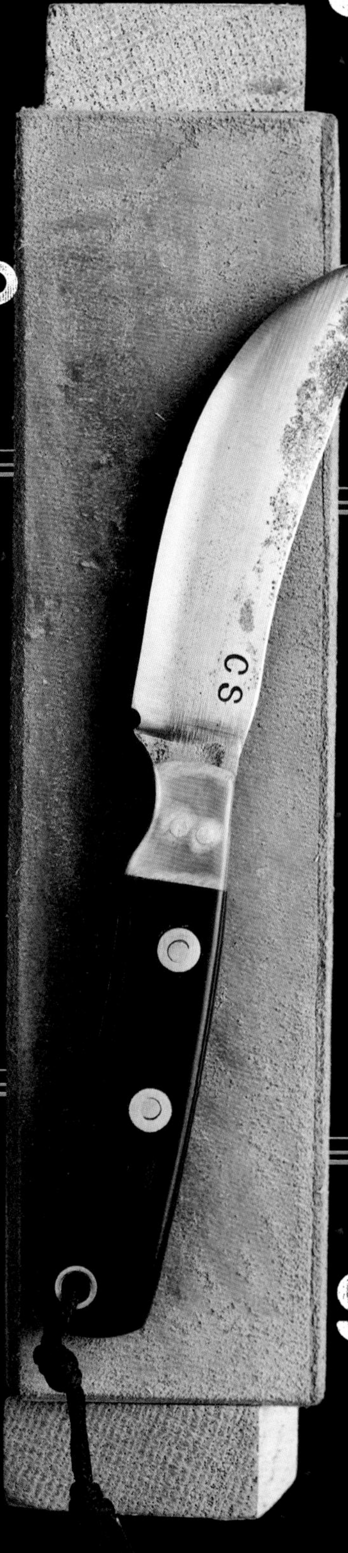

SHARPEN A KNIFE *WITH POCKET CHANGE*

(AND HALF A DOZEN OTHER WAYS)

RUST AND DUST:

BRING FILTHY KNIVES BACK FROM THE ABYSS

THE MAN WHO SEVERED HIS OWN ARM...

ON PURPOSE!

040 PERFECT YOUR SHARPENING SKILLS

There's no mystery to knowing how to sharpen a knife to a hair-shaving edge, but there is mastery. This time-honored and proven method is a good way to get started–and just might be the best way, period.

STEP 1 Place a two-sided (coarse and fine) whetstone on a damp paper towel on a countertop or table with the coarse grit facing up. The paper towel will keep the stone from sliding. Place the heel of the blade on the whetstone and establish the proper edge angle (most outdoor knives are sharpened between 15 and 20 degrees). Place the fingers of your free hand in the middle of the flat of the blade. You'll use these fingers to apply pressure to the blade and help maintain the sharpening angle.

STEP 2 While maintaining a constant angle, push the blade into the stone and draw it across the stone from heel to tip, using as much of the length of the stone as possible. Push with the fingers until the flesh under your fingernails begins to turn white. Repeat 10 to 15 times, depending on the condition of the edge. Be sure to count your strokes.

STEP 3 Run your thumb perpendicular to the blade edge to feel for the burr. When you have a consistent burr from heel to tip, flip the knife over and repeat steps 1 and 2 on the other side with the same number of strokes.

STEP 4 Repeat this entire process with the fine side of the stone. Use a decreasing number of strokes until you are able to pass the blade a single time, with only the weight of the blade providing the pressure.

041 DIAL IN THE RIGHT ANGLE

When it comes to sharpening a knife, it takes many years of experience to be able to just eyeball the correct blade angle on a whetstone. Until you get there, here are a pair of fairly simple ways to dial in on the just-right angle degree.

THE CHEAP WAY Buy a set of inexpensive angle wedges. To use them, choose the correct wedge for your desired angle, place it on the side of the stone, place the blade on the wedge to establish the angle, and sharpen. This is as foolproof as it gets.

THE FREE WAY Fold the bottom left corner of a piece of paper so that the bottom of the sheet lines up with the right edge. You've now created a 45-degree angle. Fold the creased edge to the right edge once more, as if you're making the wing on a paper airplane. That's a 22.5-degree angle, which is very close to the 20 degrees at which many working knives are sharpened. Fine-tune the fold so the angle is just a bit sharper, and you'll have a paper guide to check your edge angle when sharpening.

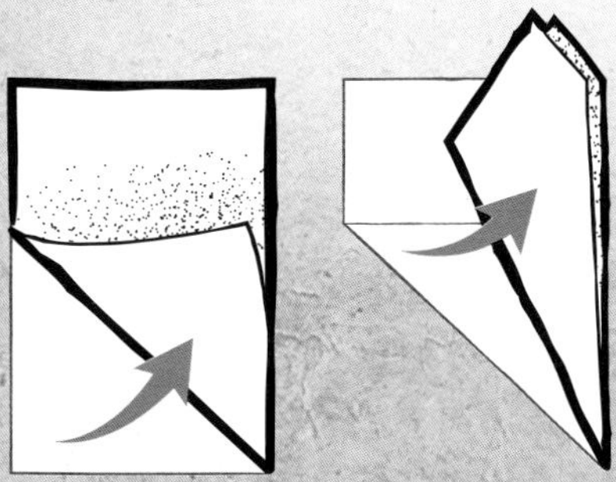

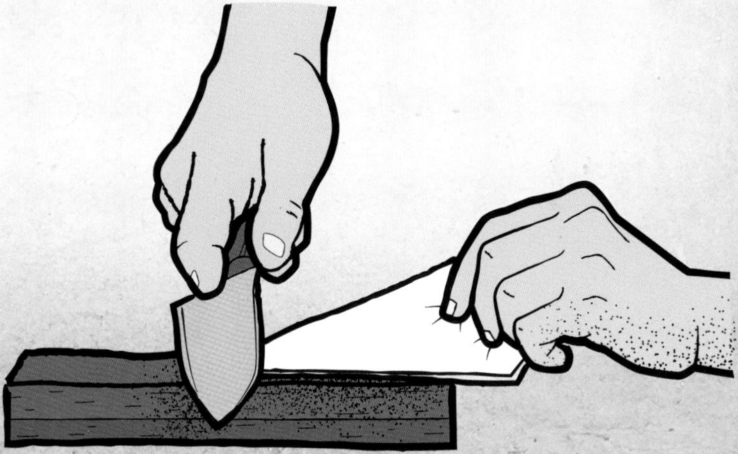

042 FINISH WITH A LEATHER STROP

Barbers finish a honing job with a leather strop to remove the tiny rolled wire edges left by even the finest-grit stones. You can use a leather belt, but you'll get better results from a dedicated bench strop constructed of fine honing leather mounted to a block of wood. First, "charge" the strop by smearing it with a thin film of honing compound. There are two basic kinds: chromium oxide and diamond paste. Diamond paste works better on hard stainless steels.

Next, lay the knife nearly flat on the strop and draw the edge backward along the leather. This compresses and conforms the leather to the profile of the knife's edge. Start with a dozen strokes to each side of the blade, using very light pressure. Increase the pressure on subsequent strokes if necessary. Once the knife is shaving-sharp, wipe the blade clean with a few drops of honing oil.

043 KNOW YOUR WHETSTONES

In Grandpa's day, choosing a whetstone for hand-sharpening a knife was simple: Soft or Hard Arkansas stone? Today, whetstones come in a mind-boggling array of types, materials, and grades. Hard whetstones cut more slowly, making a finer, polished finish. Softer whetstones fracture easier, exposing new grains in the matrix for quicker removal of metal from the blade.

Before you put metal to stone, first you will have to decide how you'll use the knife. If you require a superfine edge for delicate caping and cutting, you'll want to finish a polished edge with a Hard Arkansas or Japanese water stone. For everyday use and general camp chores, a Soft Arkansas or silicon carbide stone will do the trick. Many start with silicon carbide for edge reprofiling, then move to aluminum oxide, finishing with a Hard Arkansas stone. Here's what you need to know about sharpening stones before you fine-tune a knife edge.

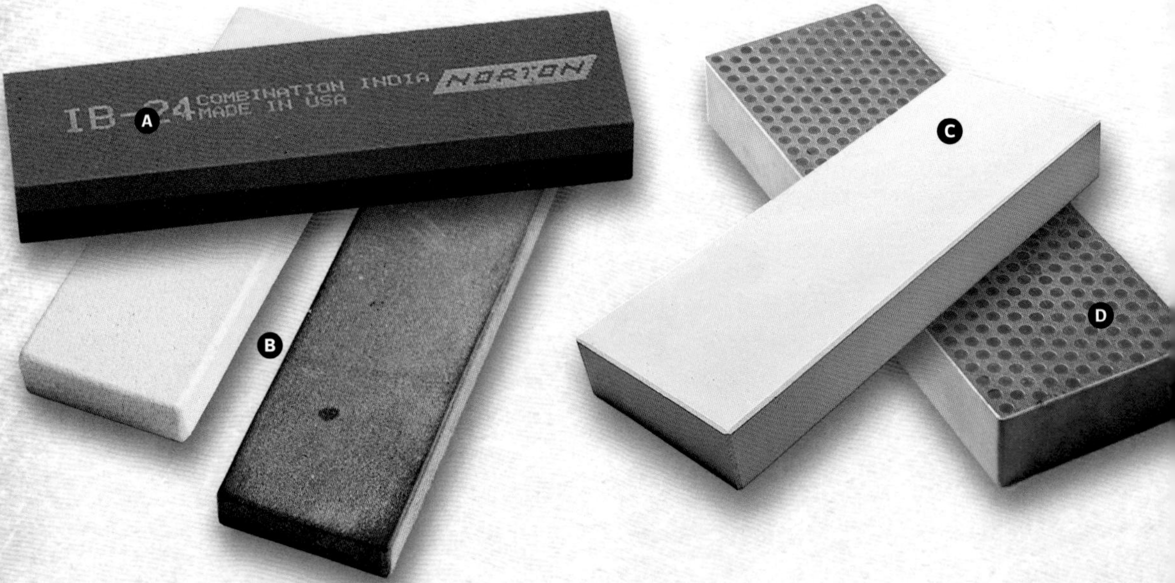

A MANMADE OIL STONES Aluminum oxide oil stones, also called India stones, cut metal quickly and still produce a very keen edge. They are typically graded fine, medium, and coarse. Silicon carbide stones (also called carborundum) cut even faster than aluminum oxide. They're exceptional for reshaping a blade profile and removing damaged edges, but they don't produce the fine edges you'll get from other, harder stones. They're also graded fine, medium, and coarse.

B NATURAL OIL STONES Arkansas stones are made from a metamorphic chert called American Novaculite, found almost entirely in Arkansas. They come in the following grades (from coarse to fine): Washita, Soft Arkansas, Hard Arkansas, Hard Black Arkansas, and Hard Translucent Arkansas.

C WATER STONES Typically softer than oil stones, water stones require wetting before use. Some must be submerged for several hours. Others need only a splash. In general, water stones are softer than oil stones and are less messy to work with, but wear unevenly, requiring a flattening process to restore to form after extended use. Synthetic water stones are typically made of aluminum oxide and cut faster than aluminum oxide oil stones. Made from a sedimentary stone in which tiny silicate particles are suspended in clay, Japanese water stones are very porous and must be soaked in water before use.

D DIAMOND HONES Diamond hones are metal plates dusted with tiny industrial diamonds. They cut very quickly for fast sharpening and stay flat practically forever. They can be more costly, but rarely wear out.

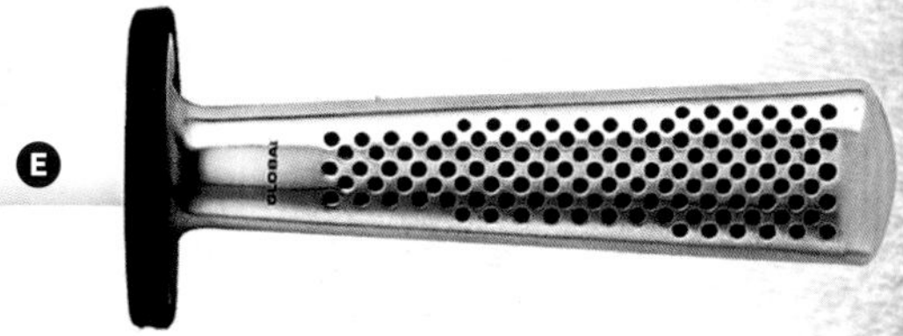

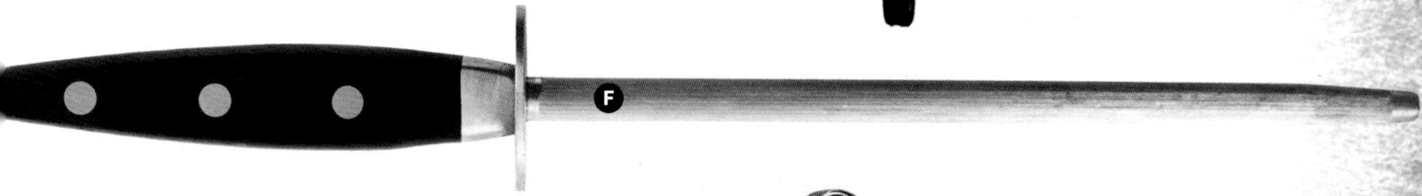

E SHARPENING RODS Ceramic rods and rods covered with diamond grit are used to put a fine edge on a knife. These slightly abrasive tools are handy for touching up an edge during use.

F HONING STEELS Also called butcher's or chef's steels, honing steels are rods used to straighten and realign a fine edge, not sharpen a blade. Ridged steels remove a tiny bit of material in the honing process; smooth steels do not.

G GUIDED SHARPENING DEVICES These ingenious honing systems hold abrasive materials in the proper sharpening positions, thus removing the need for a user to calculate edge angles.

H POWERED SHARPENING DEVICES Plug-and-play sharpeners involve powered belts and sharpening guides, enabling users to switch between grits for finely tuned metal removal. They also typically include various angle guides for sharpening scissors, working edges, culinary knifes, and axes and hatchets.

044 SHARPEN A SERRATED BLADE

Serrations work like tiny saw teeth, and they're great for cutting through tough, fibrous materials such as cattail reeds and dense cordage. They can be a pain to sharpen, however, and honing serrations incorrectly will just wear them down to useless nubs. Here's the drill.

STEP 1 Use a progressively tapered diamond hone made specifically for sharpening serrated blades. Sharpen one tooth at a time by placing the hone on the beveled edge of the serration. Match the honing angle with the bevel of the serration and align the hone with the tooth perpendicular to the deep gully of the serration.

STEP 2 Start with the serration nearest to the knife handle and push the hone down until the entire width of the gully is filled with the hone. Rotate the hone just a bit and repeat until you can feel a fine burr on the flat back side of the blade. Work your way down the blade, sharpening each serration.

STEP 3 When all serrations are sharpened, turn the knife over and grind off the burr with a ceramic rod or fine sharpening steel.

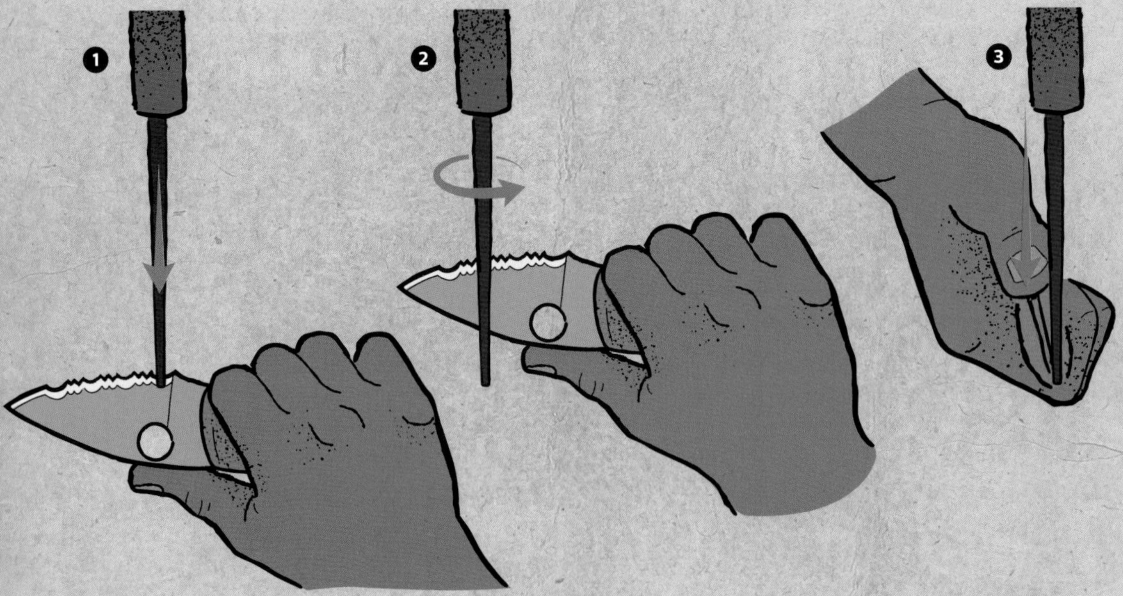

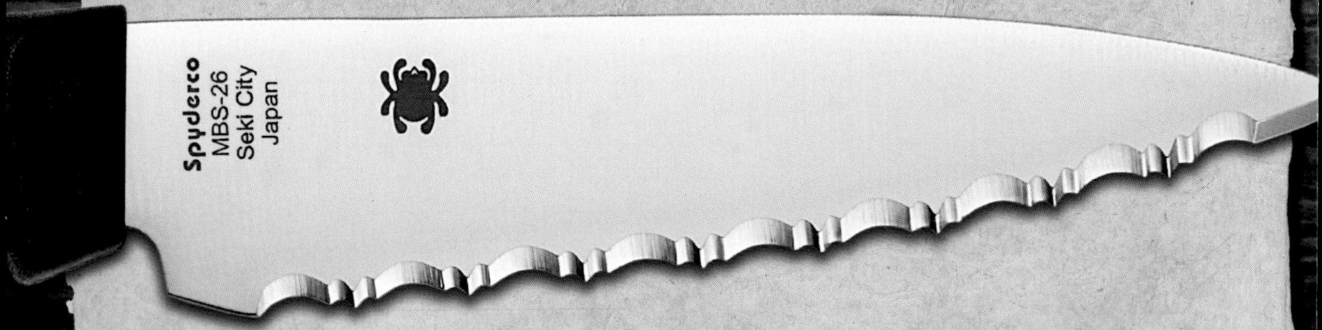

045 HONE WITH A SHARPIE

When sharpening a blade, it's critical to maintain the correct angle on the sharpening stone. This trick will help you do that. Use a wide-tipped Sharpie or other permanent marker to "paint" the knife's edge bevel with a solid stroke of black ink. Next, take a few strokes on the stone and carefully examine the knife's edge to monitor your progress.

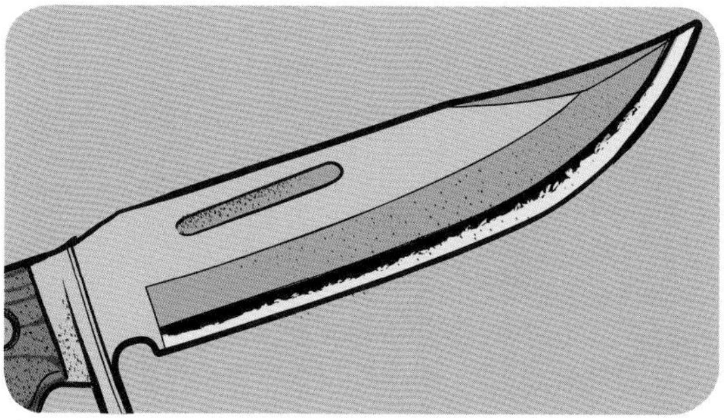

If the ink is removed at just the very edge of the bevel, you're sharpening the cutting edge too acutely.

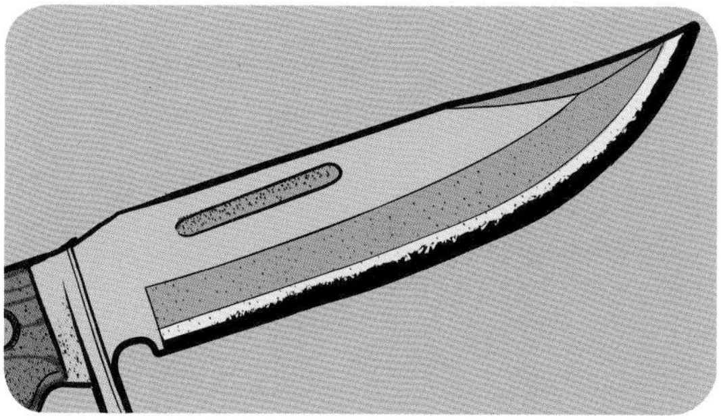

If the ink comes off at the shoulder of the bevel, leaving a black stripe on the edge, the sharpening angle is too shallow.

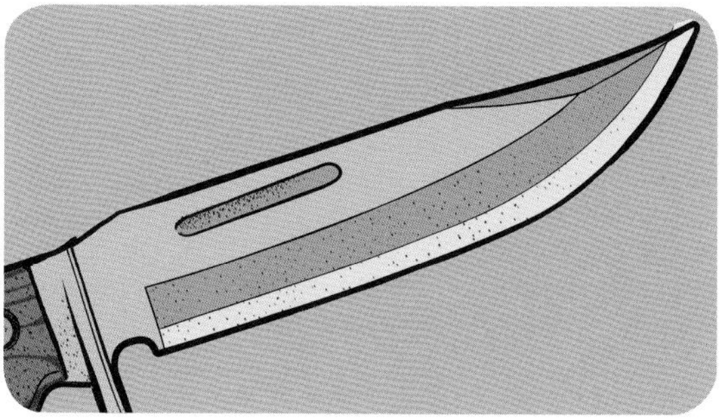

If all the ink is removed, you're reprofiling the edge bevel and sharpening the knife correctly.

FEATS *of* STEEL

SEVER YOUR ARM

For five days in April of 2003, climber Aron Ralston had been trapped inside a Utah slot canyon, his arm pinned by an 800-pound boulder. He'd run out of food and water. He'd begun drinking his own urine. He was nearly delirious. He filmed a last message to his family. But he kept his wits. And he had a knife.

He knew that his own limb was dying underneath the boulder. He'd hacked away at his thumb, feeling no pain, but hearing the hiss of gas from the decomposing flesh. On the morning of the sixth day of his ordeal, after trying earlier to sever his arm only to learn that he had no way of sawing through bone, Ralston was hallucinating, malnourished, and dehydrated. But he was prepared for one final attempt at freeing himself. He fashioned a makeshift tourniquet, and using his body weight, he snapped the radius and ulna of his own arm. Then, using the nearly blunt edge of a cheap multitool, he sawed through the ragged flesh and bone and twisted tendons. The amputation took nearly an hour. Finally freed, Ralston climbed out of the slot canyon, tied up a makeshift sling for his arm, rappelled down a 65-foot cliff, and began hiking. At the time of his rescue, he'd lost 40 pounds and a quarter of his blood. After his helicopter flight to hospital, he was still tough enough to walk into the emergency room.

046 SHARPEN CONVEX GRINDS WITH A MOUSEPAD

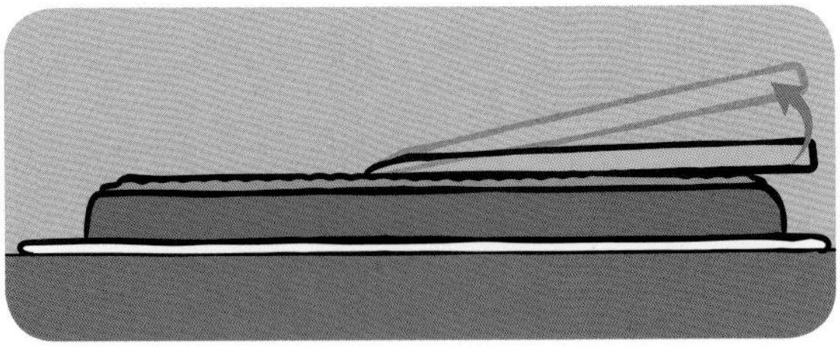

A convex grind is notoriously difficult to sharpen since the edge bevel is rounded. The fix is simple, though: Grab a mousepad with a smooth surface, 600- and 1,200-grit wet/dry sandpaper, and a wet paper towel.

STEP 1 Place the 600-grit sandpaper over the mousepad and trim the edges to fit. Place the wet paper towel on a counter or desktop and place the sandpaper-covered mousepad on the paper towel. This keeps the mousepad from sliding around.

STEP 2 Establish the sharpening angle by placing the knife blade flat on the pad, lifting the spine, and pulling the blade edge into the sandpaper. When the edge catches into the sandpaper, that's the correct angle.

STEP 3 For each stroke, pull the knife's edge away so it trails spine-first across the sandpaper. The mousepad will depress and conform to the edge bevel. Alternate sides. Finish with the 1,200-grit sandpaper for a polished edge.

047 FIND AN ANGLE WITH POCKET CHANGE

Experts tell you to maintain a 20-degree angle when sharpening a hunting or camp knife on a stone. But what the heck does a 20-degree angle look like? The answer might be jingling in your pocket.

It turns out that quarters can be used to establish a proper sharpening angle. It takes a bit of math to get right, but it's not difficult. The official height of a quarter is .069 inch. That means a stack of four quarters is just over a quarter-inch tall. To establish a 20-degree angle, divide the width of the blade (measured from spine to edge) by three to give you an estimate of how high to raise the knife's spine above the stone. Say your chef's knife is 1.5 inches wide; you'll need to raise the spine a half-inch for a 20-degree angle. That requires seven quarters. A Swiss Army Knife-style blade, about 7⁄16 inch wide, would take two quarters under the spine to set the edge for a 20-degree angle.

048 REVIVE YOUR EDGE

There might not always be an Arkansas stone or Spyderco Sharpmaker nearby when you need to touch up a knife blade, but there's nearly always a ceramic coffee mug hanging around a deer camp or fishing cabin. Turn it upside down, and you should see a raised rim with a dull finish. (When ceramic mugs are glazed in a kiln, they rest on that rim, leaving an unglazed surface.) That raw, unfinished ceramic is similar to what you'd find in a ceramic sharpening rod. Turn the mug upside down and place it on a nonslippery surface. Lay the knife blade on the rim at a 20-degree angle and stroke the edge into the ceramic with medium pressure. Count 10 strokes, then repeat on the other side.

BLADES THAT MATTERED

WYOMING KNIFE

In the late 1960s, Carl Addis was a gym teacher and big-game hunter in Calgary. While working as a guide near the Peace River in Alberta one day, Addis watched a hunter open a moose's gut cavity with a knife and knew it was going to be a long day, telling himself, "There's got to be an easier way."

Back home, Addis drew some ideas and started grinding prototypes for a gutting and skinning tool. The final design for the Wyoming Knife slit hides without nicking organs and easily peeled pelts. It was a great caping knife and would clean fish to boot. Addis quit his job, moved his family to Denver, Colorado, in 1968, and sold the knives at hunting shows across the West. Retailers soon signed on. To date, hundreds of thousands of Wyoming Knives have been sold. All parts are made and assembled in the U.S., and Addis' son, Carl Jr., still runs the company from Denver, shepherding a true American hunting icon.

049 TEST A BLADE WITH NEWSPAPER

Shaving hair from your forearm is just one way to test a keen edge. Your daily newspaper can also tell you exactly how sharp you've made your knife's edge. Use these three tests to see if your blade can hack it—but be sure to let your spouse read the front page first.

A TRY THE BITE Hold a single page of newsprint at shoulder height and rest the knife blade on the top edge at a shallow angle (always cut away from yourself). A sharp blade will bite and begin a clean cut; a dull blade will skip along the edge or tear it.

B LET IT GLIDE Your blade should also glide easily without sticking. Hold a new page vertically and pull the blade through the paper, cutting with the entire length of the blade. Any hang-ups will indicate a nick or burr on the knife's edge. Listen to the sound the knife makes while cutting, too—the higher the pitch, the sharper the blade.

C FILLET YOUR PAPER Hold the blade flat against a page on a tabletop. Press the paper firmly against the tabletop with your nondominant hand and guide the spine of the blade with that thumb. Try to slice a tiny layer from the surface of the page without cutting through—like removing skin from a fish fillet. Success? That's one sharp knife.

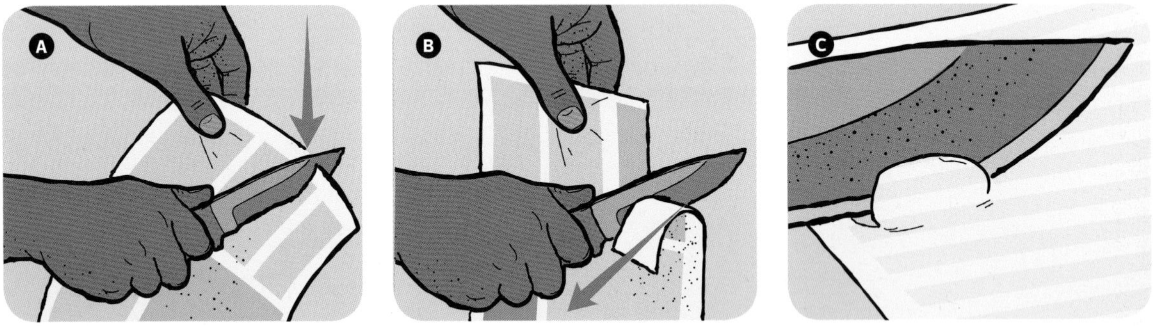

THE KNIFE I CARRY

T. EDWARD NICKENS, EDITOR-AT-LARGE

I've always preferred folders over fixed-blade knives. I've carried a folding knife every day for more than 30 years, and during that period I don't think I've worn a belt knife more than three times. Until this past hunting season. Not long ago, David E. Petzal, Field & Stream's longtime knife swami and caretaker of a certain kind of outdoorsman flame that is burning less bright these days, handed down to me a box of his personal knives. One, a DiamondBlade Summit, has a scratched and worn handle and a blade that's lost just enough sheen that I know it has seen its share of hard use. It was in a leather sheath to which was attached a handwritten note that read: "I made this sheath, by God. D.P." It's an old blade from an old friend, and it's my new hunting knife.

050 SHAVE WITH A KNIFE

If a knife is "shaving-sharp," can you really shave your face with it? In theory, yes. In practice, a very qualified yes. Even if your knife will shave your forearm slick as a skillet, beard hair is coarser and thicker than body hair. And razor blades are generally sharpened at an angle less than 15 degrees. Also, razor blades are made with some flex to follow the contours of your jaw and face. So shaving with your favorite EDC might be less a question of how your knife will fare than how well your face will hold up. But it you're determined to channel your inner mountain man and shave with a knife, here are a few ground rules.

BE STROPPY Let's assume you've given your knife a wicked edge. No matter how sharp it is, strop it on a piece of leather to remove the rolled wire edge, which can leave behind some nasty nicks.

GO SOFT Shave immediately after a hot shower or prep your face with a hot washcloth. Use shaving cream or shaving soap. Most important, take your time.

USE THE RIGHT EDGE Avoid using a knife with lots of belly, or at least use the straightest edge section on your blade. Move the blade straight across your face without pushing or pulling the knife along its length. Otherwise, you'll slash your skin.

SHAVE WITH CARE It's a bit of trial and error to determine how much pressure to apply to the skin and the angle to hold the knife. Take your time, keep bandages handy, and don't try this before a job interview.

EXPECT ROUGHNESS You won't be as smooth as a plum, and don't be surprised if you develop a bit of a rash. Razors glide over sensitive skin to minimize rash. If you're the sensitive type, you're probably not going to remove your beard with a Bowie.

051
HAVE IT HANDY

Years ago, I learned a humiliating lesson from a close friend when I needed to cut something–I don't recall, and nor does it matter, what it was. I asked him if he had a knife. He gave me a friendly sneer and replied, "Am I wearing pants?" 'Nuff said. You don't have to walk around with a knife in your hand, but a knife out of reach is no knife at all. Store a knife deep in a pack, in your toiletries kit, or worse, back at the camp or cabin, and you'll deserve a similar dressing down.

052 TAKE YOUR FOLDER TO THE SPA

The internal mechanisms of folding knives attract dirt, lint, and grime. At best, a dirty folder will be difficult to open. At worst, it will fail to lock and could injure the user. Here are five steps to keep your folder operational and safe.

STEP 1 Inspect and clean folders regularly, especially after hard use. Pay close attention to where the blade tang mates with other metal parts and look for wear on lockbars.

STEP 2 Use a toothbrush to remove all dirt and foreign matter from pivot points and locking mechanisms.

STEP 3 Try compressed air to clear interior spaces and crannies a brush can't reach.

STEP 4 Lubricate pivot points with a light oil, such as 3-in-One or honing oil.

STEP 5 Clean interior locking mechanisms with a short burst of aerosol oil through a spray tube. Open and close the blade several times to allow the oil to penetrate. Shake the knife well and wipe away any excess oil, which will only attract more grime.

THE KNIFE I CARRY

ANTHONY LICATA, EDITORIAL DIRECTOR

The knife I reach for most is a Buck 102 Woodsman. It's a rugged little knife, with a 4-inch, clip-point blade. It's kind of a do-it-all design, perfect for essential hunting tasks like field dressing a deer, skinning small game, and slicing salami. I also think it's quite handsome, with its leather sheath, black handle, and stainless steel accents. But what I really love about it is my dad had the same model, and every time I strap it on my belt, I think of him.

053 REMOVE CAKED-ON RUST

Perhaps you've inherited a neglected old family heirloom knife. Or maybe you left your own carbon-steel knife in a wet leather sheath or outside in the rain. Either way, the first step to bringing a crusted, rusty blade back to life is to clean it so that you don't grind dirt into the rust. Don't use water. Scrub with mineral oil and wipe as clean as possible with a rag. Next, soak a rag in white vinegar, wrap the rag around the knife blade, and give it a few hours. Use the rag to rub the crud from the blade again, then clean the metal with steel wool.

For next-level restoration, try a few of these strategies. Once the rust is gone, treat your blade with a light oil and promise yourself that you'll never abide another spot of rust.

GRAB AN ONION Rub a cut onion on the knife blade. An onion's natural sulfuric acids can help clean it up.

PULL OUT A POTATO Stick the knife into a large potato and leave it for a few hours. Like an onion, a potato contains a natural acid–oxalic acid–that will eat rust.

POLISH WITH ASH Rub the steel with a cork that's been dipped in cold wood ashes.

054 CLEAN A BLOOD-SOAKED KNIFE

It's all too easy to ignore a blood-soaked knife after a tough few hours of gutting and cleaning a deer, elk, or moose. Cleaning a knife gunked up with guts, hair, and blood will be twice as difficult the next morning, and it won't get any easier. Best get started.

Clean the handle first so you can hold the knife without getting grime all over your hands. Use hot, soapy water and a natural-bristle brush. A Mr. Clean Magic Eraser works wonders on heavily soiled handles. Be careful: A soapy knife is a slippery knife. Rinse and dry.

Attack built-up blood and glop in the joints between bolsters and handles, and in folding knife pivots, liners, and locks. Hair and tallow will hang on in every nook, cranny, and screw head. A cotton swab dipped in Dawn dishwashing liquid does wonders to loosen stubborn material and wipe away grease. Toothpicks won't scratch metal, and they can clear out the tightest spaces.

Once cleaned of all the icky stuff, wipe blades with a light oil and treat handles as described in the "Design Class–Handle Materials" section of this book.

055 CHOOSE THE RIGHT CARRY STYLE

Folding knives are hugely popular, but there's a decision to make in how you carry one: tip down or tip up?

STOW IT DOWN Many prefer tip-down carry for safety reasons. If the blade were to open slightly in your pocket, tip-down carry helps prevent the accidental slicing of your fingertips. Assisted-opening knives should be carried tip down for this reason. To deploy a tip-down folder, place your thumb on the knife scale facing your leg and two fingers on the clip, then draw. As the knife comes out of your pocket, grasp the pivot point between your thumb and forefinger, and use your middle finger to catch the edge of the pocket clip and rotate the handle slightly into your palm, keeping your thumb on the opening stud or hole. You're now ready to open the knife.

KEEP IT UP The tip-up position allows for very rapid deployment, especially of flipper knives. To deploy a tip-up folder, reach into your pocket and slide your thumb down the handle almost to the pivot point, with other fingers on the clip side of the handle. When the knife comes out of your pocket, it's in position to open.

056 TIGHTEN TINY SCREWS FOR GOOD

To keep a pocket clip from loosening and falling off, treat the clip screws with a thread-locker like blue Loctite 243. Before removing the pocket clip, place the knife in a small box so you won't lose the tiny clip screws as you back them out. Be sure to use the correct bit driver. Clips on most quality knives are attached with small Torx screws, but the screw head indents can get gunked up, causing you to think a smaller-size driver is the right one. Find what you think is the right size, then try one size larger. Remove the screws, clean them, then place a tiny drop of thread-locker on the threads of each screw as you replace it. The compound will set the screws with a tight grip.

057 RIG A WAVE OPENER

One slick modification for tip-up knives, especially Spyderco knives with an opening hole, is to use a cable tie (or a bit of 550 cord) to create a quick-opening feature similar to the famed Emerson Wave. Insert a small cable tie through the opening hole and cinch it down tightly so that the tie's lock is on the same side as the knife's clip. Cut the tie's tail flush. You might need a second cable tie to keep the first from wiggling around. As you pull the knife from your pocket, let the cable ties catch the back corner of the pocket seam. Pull the knife down slightly with a snap to the wrist, and the blade will open completely. With practice, deployment can be impressively instantaneous.

058 TEST YOUR KNIFE THE *FIELD & STREAM* WAY

Knives tested by *Field & Stream* must endure a real-world torture chamber before they make it into the magazine. Here are three trials you can put your own knives through to see how they measure up.

HOLD TIGHT To test grip, place the knife in a small plastic tote with three strips of bacon. Shake and shimmy for 30 seconds. Grab the knife by the handle and evaluate its in-hand feel. This test is meant to simulate field dressing an animal.

HANG TOUGH To assess cutting ability, toughness, and edge retention, slice through old carpet scraps so nasty you wouldn't walk on them with bare feet. Then, work the blade through a half-inch stack of leather.

HOLD THE EDGE Finally, test the knife to see if it will cleanly slice and lift words of type from the page of a copy of *Field & Stream*.

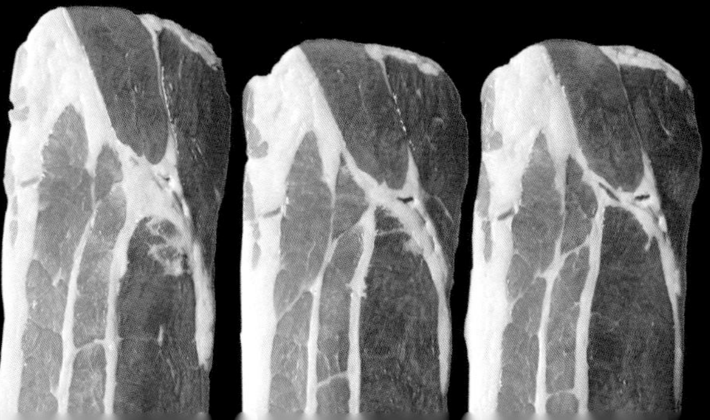

HUNTING & FISHING

→ IN THIS SECTION →

AFTER THE SHOT:

FIELD-DRESSING BIG GAME

HOG WILD:

HUNT PIGS WITH A KNIFE

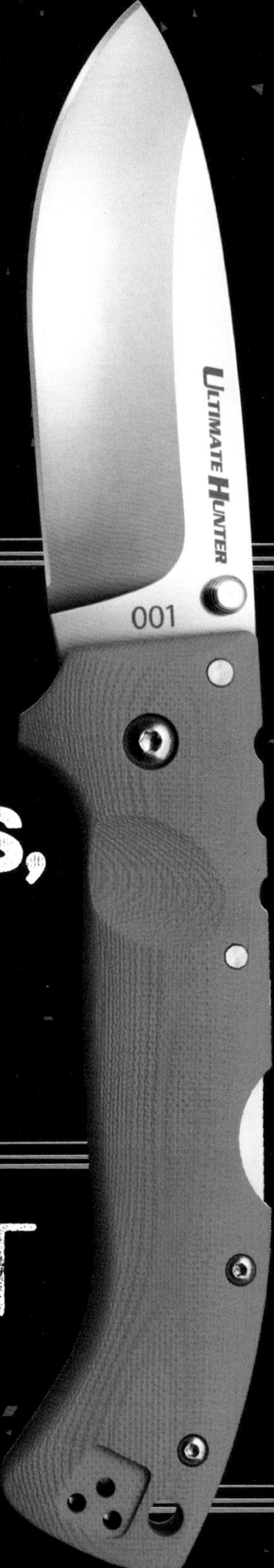

BUTCHER DEER, SQUIRRELS, RABBITS, DUCKS

AND MORE!

NOW CLEAN THIS:

BREAM, CATFISH & TROUT

COMPLETE GUIDE TO FILLET KNIVES

TO GUT HOOK

OR NOT TO GUT HOOK?

059 DRESS BIG GAME WITH ONE KNIFE

The plan came together just as you drew it up, and now there's a deer on the ground. Or maybe it's an elk or an antelope or a wild pig. Doesn't matter. The basics of field-dressing big game are the same. First, wrestle the animal onto its back–head uphill if possible. Next, pull out your knife and get to it.

You'll want a knife with a well-honed drop-point blade, a sharp tip, and a nonslip handle. You don't need a lot of belly in a gutting blade–that comes in handy later when skinning.

STEP 1 Insert your knife half an inch from the anus and cut all the way around it.

STEP 2 Starting at "X," nick the belly with the tip of your knife. Work the index and middle fingers of your off hand into the slit, make a "V," and position the knife blade–edge up–between your fingers. As you slide the knife forward, use your fingers to pull the hide and abdominal wall upward and away from the gut cavity to prevent cutting into the innards. Do the same for a doe, but cut around the udder.

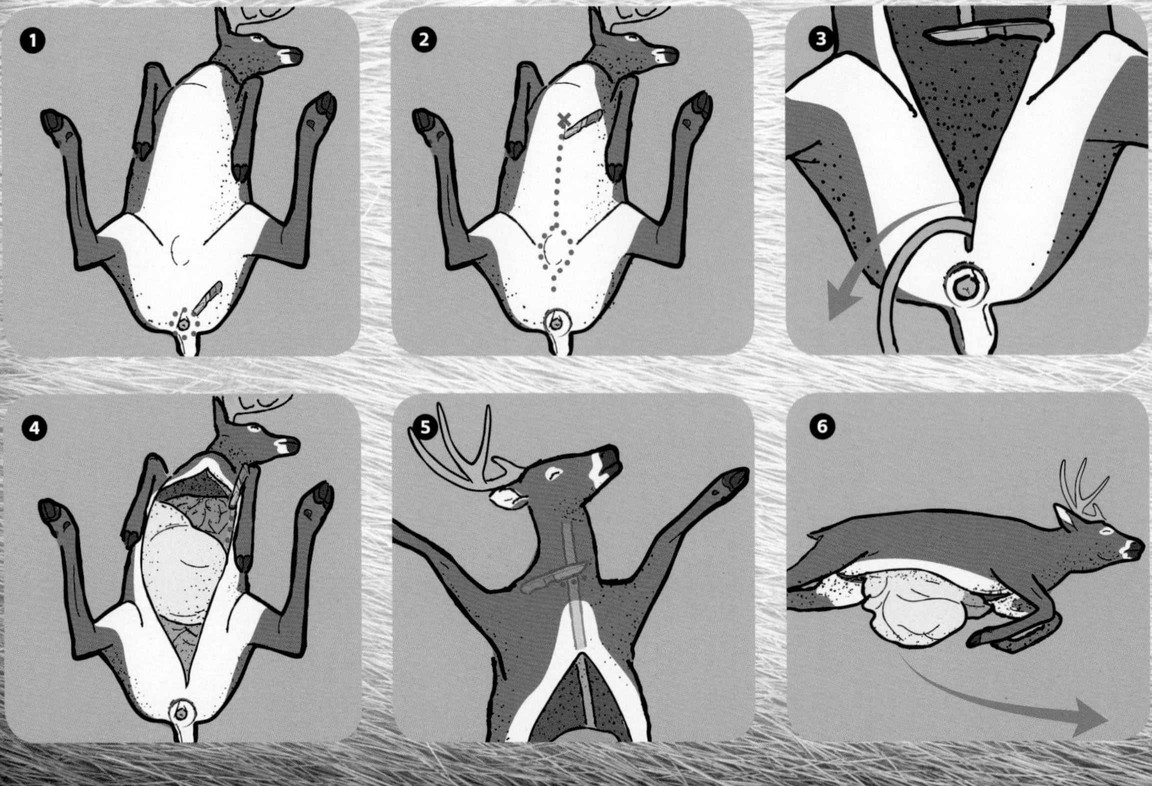

STEP 3 Pull down on the urethra as you make careful cuts on either side to free it. Stop just above the anus without severing it.

STEP 4 Cut all the way around the diaphragm to free it from the abdominal wall.

STEP 5 Reach into the chest cavity with your non-knife hand and grasp the windpipe. You'll likely have to get elbow-deep. The windpipe will feel like a ridged hose. Carefully bring your knife up and sever the windpipe.

STEP 6 Roll the animal onto its side. Pull the windpipe, lungs, and heart free, cutting away any connective tissue. Pull and roll the guts out of the belly. Carefully pull the rectum and urethra from the pelvic canal, using your knife to free it from any remaining connective tissue. Finally, lift the head and chest off the ground to drain the blood. Rinse the cavity or wipe it free of blood.

060 DECIDE IF A GUT HOOK IS RIGHT FOR YOU

Some game knives feature a gut hook, which is an oval or C-shaped semicircle ground and sharpened into the spine near the blade tip. It's designed to be hooked into a small incision in the belly hide and easily pulled like a zipper through the hide without nicking or cutting the animal's entrails. A sharp, well-designed gut hook will open up an animal quickly and cleanly, but it's a specialized feature with few other uses. On the downside, a gut hook can be difficult to sharpen and weakens the overall strength of the knife blade. In addition to knives with integral gut hooks, there are many dedicated gut hooks available. These sharp, slim, specialized tools are often more efficient than gut hooks found on knife blades. Some bird-cleaning knives come with a different kind of gut hook: a wire bent into a J-shape. To use a bird gut hook, the hook is pushed into the bird's vent, twisted inside the gut cavity, and then pulled back out of the vent. Done correctly, the bird's entrails are easily pulled free of the body.

061 SPLIT A RIB CAGE WITH A KNIFE

If you're not saving an animal's cape for a shoulder mount, splitting the rib cage makes it easier to remove the windpipe (which can spoil quickly) and allows you to wedge the rib cage open with a stick to aid in cooling the meat. A stout hunting knife and an off-center cut gets the job done.

STEP 1 Start with the animal on its back. Make a cut along one side of the breastbone, where the costal cartilages connect the ribs to the sternum.

STEP 2 Face the critter's head and straddle the carcass so that the bottom edge of the sternum is between your knees. Grip the knife firmly with your strong hand (blade pointing up), and your off hand positioned aft of the pommel like a saucer under a cup.

STEP 3 Insert the point of the knife under the sternum an inch to the side of the bony edge. Keep your arms relatively straight and pull the knife up and away from your face. It should slice though the cartilage of a rib or two. Continue through the last rib.

STEP 4 Finally, prop the rib cage open with a clean stick.

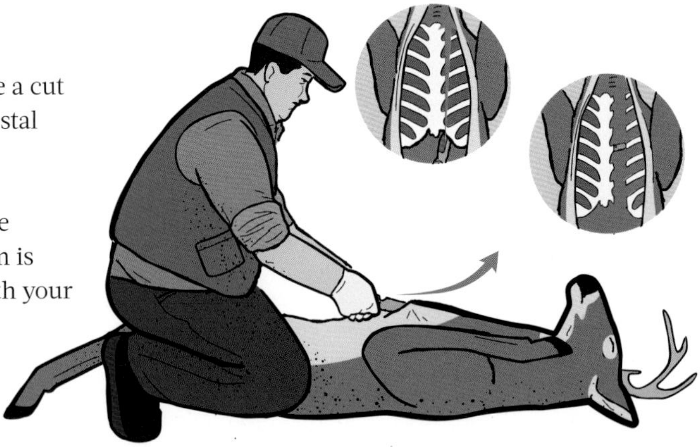

062 BUTCHER A DEER HAM

Boning out an entire deer ham is quick and easy, and results in tender cuts of meat void of the bone meal and marrow you get when sawing through bone.

STEP 1 Place the skinned leg of a deer on a sturdy table, with the outside of the leg facing up. Slice through the silverskin along the natural seam between the top round and the sirloin tip. Use the top of the knife to free the muscle from the bone. Cut the top round off at the back of the leg.

STEP 2 Remove the remaining silverskin. Cut the rump roast away from the top of the hip bone.

STEP 3 Turn the leg over. Using your fingers, separate the bottom round from the sirloin tip at the natural seam. Cut the bottom round from the bone. Then, cut the sirloin tip from the bone.

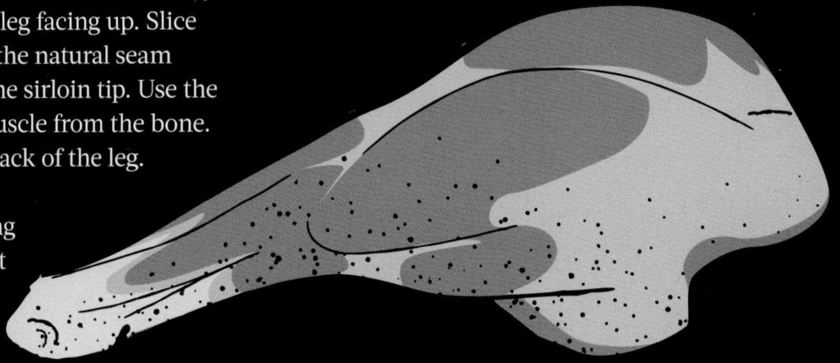

063 REMOVE THE BACKSTRAPS

Backstraps are the real trophy of any deer. To remove them cleanly and easily, start by hanging the animal by its hind legs and removing the shoulders. You'll want a boning knife with a slightly flexible blade for claiming the straps.

STEP 1 Insert the knife to one side of the spine right in the middle of the deer. Keep the blade tight against the vertebrae and cut down to the neck. Turn the knife around and extend the cut to the hindquarters until the knife hits the pin bone of the hip.

STEP 2 Cut across the backstrap at the top of the hip. Insert the knife tip into the top of the backstrap where it meets the vertebral processes and free a couple of the topmost inches from the bone, moving away from the spine. Establish the full width of the backstrap and use one hand to hold the freed backstrap away from the bone. With the blade pointing down, carefully fillet the backstrap from the spine, using the flexible blade tip to retain as much meat as possible.

STEP 3 Make the final cut across the backstrap near the front shoulder. It should fall into your hands. Repeat on the other side.

064 CUT OUT THE TENDERLOINS

The tenderloins lie underneath the backbone and extend from the last ribs to a point between the hams. Some people try to pull these tender cuts out with fingers, but doing so increases the risk of leaving a few morsels behind. It's easiest to cut the tenderloins from a gutted, hanging deer. You'll want a thin, flexible blade to ride close to the bone, with a sharp tip that will slide easily along the rounded pelvic bone.

STEP 1 Use your fingers and a knife to clear away fat and connective tissue from the two tenderloins, which are 10 to 14 inches long.

STEP 2 Use a forefinger to free the tenderloin from the side of the backbone. Cut across the top.

STEP 3 Work the knife tip underneath the tenderloin, which lies along the 5 short spinal processes behind the last rib. Slice it free.

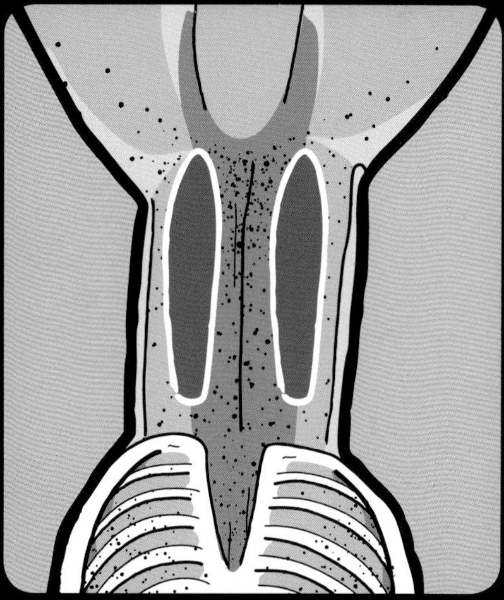

065 CUT UP A DUCK (OR GOOSE OR SWAN)

The best knife for fowl is a short fillet knife or a larger paring knife to retain as much meat as possible. Set the bird on a cutting board, breast side up, legs down.

REMOVE THE LEGS Push the top of the drumstick away from the breast and cut through the skin and thigh to the socket at the hip. Snap the leg joint. Work the knife tip into the joint, then orient it to slice under the oyster of meat atop the thigh and cut the leg free.

REMOVE THE WINGS Turn the bird over and cut each drumette free behind the shoulder blade.

REMOVE THE BREAST Turn the bird over again. Insert the knife tip just under the wishbone between the breast meat and the keel. Draw the knife to the bottom of the breastbone, blade as close to the keel as possible, and peel the bottom of the breast away from it. Work up to the wishbone and angle the knife point under it to capture as much meat as possible. Cut down to the armpit to free the entire fillet.

FINISH UP Repeat the leg and breast cuts; save the carcass for stock.

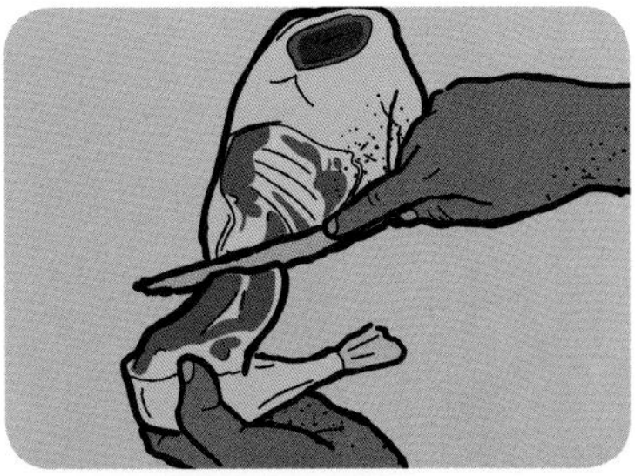

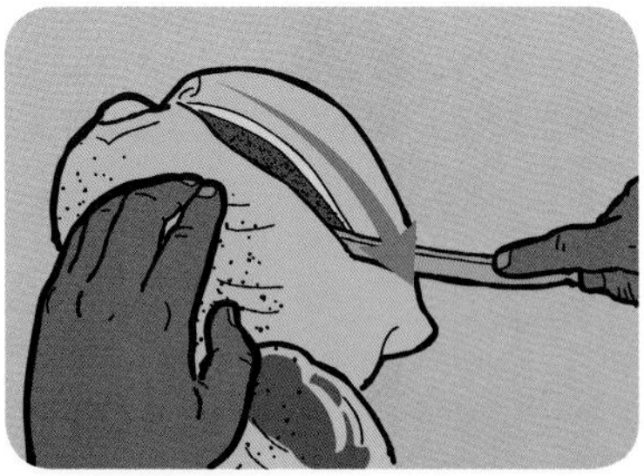

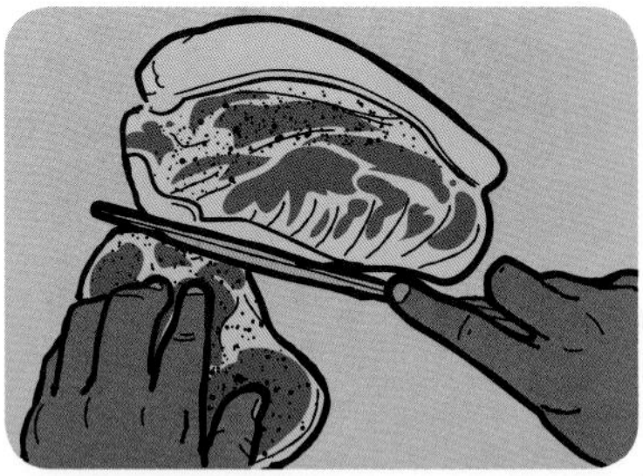

066 BUTCHER A SQUIRREL (OR RABBIT OR RACCOON)

Squirrels, rabbits, raccoons, opossums, beavers, groundhogs, and most other medium-size, four-legged mammals can be butchered into six separate pieces for easier cooking. Here's how.

STEP 1 Place a skinned and cleaned squirrel belly-up on a cutting board.

STEP 2 Gently press a back leg flat against the cutting board and slice through the inside of the leg to expose the ball-and-socket joint. Snap the leg joint. Use the tip of the knife to sever the joint, then flip the squirrel over. Pull up on the leg and slice downward against the backbone to free the leg. Repeat with the other leg.

STEP 3 Lift a front leg and cut behind the shoulder blade. You can free the entire leg without cutting bone. Repeat.

STEP 4 Hold the remaining carcass in two hands and bend it sharply to crack the spine. Use a sharp knife to sever the saddle into two pieces.

067 PREP A TURKEY FOR THE TABLE

Butchering a wild turkey isn't much different than cutting up a duck or goose, though you're left with a much larger pile of meat and more options for the cook.

A Leave one boneless breast fillet whole for smoking, grilling, or slow cooking.

B Slice one boneless breast fillet into cutlets for frying.

C Braise the legs low and slow for maximum tenderness. Or grind the dark meat for grilled wild turkey sliders.

D Fry turkey wings like chicken wings and you'll lose a couple teeth when you bite into them. Instead, season, batter, pan-fry, smother with gravy, and bake in an oven.

BLADES THAT MATTERED

OLD TIMER SHARPFINGER

Introduced in 1973, the Schrade Cutlery Model 1500 OT Sharpfinger was a sleek, wicked-looking, and affordable knife that doubled as a very useful field tool. In a break from a long string of large, Bowie-esque knives, the Sharpfinger was a special-purpose blade made for stripping the hide and removing the entrails from dead beasts. Its sharp tip was perfect for piercing soft belly tissue and tough outer hide. The sweeping belly of the blade made for a serviceable skinning tool. Early advertisements crowed that it was built "for small elephants and large squirrels." For a while, it seemed that half the hunters in America kept a Sharpfinger on their belt. The founder of the Hell's Angels motorcycle gang was a fan, too, which didn't hurt sales one bit. Schrade made Sharpfingers for nearly 30 years, and for most of that time the relatively short sheath knife was as much a staple of deer camp as red-and-back plaid and a Remington rifle. Eventually it was supplanted by the welcome embrace of the drop-point blade–a sort of new kid in knife town. When the Sharpfinger's trademark expired, plenty of Chinese knifemakers stepped up to the forge. Thankfully, Schrade is at it again, producing Sharpfingers in both original and larger versions.

068 KILL A WILD PIG WITH A KNIFE

The explosion of feral hogs across the country has given rise to great interest in that most primal of knife feats: Killing a dangerous animal with nothing but a blade. Sticking a wild pig with a knife is gruesome and edgy. Proceed with caution, but give it all you've got. Crawling up the body of a wild hog pinned down by raging dogs is no time for second thoughts and timidity.

APPROACH WITH CARE In most cases, the hog will be either bayed by dogs or fighting off hounds that already have hold of an ear or two. Assess the situation quickly. Dog handlers should pull hounds off the animal's rear quarters, giving you room to work. Approach from behind while the hog's attention is focused on the dogs, moving slowly so it won't sense danger. Be aware of trees, rocks, water, and thick vegetation–you don't want anything to prevent you from backing up quickly if things get out of hand. At this point, keep your knife sheathed.

GRAB ON QUICK In a swift, decisive move, grab both of the hog's hind legs above the hooves. Lift the animal like a wheelbarrow. And don't let go. The pig

will thrash, but most of its leverage and strength will have been taken away. Flip the animal on its side and immediately let go of the leg in your strong hand. Move up the body, pinning the hog down with your weight. Release the other hand and get a knee on the hog's shoulder. Remain aware of the dogs at all times, for your safety and theirs.

DELIVER THE COUP DE GRACE Unsheathe the knife and grasp the handle in your fist. Don't stab. With younger hogs, place the tip where you'd aim for a heart shot and use both hands to sink the blade to the hilt. Older hogs have a shield of gristle over their vitals, so insert the blade tip under the front armpit and angle it back toward the heart. Lever the blade back and forth; the heart will feel like a hard knot. Once the heart is cut, remove the knife to aid in bleeding. Stay aware of the dogs as the pig stills beneath you.

069 BRING THE RIGHT BLADE

Bringing down a hog with a knife demands not just the right approach, but the right knife–and a fairly big one at that. Look for a full-tang knife that has a sharp blade that's at least 5 inches long. In addition, it needs to have a sharp piercing tip, and the handle should be made of a material with a texture that won't slip, even in your blood-slicked hand. If you're choosing a knife strictly for putting down wild hogs, this is one instance when a sharpened spine can be a bonus. It will help with initial penetration and interior damage alike.

070 TAKE A KNIFE INVENTORY

These hunters have done their part–they are tagged out and headed back to a remote camp on Michigan's Upper Peninsula. The deer is field-dressed, but they're not finished with edged tools quite yet. They have more knife work to do, and they better hope they have the proper tools available. Before hunting season, take inventory of the knives and other tools on hand at camp and determine what knives, axes, hatchets, and saws you'll need. There's nothing more aggravating than learning that some camp member took off with the bone saw when there's a deer pelvis that needs splitting.

071 CLEAN A TROUT STREAMSIDE

There's no experience quite like eating a freshly-caught trout streamside. Of course, you'll need to clean it first, but these four steps should make that a snap.

STEP 1 Insert the tip of a pointed knife into the trout's anal vent and make a shallow slice up to the jaw at the gills.

STEP 2 Stick a finger from your nonknife hand into the trout's mouth and push down to make the jaw protrude. Work the knife tip through the thin skin under the lower jaw and slice toward the mouth to create a V-shaped tab across the chin.

STEP 3 Insert your finger through the chin cut and into the throat. Grasping the gills from the inside, pull firmly toward the tail. The gills, guts, and pectoral fin should come out in one clean shot.

STEP 4 Scrape the dark blood line away with your thumb. Give the fish a good rinse, and it's ready to cook.

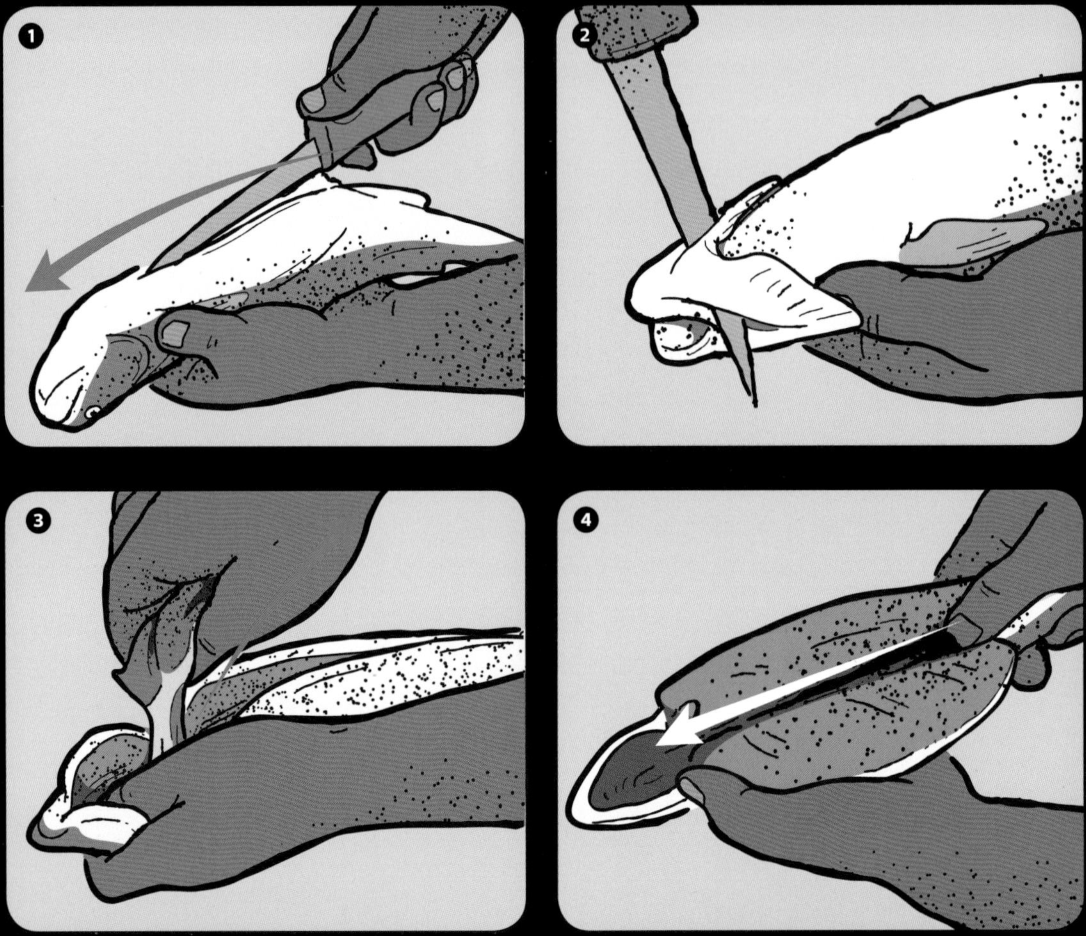

072 CLEAN A PANFISH WHOLE

This cleaning method works for just about any fish (though it's especially useful for panfish) and is the quickest route between pond and frying pan. The result is a whole, headless fish that retains the delicious skin and perhaps the best part of a fried bream or crappie–the crispy fins, a.k.a. Mother Nature's potato chips.

STEP 1 Scale the fish with the back of a fillet knife (the edge of a spoon works, too). Hold the tail firmly to a tabletop or counter and scrape toward the head. Don't overlook the belly and the top of the back. Rinse well.

STEP 2 Slip the knife blade under the pectoral fin and orient the knife at an angle in order to retain the fat meat behind the eye. Position the blade at a 45-degree angle to the fish's head and cut to the spine. Flip the fish over, cut, and repeat, but continue through the spine to completely sever the head from the body.

STEP 3 Gut the fish. Insert the knife tip into the anal vent and make a shallow cut all the way up the belly. Insert a finger and scrape away the entrails. Rinse and pat dry.

073 FILLET A PANFISH

If you're looking to fillet a panfish, scale it as described previously in item 072 and complete the steps up until you've cut to the spine. Then, continue with the steps below.

STEP 1 Without removing the knife, turn the blade so it lies flat along the spine with the cutting edge facing the tail. Cut with a slight sawing action toward the tail, severing the ribs. Lift the knife point slightly so the blade cuts as close to the top of the fish's back as possible. Run the knife blade all the way to a point a half-inch from the tail.

STEP 2 Leave this loose fillet attached and flip it so it's skin side down. Place the knife blade nearly flat on the tail portion of the fillet, press down, and slice between the meat and the skin to remove the fillet.

STEP 3 Remove the ribs by using the knife tip to free the rib cage from the meat, slicing carefully and as close to the bone as possible.

STEP 4 Flip the fish over and repeat on the other side.

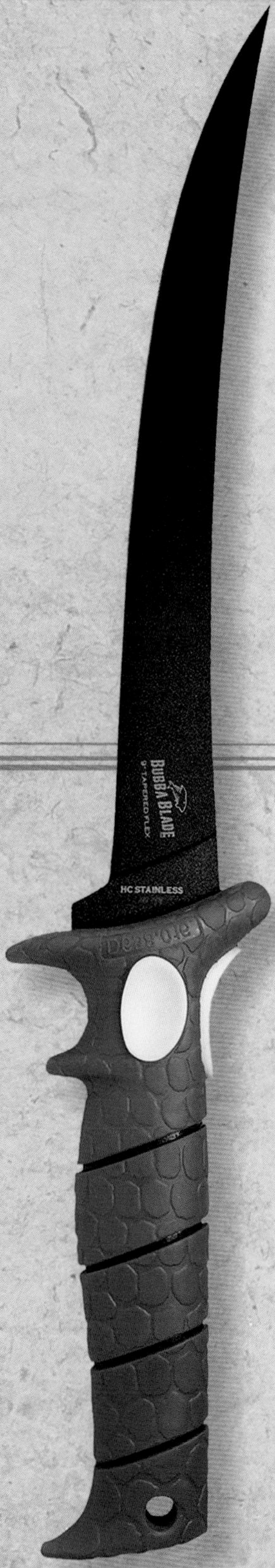

074 FIND YOUR FILLET KNIFE STYLE

It seems like a simple tool, but there's more to a fillet knife than a long, sharp edge.

TRY THE CLASSIC More than 40 million Rapala Fish-N-Fillet knives have made their way to riverbanks, lakeshores, and coastlines around the world. This classic birch-handled beauty comes with a tooled Laplander leather sheath and handy sharpener.

MEET THE UPSTART A growing favorite of guides and mates, Bubba Blade fillet knives aren't subtle, especially with a bright red handle. The flexible blade is coated to glide through meat, and thumb and finger pads in the rubberized handle give a sure grip no matter how many crappies you clean. Bubba Blades come in both flexible and "Stiffie" blades in varying lengths.

HANG ONTO AN HEIRLOOM The Rapala Marttiini Witch's Tooth Collectors Fillet Knife is made at the Marttiini knifeworks in Finland. This beauty is built with a premium, hand-ground stainless-steel blade and a handle of curly birch and reindeer antler. A rattle in the handle is said to drive evil spirits away, leaving the knife user in peace.

075 PLUG IT IN

When you've loaded a cooler with a few limits of walleyes, going electric saves time and hassle. There are plenty of cheap electric fillet knives, but you're better off with an upgrade.

POWER UP The heavy-duty motor in a high-end model drives the blade through tough skin and bones, and keeps the knife from overheating when you're working through a pile of fish worthy of a church supper.

GO PORTABLE Knives powered with rechargeable batteries are super convenient for camp use, but make sure the knife motor is beefy enough to handle more than just a single serving of fish.

SWAP BLADES Electric knives that come with blades of different sizes enable you to fillet both perch and wahoo with ease.

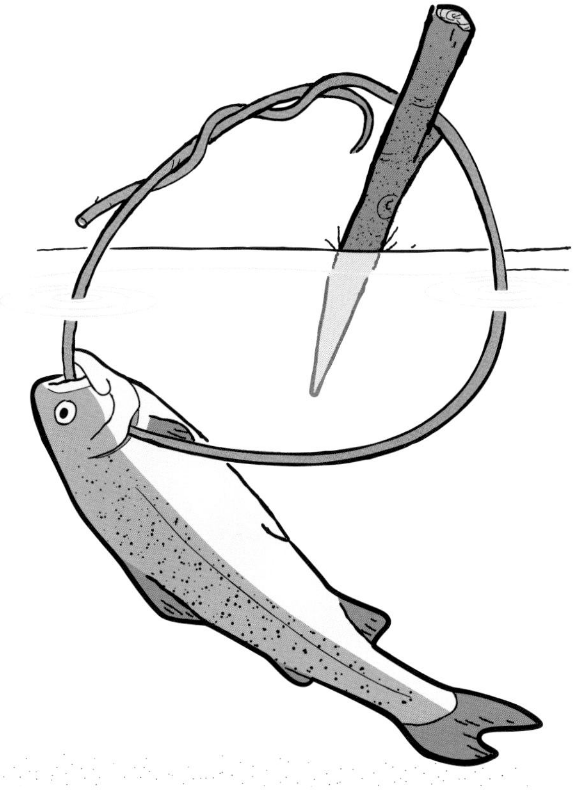

076 MAKE A STRINGER ON THE FLY

Left your fish stringer at home? As long as you have a knife and you're not fishing on the moon, you can easily make a stringer on the fly. Cut a wooden stake about a foot long and sharpen one end. Then, cut a 3-foot-long piece of a thin green tree branch. Bend it into a circle, twisting the ends around each other so they hold the round shape. Drive the stake into the ground beside cool, shallow water. When you catch a fish, unwind the tree branch, thread one end through the fish's gills and out the mouth, and retwist the ends. Hook the round branch over the wooden stake so the fish remains in the cool water. It's that easy.

BLADES THAT MATTERED

D.H. RUSSELL CANADIAN BELT KNIFE

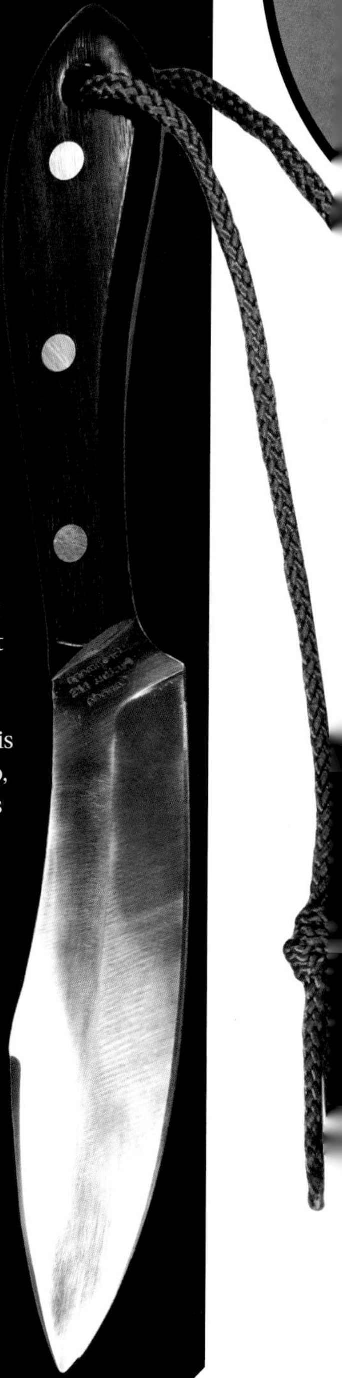

In 1957, a Czech immigrant and a Toronto cutler teamed up to produce a curious knife with an elliptical blade and an offset handle that has become a Canadian icon and one of North America's finest all-around knife designs. The knifemaker was Rudolph Grohmann. The cutler was D.H. Russell. The blade they created is known by two names: the D.H. Russell Canadian Belt Knife and the Grohmann #1. It's been copied by dozens of manufacturers, but the original has been in constant production in Nova Scotia for more than 60 years.

There's a great story about this knife that has, as great stories do, as least some truth to it. It seems that someone took an ill-used Grohmann to a bladesmith for a rebuild and ordered a custom knife to handle camping and skinning work. When he returned to pick up his new knife, the bladesmith gave him his reworked Grohmann with the admonition: There is nothing better I could do. Honest words. The Grohmann #2 Trout and Bird Knife is slightly smaller than the original, with the same materials and build, and is an even better fish-cleaning blade.

077 CLEAN A CATFISH

They say there's more than one way to skin a cat. A knife, pliers, a 2×6, and a tailgate or picnic table are all you really need to skin a catfish.

STEP 1 Use a sharp knife to score the skin around the head in front of the gill plates. Make another slit down the back to the tail. Drive a nail through the fish's skull and into the board. Cut off the dorsal fin.

STEP 2 Brace the board against your waist, with the fish's tail near your body. Grasp the skin near the head with your pliers and peel it back toward the tail. The skin may come off whole or in several strips.

STEP 3 Remove the fish from the board, grasp the head in one hand and the body in the other, and bend the head down sharply to break the spine. Bend the body up and twist to separate the head from the body. Most of the guts will come out with the head, but use your knife to split the belly open and clean any that remain inside.

078 LEARN FISH FILLET ORIGAMI

The inconsistent thickness of many fish cuts makes cooking a challenge. The tail portion of a fish fillet is thinner than the body meat, as are the belly flaps on larger fish such as salmon. A sharp knife and a bit of piscatorial origami will fold a fish fillet into a single piece of flesh with a similar thickness for cooking perfection. Here's how.

FULL-LENGTH FILLET Skin the fillet–otherwise the skin will be trapped inside the fold and create a mushy layer. Make a deep, crosswise scoring cut a little past the halfway point of the fillet toward the tail. Fold the tail portion under the thicker portion to create a single thickness.

SALMON-SHAPED CUT The belly flaps are a fraction of the thickness of the body meat. Score each belly flap lengthwise where it begins to thin and fold it under the body meat.

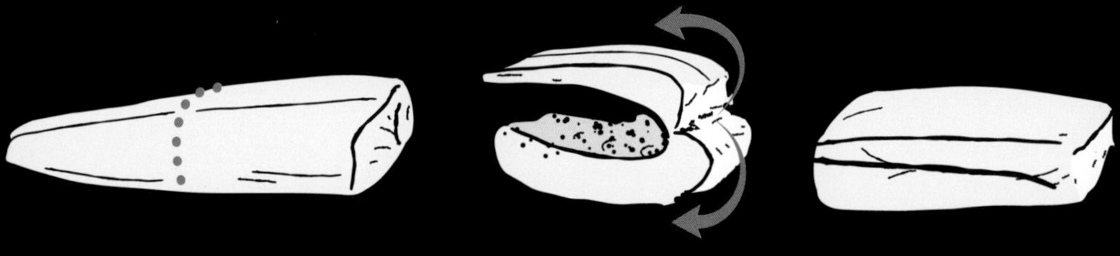

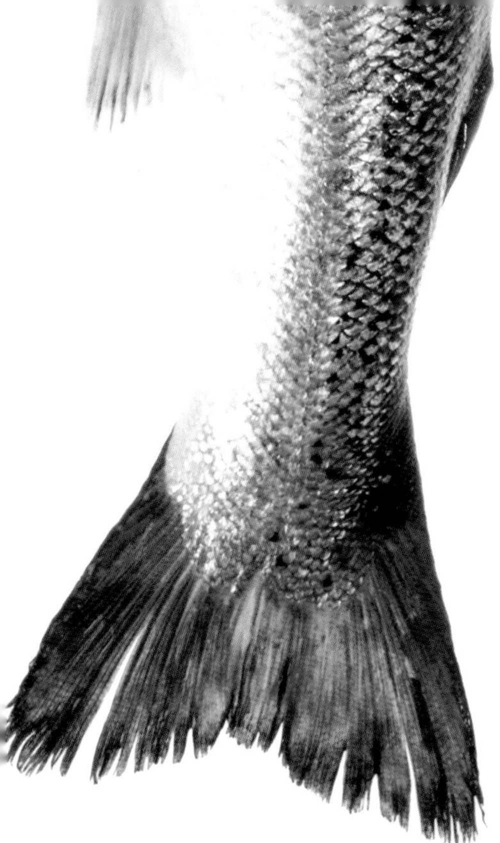

079 TURN A FISH FILLET INTO A STEAK

Thick, skin-on chunks of large fish are often too thick to cook. Butterfly the fillets by splitting the thick steak lengthwise without cutting through the skin. Then, simply fold each piece to the outside to capture the skin in the middle of the steak.

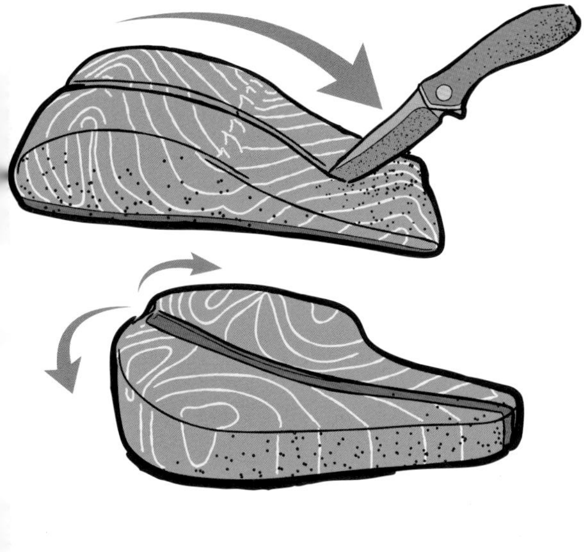

080 REMOVE A NORTHERN PIKE'S Y-BONES

A northern pike's Y-bones, embedded in the dorsal part of the fillet, discourage many anglers from dining on one of the tastiest fish around. A sharp knife is all you need to remove them.

STEP 1 Fillet the fish and remove the ribs from the fillet as you would with any other fish.

STEP 2 Find the row of white dots visible midway between the spine and the top of the fillet. These are the tips of the Y-bones. Slice along the top of these dots, nearly through the fillet, following the curve of the bones.

STEP 3 Next, slice along the bottom of the Y-bones, following their shape, while aiming the knife tip toward the first incision.

STEP 4 Connect the two cuts at the tail of the fish, remove the bony strip, and then get the grease popping.

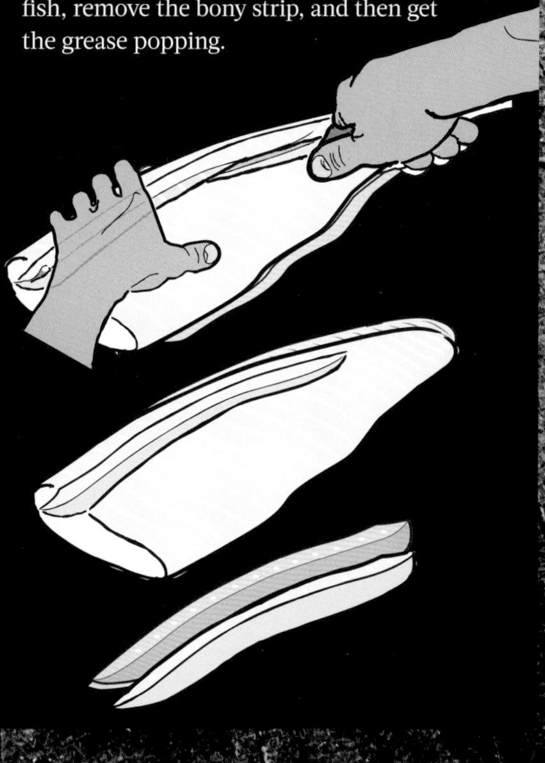

WILD KITCHEN

→ IN THIS SECTION →

GET GRAINY:
HE SCIENCE OF LICING JERKY

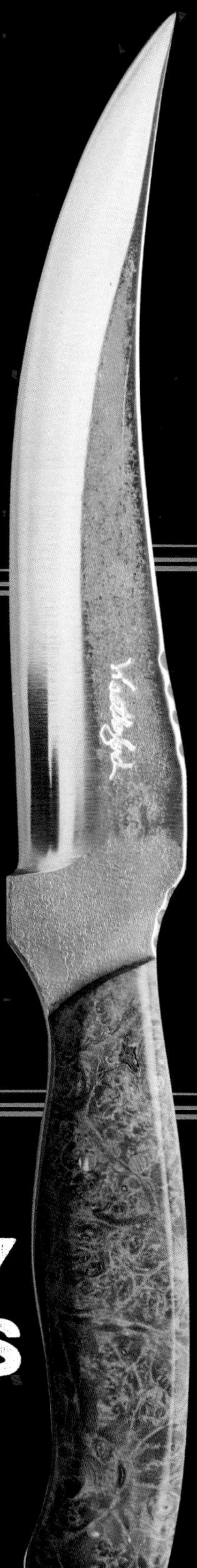

THE BEST CUTS FOR FISH & GAME
PLUS: PREPARATION TIPS AND TRICKS

DOS & DON'TS
OF WILD FORAGING

BLADE +FISH +FIRE= FEAST

STICK FIGURES
CARVE DIY ROTISSERIES
(LET'S EAT.)

THE HISTORIC LAGUIOLE KNIFE

081 SPIT-ROAST A BUNNY

Roasting a whole rabbit–or any small-game animal–on a horizontal campfire rotisserie is about as easy as throwing an atlatl. The biggest issue is that the legs and loins cook at different rates. The key is to stuff the rabbit with a moist dressing, wrap it with bacon to keep it from drying out, and lock the rotisserie in place for minutes at a time for even cooking of each side.

STEP 1 Use a sharp knife to cut three green sticks: two forked uprights and another for the spit.

STEP 2 Stuff a cleaned rabbit with a mixture of figs, thyme, and olive oil; secure the legs and torso with kitchen twine.

STEP 3 Wrap with bacon and truss with twine to keep the bacon in place.

STEP 4 Roast each side. To prevent the rotisserie from spinning, knot the spit with kitchen twine to one side of the V of the forked stick.

082 BUTTERFLY A BACKSTRAP

When most folks think of butterflied loin, they imagine chops sliced nearly all the way through and spread out in a steaklike fashion. That's not what we're talking about. To butterfly an entire backstrap–or least a sizable 10 inches or so–allows the cook to stuff it with cream cheese, jalapeños, fruit chutneys, and other blissful items, then close it up with butcher's twine and grill or roast. There's nothing better.

To butterfly a backstrap, you'll want a sharp knife with a long, thin blade, like a boning knife. With the backstrap laid flat on a table, place the palm of your free hand on top of the meat, press down slightly, and slice horizontally through the middle of the backstrap, almost but not quite all the way through. Stop a half-inch from the far side. Now you can open the cut like a book and fill it with awesomeness.

083 COOK DUCK ON A STICK

Cook a whole duck on a stick and the bird self-bastes in its own dripping fat, which scorches in the fire and sends plumes of seasoning smoke wafting around the meat. The only utensil you need is a knife.

STEP 1 Cut an inch-thick green stick about 18 to 24 inches long. Sharpen one end.

STEP 2 Gut and pluck the duck. Remove the feet and wings.

STEP 3 Butterfly the duck through the breast, not the back. To do this, insert a stout knife along one side of the breastbone keel, cutting all the way to the backbone. Loosen up the bones and flesh by working the duck back and forth in your hands, like you're trying to break a stick. Place it on a flat surface and press down with the palm of your hand.

STEP 4 Skewer the duck by running the stick in and out of the breast meat on one side of the keel, then the other.

STEP 5 Anchor the stick in the ground at a 45-degree angle to the fire, 6 inches to a foot away from the heat source. Cook with the breast side to the fire first and rotate once.

084 CUT JERKY MEAT

Jerky aficionados have been known to come to blows when discussing the "correct" way to slice jerky meat–with the grain, or across it. But really, there's no argument. Do it both ways.

The grain of the meat is easy to see: It's the direction the muscle fibers run within each cut of meat. Slicing meat parallel to the grain results in jerky that won't fall apart, though it will tend to be chewy. Slicing jerky meat across the grain results in more-tender jerky, but if it's too tender the pieces tend to crumble. When prepping your next batch of jerky, cut half the meat with the grain and the other half across it. Then you'll have the choice of a quick bite of tender jerky or a long, satisfying chew.

No matter which you prefer, there are two tricks to getting evenly sliced pieces of jerky meat for the smoker or dehydrator. First, wrap the meat in plastic wrap and place it in the freezer for 30 minutes. Chilled, firm meat will be much easier to slice. Second, keep a small dish filled with canola or olive oil handy. While slicing, smear an occasional dab of oil on the blade to help it slide through the meat.

085 SPATCHCOCK A DUCK

The best way to grill a whole duck–or any game bird–is to first spatchcock the carcass. Don't worry; it only sounds illegal. What you're doing is flattening the bird so that it can be grilled or otherwise cooked whole in one relatively uniform piece. And it's easy: Clean and rinse a plucked duck and place it breast down on a cutting board. Insert the tip of the knife into the gut cavity to one side of the tail, with the edge facing up. Cut all the way up one side of the backbone to the neck, then repeat on the other side of the backbone. Dispose of the backbone and tail. Next, flip the bird over so it's breast side up. Pull the two sides of the back out to either side and press the breast firmly with your hand or flatten it with a heavy plate.

086 USE A KNIFE TO PLANK A FISH

PREP THE PLANK Soak a ¾- to 1-inch-thick plank of aromatic wood in water for one to two hours (if you don't have a plank, split a log in half and use the flat surface for cooking). Cedar is the classic choice, and hardwoods such as oak and hickory work great, but avoid resinous pines and firs. Whittle half a dozen two-inch wooden pegs, each with one sharp end. Toss the pegs into the water with the plank. Preheat the plank or log by placing it upright near the fire until it is very hot.

READY THE FISH Season the fish to taste and lay it on the plank, either whole or skin side down. Use the point of a knife to poke through the fish to mark where the pegs will go. Remove the fish, then use your knife point to auger a starter hole for each peg. Replace the fish and tap the pegs into place with the knife handle.

PROP THE PLANK Push the plank or log into place, chocking with rocks or sticks so that the fish stays vertical. Cook until the flesh flakes in the thickest part of the fish.

087 SCORE A FISH FOR FRYING

Using a sharp knife to score the flesh of your fish can help it fry more quickly and with a more satisfying crunch. Spices and seasonings penetrate more deeply, and the cuts allow rendered fat to drain away, making the skin crispy.

First, make cuts perpendicular to the backbone, an inch apart, from head to tail. On firm-fleshed fish you can cut all the way to the spine. On less meaty fish, such as panfish and trout, cut just a quarter of an inch into the flesh. Season and bread the fillets, then fry in hot oil.

088 OPEN A BREW

With a minute's practice you can open a beer bottle with most any knife blade, though one with a narrow, sharp blade like a fillet knife isn't safe to use with this technique.

Hold the neck of the bottle firmly, with the top of your hand just under the bottom of the cap. Place the back of the knife blade across the top of the third knuckle of your index finger and wedge it under the cap. Pry the cap off with a satisfying "pop" and enjoy!

089 COOK A FISH ON A SWORD

Espeto de sardinas–fish on a sword–is a famed Spanish cooking technique, and it's still common to see fish prepared this way along Spain's coast. Traditionally, whole, clean fish are threaded onto a sword, which is propped–handle down–over an open fire. The fish then cook and baste in their own juices. However, swords aren't very prevalent these days, especially ones suited to be stuck into a fire handle first. But you can fake it by using your knife to cut a green stick with a branch stub near the "handle" end. Skewer seasoned fish onto the "blade" and prop the "sword" over hot coals.

090 HARVEST WILD RAMPS

Ramps are one of the first wild greens to appear in spring in eastern North America, and these onionlike leeks are hugely popular with foragers. That makes sustainable harvest all the more important, because it's easy to wipe out an entire ramp patch for good without even realizing it if you're careless.

DIG IN Use a stick or trowel to carefully scrape away the dirt at the base of each individual ramp plant, one at a time. Your goal is to expose the bulb without disturbing its roots .

CUT CAREFULLY Use a foraging knife or similar short-bladed knife to slice through the bulb, leaving the bottom third still rooted in the ground.

LEAVE NO TRACE Move the dirt back over the bulb, tamp it down slightly, and cover the site with leaves.

091 CUT WILD MUSHROOMS

Foraging for wild edibles is a logical next step for hunters and anglers. After all, gathering food from the wilds is another expression of self-reliance and outdoors capability. It makes sense that there are knives made specifically for foraging.

When it comes to harvesting wild mushrooms, there are two schools of thought. One camp holds that it is best to twist and pull the entire mushroom from the ground. This keeps the mycelium–the mass of reproductive structures attached to the mushroom stalk–embedded to the stalk. Others believe it's best to carefully cut the stalk and leave the mycelium in the soil. Each approach has pros and cons, and discussions among ardent foragers can get heated over which approach is better. For knife fans, however, it's a slam dunk: Any chance to use a cool knife is worth the taking. A dedicated foraging knife is made with a curved blade to hook around the plant stalk and an attached brush on the other end of the knife that is used to tidy up the mushroom.

BLADES THAT MATTERED

LAGUIOLE KNIFE

The esteemed Laguiole is not a brand or a manufacturer, but a style of knife rooted in the French knife-making region around the villages of Laguiole and Thiers. Originally designed for shepherds in the 19th century, the traditional Laguiole knife has a single blade that folds into a slim, sinuous handle. The knife's backspring is tipped with a welded or forged bee. Set into the handle scales on one side of the knife are tiny metal pins inlaid in the form of a cross.

When traveling in remote regions, shepherds would plant the knife in a piece of bread and face the cross for their prayers. There may be no finer waterfowling blade, as the spear point and flexible steel will separate breast meat from bone like nobody's business. But buyers beware: Knockoffs abound. Authentic Laguiole knives bear the words "France" or "Made in France" on the blade.

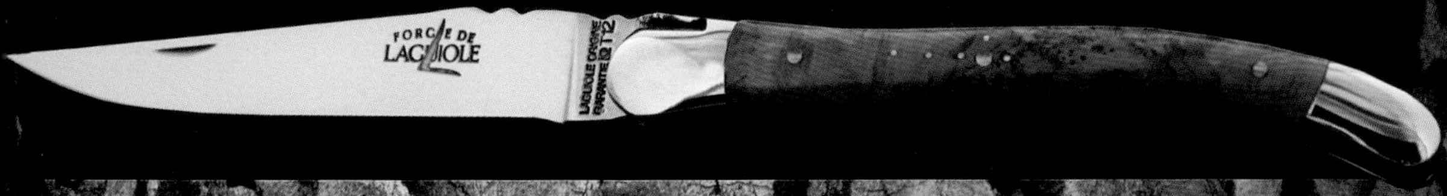

CAMPING

→ IN THIS SECTION →

YOUNG BLADES:

CHOOSE THE RIGHT KNIFE FOR EVERY AGE

SIGNAL A PLANE WITH A KNIFE

(AND A PINE TREE AND A MATCH)

THE TWO WHITTLING STROKES YOU MUST KNOW

MAKE A KNIFE OUT OF POOP

THE KNIFE AS AX:

SPLIT LOGS, CARVE TINDER, FELL A TREE

MAKE THE COOLEST WOODEN TOY EVER

092 MASTER THE CHEST LEVER GRIP

The chest lever knife grip is a controlled stroke that allows you to direct serious power when sharpening stakes, trimming branches, or cutting notches into sticks too thick or tough for simple whittling. The grip gets its oomph from the simultaneous use of arm, chest, and back muscles, but since the knife stays relatively stationary, this is one of the safest cutting techniques.

STEP 1 Start by holding the knife so that the edge faces away from you. Bring your knife hand to your chest and support it against your lower rib. Your other hand holds the stick.

STEP 2 Bring the stick under the blade as your hands nearly meet at chest level.

STEP 3 Bite the blade edge into the wood, lock your elbows, then contract your back muscles as you push your chest forward. This will allow your chest to act as a lever and increase the force on the cutting edge of the blade.

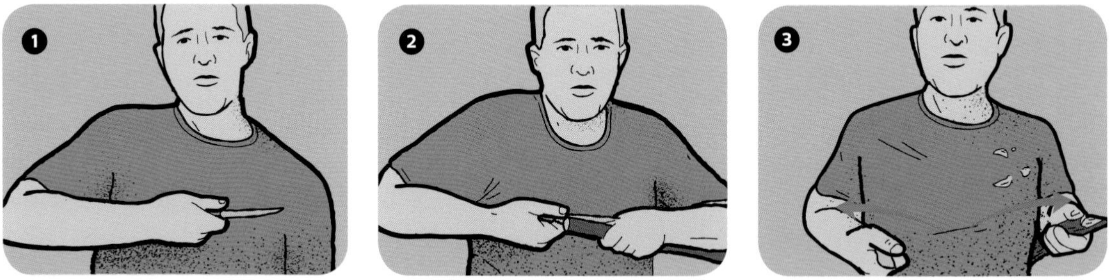

093 CARVE A FUZZ STICK

A fuzz stick, also called a feather stick, is a super tool for starting a blaze, but making one requires a little work. Here's how to carve a mass of thin, spark-catching curls. Flat-ground blades work better than hollow-ground blades, but experiment to find a knife you can control with steady pressure.

STEP 1 Split a foot-long length of knot-free, straight-grained wood from a larger chunk of pine, spruce, or aspen. Its sides should be 1 to $1^{1}/_{2}$ inches wide.

STEP 2 Place one end of the stick against a tree. Hold it in place with your chest at a 45-degree angle or press it firmly against a chopping block. Lock your wrist and use slow, steady pressure to push the blade down a corner edge of the stick to shave a thin, curly strip, being careful not to remove the strip.

STEP 3 Bring the knife back to the starting point, rotate the stick slightly, and carve another strip. Avoid sawing back and forth. Point the knife tip down and curls will come off to the right. Point the tip up and those curls will shave off to the left.

STEP 4 Create curls along most of the length of the stick, finishing with short, superfine curls to help catch a spark.

094 SPLIT A LOG WITH A KNIFE

A strong knife can be used to split a round of firewood in a pinch. You'll need a stout blade with a full tang that can take some pounding. Use it to cut a dense wood baton, then bring it to bear on the log.

Set the blade on the end of a log round a few inches from the edge. Press it into the wood and use the baton to chip U-shaped shingles from the log. Use the knife to form each shingle into a wedge. Insert the wedges into an existing lengthwise crack in the log. If no crack exists, you'll have to make one with your blade and baton. Hammer the wedges with the baton until the log splits. You can then split each half to create four log quarters. Use the knife and baton to split kindling and shave tinder.

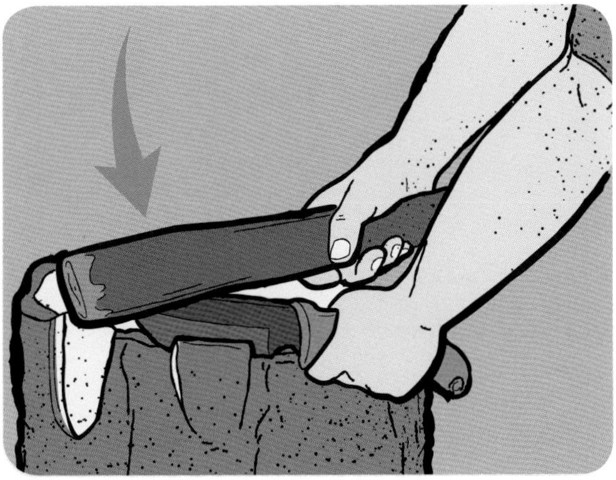

FEATS of STEEL

MAKE A CRAPPY KNIFE

If you've ever wondered if you are as tough, cunning, and resourceful as an Inuit, here's your answer. Residents of Arctic Bay, in Nunavut, Canada, told the adventurer and ethnographer Wade Davis about a man who had a rather impressive reaction to forced relocation. When the Canadian government was moving the Inuit into settlements in the 1950s, one old man said, essentially, "Bite me." His family was afraid he might do something rash, so they gathered up all the old man's tools and gear as a way to force him to move to the Arctic suburbs with the rest of the family.

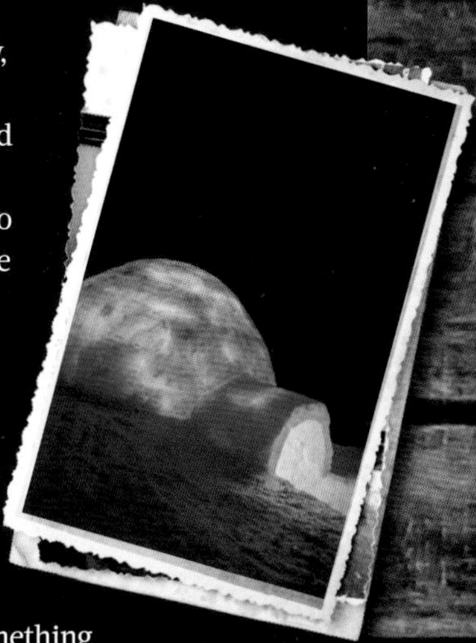

As one might imagine of a man who had long made a living in the harshest environment on the planet, the Inuit elder wasn't keen on leaving his home and was less enamored of being told what to do. So, he bolted from the family igloo in the middle of the night. Once outside, he dropped his caribou and sealskin drawers. The man had a plan. He shat into his own hand. He molded the freezing excrement into the shape of a blade and let it harden. He then spread saliva along the edge and let it freeze for an even sharper bevel. He used the poop knife to kill and butcher a dog. He made an improvised sled from its ribs and leather traces from its hide. He used the laces to harness another dog, hooked up his dog-rib sled, and slipped off into the Arctic night.

That's a helluva story, and even if it's only partly true, it's an impressive tale.

095 BUILD A MASSIVE SIGNAL FIRE

A knife can make quick work of building a signal fire. For darker smoke, cut green coniferous vegetation and strips of any petroleum-based gear you can dispense with, such as boat cushions, oily rags, and vehicle floor mats. In areas with extensive green vegetation, white smoke might be more visible to rescuers in an airplane. For white smoke, cut wet grasses and foliage and nearly smother the fire with the fuel.

096 FELL A TREE WITH A KNIFE

When it comes to chopping down a tree, a knife won't work as quickly as an ax or hatchet, but it will bring down a 4- or 5-inch-diameter tree with surprising ease. You'll need a fixed-blade knife with a full tang that will stand up to serious pounding, as well as a stout baton.

DO WEDGE WORK Hold the knife's edge horizontally against the tree trunk, with the blade angled slightly downward. Pound the full width of the blade into the trunk. Extract the blade and make a second cut, angled slightly upward, directly under the first one. This will remove a wedge of wood.

GIRDLE THE TREE Extend these wedge-removing cuts completely around the tree. Don't bend the tree over until you've girdled it entirely; doing so will splinter the wood, which makes it harder to cut.

PUSH IT OVER Once you're girdled the tree, shove it over. If it won't go, remove more wedges as needed.

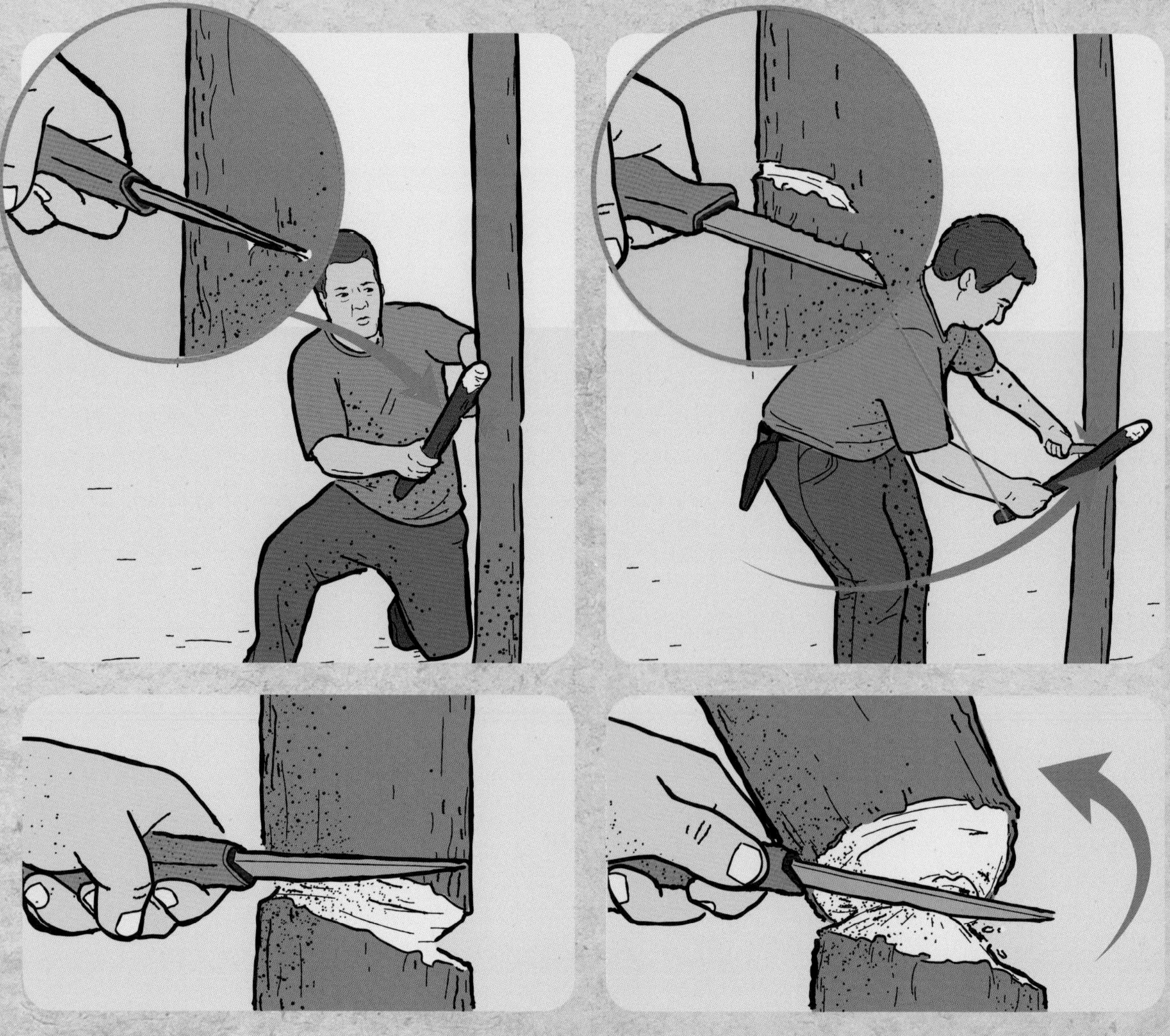

097 SPLIT KINDLING WITH A TWO-MAN BATON

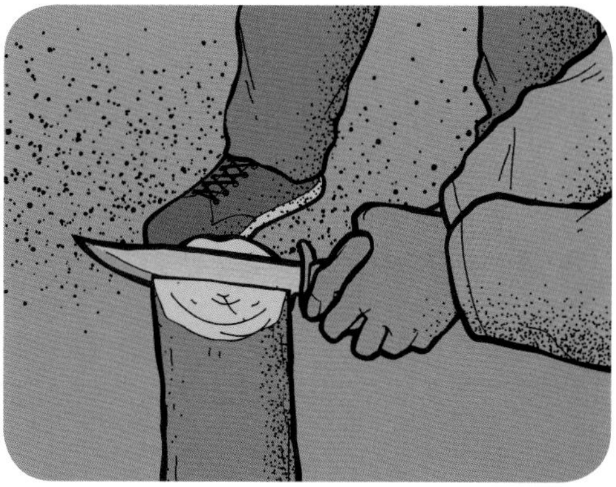

Large fixed-blade knives can be used to split logs 3 to 8 inches in diameter into usable kindling. When batoning kindling with a buddy, it's a good idea for both people to wear gloves to protect hands from a missed strike or splintered wood.

GET IT SET Set the log to be split upright. One person kneels and centers the knife blade across the end, with as much of the blade point as possible extending beyond the edge opposite the holder. The holder applies downward pressure to the knife blade to "set" the bite and prevent the knife from slipping off the log. A two-handed knife grip is safer; it not only enables greater pressure to be directed to the log face, but it keeps hands and fingers out of the way of the baton.

BEAT DOWN With the knife in place, the second person pounds the knife spine with a strong baton. Make this strike as close to vertical as possible. When the blade spine is driven below the face of the log, bring the baton to bear on the point of the blade extending beyond the wood.

BLADES THAT **MATTERED**

OPINEL NO. 8

Sure, over the last few years this 125-year-old French folding classic has taken on a bit of a hipster vibe, but don't let that spoil it for you. Inexpensive and sharp, with a trick little safety ring to lock the blade open, there are few better goose-breasting, fish-filleting, general-purpose camp kitchen knives than an Opinel.

Designed in 1890 by Joseph Opinel, the son of a sickle maker in Savoie, France, the knife gave rise to a family dynasty that is still managed by the ancestors of its founder. Each knife carries the Crowned Head emblem, with the blessing hand of Saint Jean-Baptiste. John the Baptist, of course, was the Biblical wilderness prophet who lived off locusts and honey, and he might suggest that you man up and opt for an original carbon-steel blade, which requires a bit more TLC than a newer stainless steel one.

098 TEACH A KID KNIFE KNOW-HOW

How old is old enough for a knife? That depends on the maturity and physical dexterity of the child, but it's never too soon to talk about knife safety and demonstrate how to correctly use a blade. Here's a step-by-step guide to bringing up a knife-savvy child, one ready for a lifetime of learning the knife skills that make life in the outdoors more fun.

START WITH WOOD Companies such as W.R. Case, CRKT, and Spyderco sell wooden knives and knife kits. For kids too young to handle the real thing, they're a great way to introduce the safe and fun use of knives.

DO A HACK JOB Use a rotary tool to grind down the blade on a Swiss Army Knife and let your 5-year-old putter around camp at will. That will spark plenty of early conversations about knife safety and pay off later when he's ready for a real blade.

GET KITCHEN HELP Cooking with a child is a great way to introduce safe cutlery skills. It's easy to provide close supervision, and there's plenty of knife work to be done in the kitchen, which keeps boredom at bay.

099 CHOOSE A BLADE FOR ANY AGE

A MORAKNIV WOODCARVING JUNIOR Made specifically for smaller hands, this is a great first fixed-blade knife for kids up to age 10. The birch handle is appropriately sized, and there's an extended finger guard that provides a barrier between handle and blade. The blade is carbon steel, so it will rust if abused. But that assists in another valuable lesson–knife care.

B W.R. CASE LEATHER MINI FINN HUNTER A perfect blade for kids aged 14 and up, with a finger guard to keep hands from sliding off the handle, a smaller Finnish-style blade or easier handling, and its clip point blade is safer than sharper trailing point designs.

C VICTORINOX EVOLUTION GRIP S18 This new classic is better than ever for kids 11 to 13. All the cool stuff is there–tweezers, toothpick, screwdrivers, saw–but its ergonomic, dual-material handle and locking main blade ensure improved safety.

A

B

C

100 TEACH THE HAND-OFF

One of the first knife skills anyone must learn is how to pass a knife to another person. It's no time for indecision or wishy-washiness–someone could end up bleeding. It's easy with a folding knife: Close it up and hand it over. But a fixed-blade knife is a bit trickier. Here are three ways to safely pass a knife that you can practice with young knife users.

PUT IT DOWN The best way to pass a knife is to not pass the knife at all. Place it on a table or counter, and let the other person pick it up.

USE A CRADLE HOLD Hold the knife by the handle, edge down (A). Next, pinch the bolster between thumb and index finger and swing the handle forward (B) at a slight angle, away from your palm. The knife handle should end up canted toward the other person, with the spine resting safely between the base of your thumb and your forefinger (C). As the other person takes the knife from your hand, ask, "You got it?". When the reply is affirmative, gently move your hand downward.

HAND IT OFF HANDLE FIRST Hold the knife blade with the tip pointing toward you, edge facing away from your palm, between your thumb and fingers. As the other user grasps the handle, ask, "You got it?" Upon confirmation, gently move your hand away from the knife.

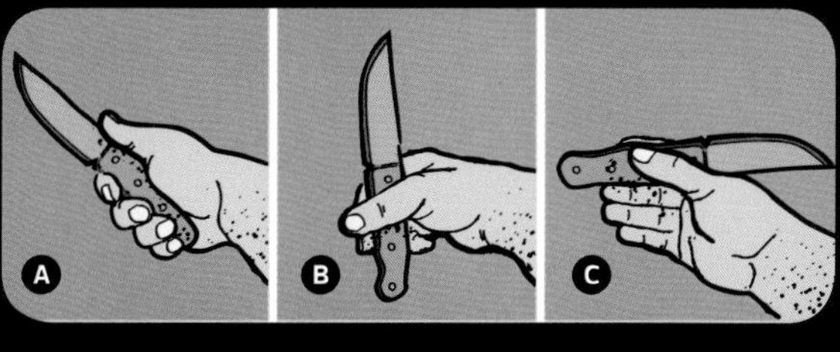

101 WHITTLE LIKE AN OLD-TIMER

Whittling is one of those things that's about 10 times harder than it looks, so don't think you and your Barlow knife are going to turn the butt end of a 2×4 into an award-winning wood duck head right off the bat. When you're ready to move beyond making fancy cedar toothpicks, step up to a decent whittling knife and a good piece of wood.

Start with a soft, straight-grained wood such as basswood or balsa. Skip pine unless you're suddenly inspired by the campfire and there's no Hobby Lobby in sight–the sticky sap will gum up a knife blade. Find a comfortable seat to give you a stable platform. If you're a rank beginner, armor the thumb of your knife hand with 3 or 4 wraps of duct tape. Often, you'll use that thumb to push the blade through the wood, and the tape will help prevent blisters. Other times, you'll draw the blade toward your thumb, and the tape can help protect against an errant stroke. Carve with the grain to keep the blade from sticking and skipping.

102 STEP UP TO A WHITTLING KNIFE

The best pocketknife blade for whittling is a clip point. The straight edge is perfect for push and paring cuts, and the sharp point works well for scoring and fine marking. There's not a thing wrong with whittling with your favorite EDC knife, especially a model with multiple blades for different cutting strokes. But a dedicated whittling knife is built with an ergonomic handle to help reduce hand fatigue. The short, often stout blade can be used to bring both force and finesse to a whittling job. These specialty knives come in both single-blade and multiblade models, and they'll take your craftsmanship up a notch or two in short order.

103 LEARN TO PUSH AND PULL

You won't get far with that standard pencil-sharpening stroke. Instead, work on these two basics.

PUSH STROKE This is a whittler's take on the standard weenie-stick stroke, but with greater power and control. If you're right-handed, hold the wood in your left hand and the knife in your right. Place the knife edge on the wood facing away from you. Now, line up both thumbs on the spine of the knife blade and push the blade forward with your left thumb, using your right-hand fingers and thumb to guide the blade to make the desired cut.

PARE CUT STROKE This is a pulling stroke, like you'd use to pare an apple. With the wood in your left hand, hold the knife in your right hand, edge facing you and right thumb against the wood. Use thumb pressure to guide the knife blade while drawing in the fingers of your right hand. This pulls the blade into the wood for short, precise strokes.

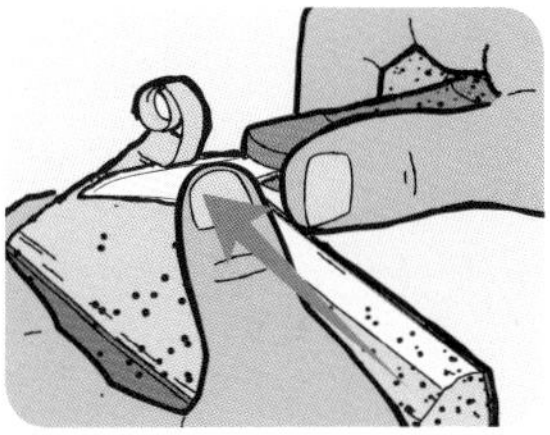

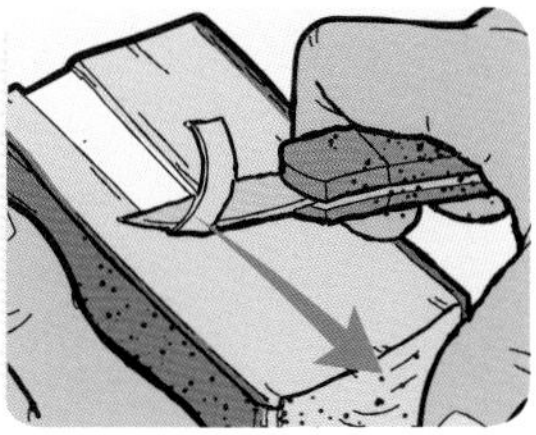

104 WHITTLE A WHIMMY DIDDLE

Few camp toys have intrigued kids more than the ancient gee-haw whimmy diddle, whose spinning propeller appears to magically change direction. Spoiler alert: The age-old secret is revealed below.

STEP 1 Gather three sticks of straight, dead wood (rhododendron and mountain laurel are the traditional species): stick A, approximately 8 inches long and the diameter of a pencil; stick B, about the same length but slightly thinner; and stick C, $1\frac{1}{2}$ inches long and the same diameter or slightly thinner than stick B. Whittle away most of the bark from all three pieces.

STEP 2 Carve 9 to 12 notches on the top of Stick A, starting an inch from one end. The notches should be approximately ⅛ inch deep, with ⅛ inch between each notch. Stick B requires nothing special.

STEP 3 Stick C is the propeller. Carve flat planes on two sides of the stick. Use a drill or awl to bore a small hole in the exact middle of the propeller. Bore a pilot hole into the notched end of stick A. Attach the propeller with a small brad or screw.

STEP 4 To work the whimmy diddle, hold stick A in your left hand, notches up. Hold stick B in your right hand, place it on stick A, and crook an index finger over the far side of stick A. Vigorously rub stick B back and forth along stick A. Shift your right hand so that your index finger rubs stick A on the far side, and the propeller will spin. Subtly shift your grip so that your thumb rubs stick A on the near side, and the propeller will stop and spin in the opposite direction. Perform this switch with enough nuance, and no one will notice your sleight of hand.

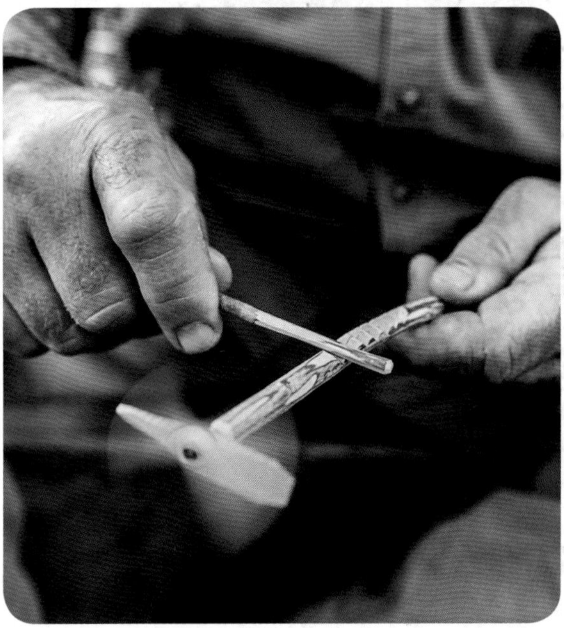

SURVIVAL

→ IN THIS SECTION →

MAKE SHELTER *WITH A KNIFE*

FLAME ON: SPARK FIRE WITH A BLADE

TOOTH AND NAIL: FIGHT AN ANIMAL TO THE DEATH

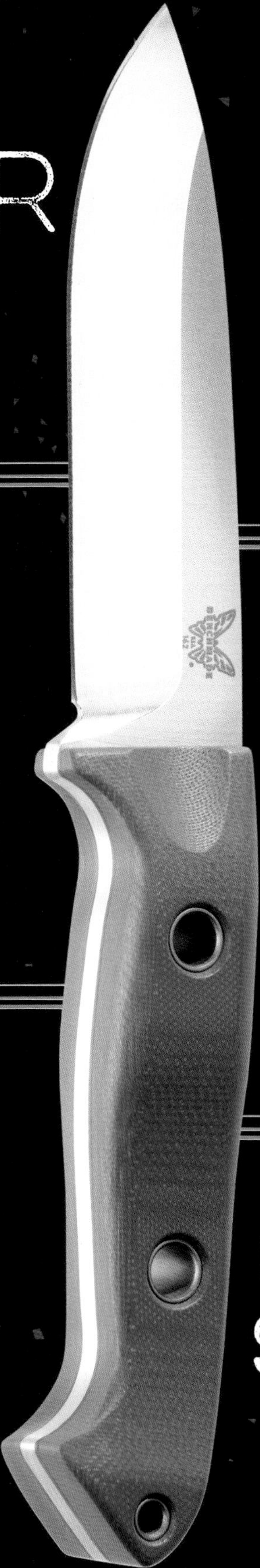

CARVE A JAW SPEAR FOR FISH & FROGS

TURN A KNIFE *INTO A SPEAR*

WHITTLE THE ULTIMATE SURVIVAL TRAP

105 MAKE SHELTER

One dark, cold night coming. One sharp knife in hand. A debris hut contains body heat better than any other emergency shelter. You can do this.

STEP 1 Cut a ridge pole as thick as your arm and twice as long as your height. Then, cut saplings for the shelter's side walls. You'll need several dozen, from 5 to 3 feet in length.

STEP 2 Prop up one end of the ridge pole on a stump or fallen log about waist high. In a pinch, use two shorter poles with a Y at one end of each to hold the ridge pole in place. Check the dimensions by lying down under the ridge pole with your feet at the low end. You want 1 to 2 feet of space between your toes and the end of the pole to provide enough room for insulation.

STEP 3 Next, you're going to create your side walls by leaning wrist-thick saplings and branches against the ridge pole to form a series of A shapes. Next, add a layer of smaller branches and fine brush parallel to the ridge pole; this layer provides structure that will help hold the insulation in place.

STEP 4 Cover the entire framework with dry leaves, grasses, and other debris. Then, place more upright branches and sticks on top of the debris layer to anchor the insulation in place. Your walls should be at least 2 feet thick.

STEP 5 Stuff the shelter with more debris and pile up enough at the entrance to plug the door once you crawl in.

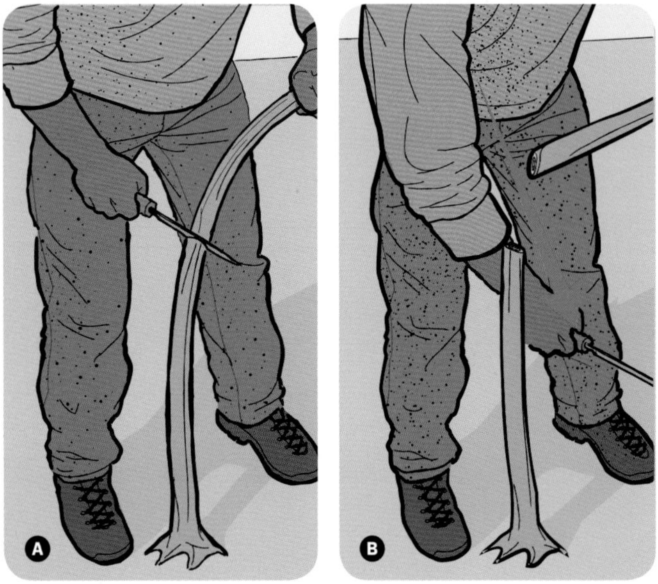

106 CUT THICK SAPLINGS WITH A KNIFE

If you can bend a green sapling, you can cut it. Smaller saplings can simply be bent and sliced through. To shear larger ones, bend the sapling back and forth to weaken the wood fibers. Next, bend it over with one hand and press down on the outside of the curve with your blade angled slightly (A). Rock the blade as you cut, maintaining steady downward pressure (B) until the blade slices through.

107 GLEAN FIRE STARTERS

The low, dead branches and sucker twigs of conifers make excellent fire-starting material. Carve a feather stick from the thickest branch; create wood shavings from the others by scraping them with the knife blade held at a 90-degree angle.

BLADES THAT MATTERED

FÄLLKNIVEN F1

There was a time when knives designed for survival situations prioritized flash, gimmick, and excessive size to toughness and usability. The introduction of the F1 helped quiet that trend. Fällkniven (pronounced "felk-nee-ven") is a Swedish-based manufacturer of highly regarded knives, and the F1 is the company's pièce de résistance. Since 1995, it has been the official survival knife of the Swedish Air Force and was tested and approved for use by air crews in the Marines and U.S. Navy. It's neither large nor complex. The 3.8-inch drop point blade is made of laminated steel–two slabs of 420J stainless steel sandwich a VG-10 core–with a full convex grind. A durable Thermorun handle provides a near rubberlike grip. The exposed pommel can be used to beat and smash. It is everything you need when a knife is what you need most.

108 MAKE FIRE FROM FATWOOD

Pine fatwood is famed as a fire starter, but it takes an all-out flame to get the stuff burning. However, process a stick of fatwood into resin-rich fatwood dust, fatwood shavings, and fatwood kindling, and mere sparks will have your blaze going in a jiffy. The best knife to use for this is a bushcraft-type blade with a 90-degree squared spine that will file dust and shavings from a fatwood stick, though a sharp knife edge will work, too. Start with a foot-long, inch-square piece of fatwood with squared corners.

MAKE SOME DUST Hold the fatwood against a firm surface. Place the knife's spine or edge along a corner of the stick at an angle so the squared corner of the spine rests against the fatwood. Use a rasping motion to grind off spark-catching fatwood dust.

CUT THE SHAVINGS Use your knife's blade to shave thin slivers of fatwood from the remaining corners.

CREATE KINDLING Split the fatwood in two lengthwise, then break each length in half to create four pieces of fatwood kindling about six inches by half an inch.

109 MAKE A BOUGH BED

Use a sturdy, fixed-blade knife to turn a conifer into a decent overnight bivvy. First, cut down two 8-foot-tall evergreens by batoning the knife through the trunk. The bushier the tree, the better. Cut off all the branches as close to the trunk as possible. Cut one of the main trunks into two 4-foot-long sections and the other into 2-foot-long sections.

To make the bough bed, first cut the branches to foot-long lengths. Use one of the trunk sections, held in place with a couple of wooden stakes, as a head log. Shingle the boughs at a 45-degree angle away from the head. Use the two 4-foot log sections as side rails to help hold the boughs in place. Compress tightly as you work your way down. Anchor with a foot log.

110 START A FIRE WITH BIRCH BARK

The papery curls of birch bark make a fantastic fire fuel. It won't catch fire with a spark, but the bark burns wet or dry, so use it as a great intermediary step between tinder and kindling. Make shallow, parallel knife cuts and pry the outer bark away from the inner bark to help protect the tree.

111 HARNESS THE MAGIC OF MAGNESIUM

A magnesium rod or block is a great addition to a fire-starting kit. When lit, the shavings burn at 5,600 degrees Fahrenheit. Shave flakes of magnesium into a quarter-sized pile and ignite with a spark. To supercharge, shave the magnesium onto the sticky side of a strip of duct tape. The adhesive will hold the shavings in place, and the duct tape will burn like crazy.

112 SPARK FIRE WITH A KNIFE

Starting a fire with blade and stone is as classic a knife skill as there is. Aim a shower of sparks at delicate tinder. Shelter the smoking ember. Tease it to life with your very breath. Sounds simple, but don't think you can pull this off without preparation. Practice first and always have the right tools for the job.

GET THE BLADE You'll need a knife with a classic carbon-steel blade to get the job done. Stainless steel is incapable of producing the sparks needed to birth a flame. The sparks produced by striking steel against flint, quartz, quartzite, or chert are actually tiny molten slivers of metal. The best steel for the job is high-carbon steel with a Rockwell C-scale hardness of at least 58. That's one reason bushcraft knives typically excel at throwing torrents of sparks. Most are made of the proper steel, with a sharp, 90-degree edge to the spine that aids in shaving metal.

GATHER TINDER Since the sparks are relatively cool and burn out quickly, you'll need highly flammable tinder. Traditional tinders are char cloth–made by burning cotton fabric, which requires a fire to begin with–and tinder fungus, which doesn't grow everywhere and requires know-how to properly collect. But cotton balls smeared with petroleum jelly will work just fine. Pick at the ball with your fingers a bit to fuzz up some spark-catching fibers.

WRAP AND TAP If you're using a fixed-blade knife, wrap the sharp edge with a piece of leather or cloth. Hold the stone with a sharp ridge on a horizontal plane extending from your hand. Give it a few strikes to see where the majority of sparks will land, then set the fire-starting material in the hot spot.

STRIKE AND SPARK Next, aim the sparks toward the tinder and strike the stone with sharp, glancing blows. Then, gently blow any embers or coals into a flame and transfer to a premade tinder bundle.

113 CARVE A JAW SPEAR

Pacific Northwest natives devised salmon spears, made from sinew and bone, that were brawny enough to hoist kings and cohos from roiling rapids. You can channel your inner Suquamish with this survival spear capable of snagging frogs, fish, and small rodents. All you need is a sharp knife and a bit of paracord. A bone from your last squirrel dinner isn't required, but it will make for a beefier spear.

STEP 1 Cut a 2-foot length of paracord and tease out the inner core strands. They're a perfect twine for lashing.

STEP 2 Cut a straight, green sapling of hard wood, such as hickory or maple, a foot longer than your height and with a strong fork at one end. Remove the bark from the fork tines. Trim the fork to 4 or 5 inches in length and angle each fork tip by removing a few slivers of wood from the inside of each tine.

STEP 3 For a center spike, carve a 2-inch-long sharp stick–or, better yet, a sharp spike of bone–and lash it to the inside of the fork. Start with a clove hitch a half-inch below the V of the fork and wrap the windings tightly toward the fork. When the lashing reaches the fork, continue with a few more wraps to create a pocket for the butt of the spike. Place the spike in this pocket, then continue lashing by alternating the cord under and over the spike, tightening with each lash. Secure the lashing.

STEP 4 For the backward-pointing spikes, carve a pair of 2-inch-long spikes of wood or bone. Begin with a clove hitch lashing ½ inch from the jaw's end and continue with a half-dozen winds. Place the spike so it points backward, resting on the angle carved into the jaw tip. The initial winds aid in setting the spike angle. Lash the tip down and secure. Repeat on other jaw.

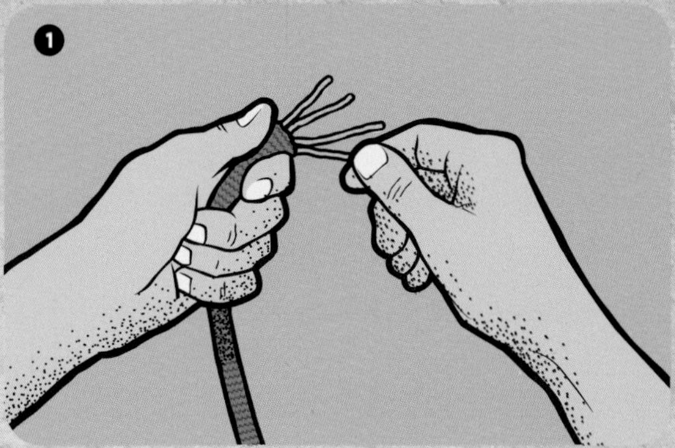

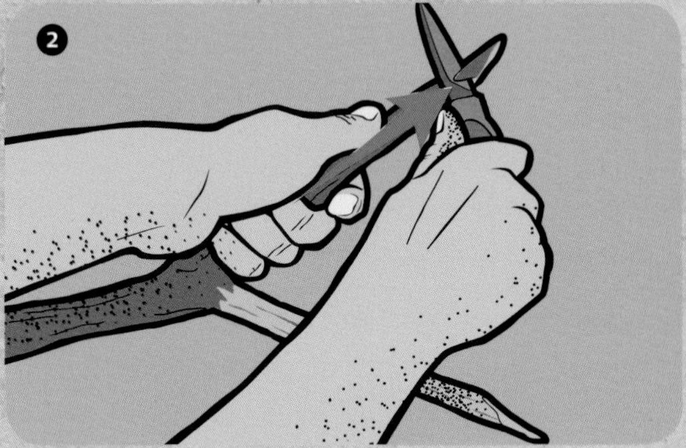

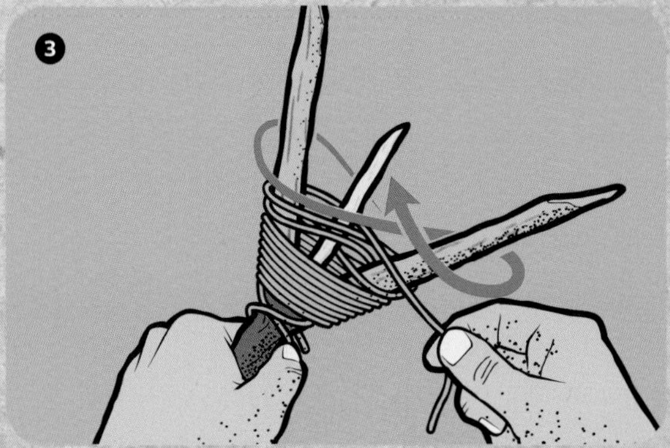

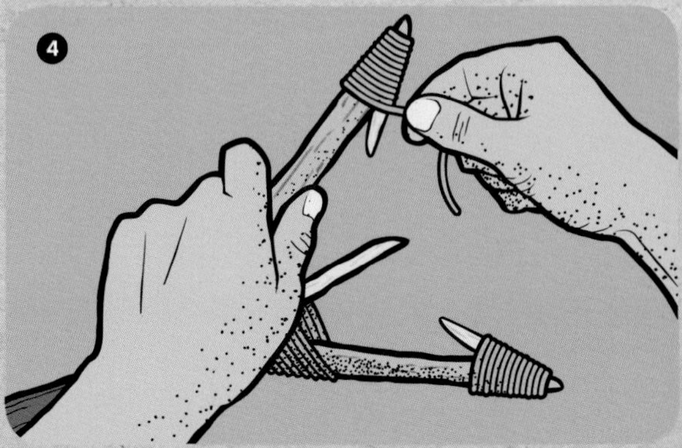

114 MAKE A FIGURE-4 TRAP

The figure-4 deadfall is the go-to grocery getter in a survival scenario. It works, but it's tricky to make. As with any survival skill, practice it before you need it.

PLACE THE POST Carve a chisel point into one end of the upright post and square off the other end. In the center of the post, carve a flat facet in the same plane as the chisel point and another at a right angle to it.

LINE UP THE LEVER The diagonal part of the "4" requires a notch carved in the side near one end and a chisel point at the other. To make a notch, cut straight down into the stick and carve off a 1-inch shaving from the center of the stick toward the end to meet your downward cut. The notch sits atop the chisel-topped post; the chisel end of the lever locks into a notch at the end of the trigger stick. The lever should be the same length as the post stick.

TEST THE TRIGGER A few inches longer than the other two sticks, it needs a notch carved in the side and another carved near the stick's thicker end. The notch at the end faces upward in the finished trap, and the notch on the side of the trigger stick will face the post. Carve a point in the free end to skewer bait.

TUNE THE TRAP Place the lever on top of the post, set the edge of your rock on the tip of the lever, then lock in your horizontal trigger stick (first against the end of the lever, then against the square edge on the post).

115 LASH A KNIFE SPEAR

The first thing to consider when using a knife to make a spear is to reconsider. In a survival situation, a knife is your most important tool. Binding it to a stick and then poking at things can damage the blade—worse, you might lose it. If you're determined to make a DIY spear, here's how. Got a second knife? By all means, spear up.

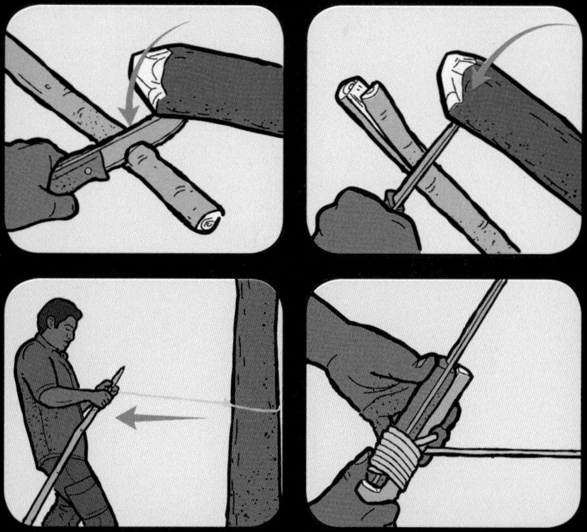

STEP 1 With a baton and knife, cut a pole to length. The slim end's diameter should be at least 1.5 inches.

STEP 2 Lay the pole on the ground and mark the distance from the end to match the length of your knife handle. Baton the knife halfway through the pole at the mark. Next, split chips from the end of the pole to the batoned cut to create a flat shelf for the knife.

STEP 3 Tightly tie one end of a length of paracord around a tree. Walk back from the tree about 10 feet

Wrap the end of the paracord around the pole and knife below the bolster. Lean back and pull tightly. While leaning back with your full body weight, turn the pole to create lashings all the way to the pommel and then back to the bolster. Finish with half hitches.

116 HIT YOUR MARK WITH A THROWING KNIFE

The American Knife Throwers Alliance–yes, such a thing exists–suggests using a throwing knife between 12 and 16 inches long and weighing about 16 ounces. Since no two people bring to the motion the same height, arm length, strength, and other variables, there's a lot of trial and error in getting the throw down pat. But that's part of the fun.

The first phase is to learn a single-turn throw, in which a knife, released by the handle, makes one full revolution in the air and hits the target point-first. Tack a playing card to a soft-wood target and make sure your knife tip is sharp.

STEP 1 Choose your grip. With the McEvoy grip, the knife is thrown with the blade in a vertical orientation. Grip the knife by the handle as you would a hammer, resting your thumb along the top of the spine. For a vertical pinch grip, turn the knife blade parallel to the ground, place your first three fingers in the center of the handle on underside, your thumb in the center on the top side. Both styles allow the knife to slip out of the hand with little friction.

STEP 2 Stand 12 feet from the target. Keep your eye on the bull's-eye and throw the knife with an overhand motion, releasing the knife just before your arm becomes horizontal. Keep your wrist straight through the motion and allow the knife to slip out of your hand. No flicking. Watch the point of impact carefully and make adjustments. If the knife sticks with the handle in a downward slant, you're too close to the target. Back up a half step and try again. If the knife sticks with the handle slanting up, you're too far back. Keep practicing until the knife sticks close to horizontal.

STEP 3 Time to stretch it out for a two-turn throw. Take five full paces from the 12-foot mark. Adjust your distance from the target as needed until the blade sticks.

STEP 4 Experiment with force. Throw the knife harder and harder, replicating the throwing motion and release as closely as possible each time.

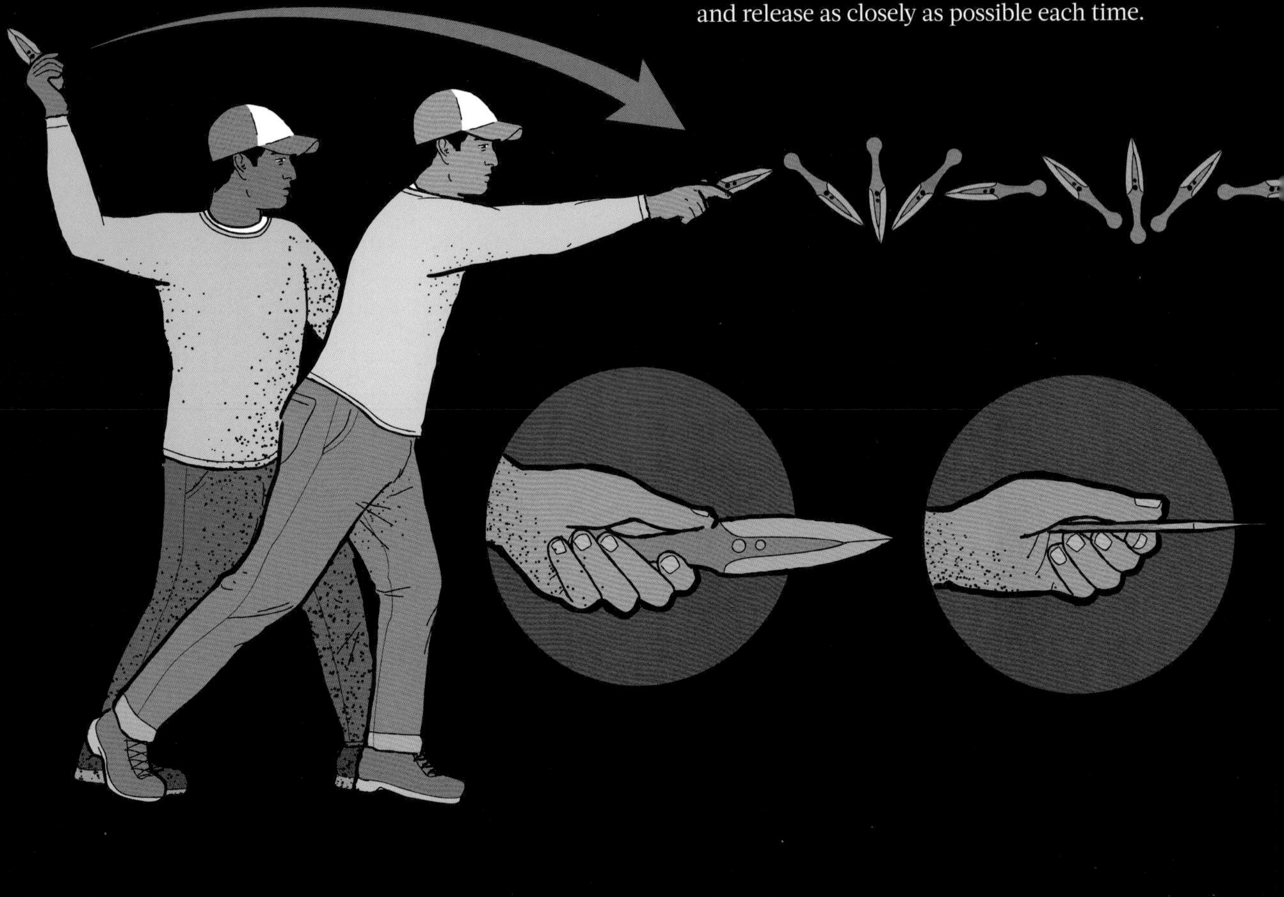

117 BREAK OUT A CAR WINDOW

Some knives have a glass breaker built into the handle, but any stout knife can smash a car window if you know how to wield it. For fixed knives, use the pommel. For folding knives, use the pointiest part of the handle. Choke up to keep your palm as far from the window as possible. Forget the windshield, which is made of laminated glass to prevent shattering. Instead, target a side window, which is made of glass tempered in a way that it shatters into tiny, relatively dull shards. Aim at the window's edge–often easier to break than the center–and give it a solid, smashing blow. Focus your energy to the tiniest point of the knife's handle. If you have an extra few seconds, slip on a glove or grab a batonlike a piece of wood or a brick and use it to pound the knife through the glass and keep a bit of distance between your hand and the shards.

118 MAKE CORD WITH A KNIFE

Cord is a primary survival item, essential for lashing gear, strengthening poles for makeshift shelter, and constructing survival spears and gigs. Strips of leather can be cut into thin laces for lashing by using a circular cutting technique. Drive your knife point into a flat wood surface with the edge pointing toward you. Carefully push the leather into the sharpened edge. Grasp the end of the resulting lace with the fingers of one hand, hold it off to one side, and continue cutting the leather lace.

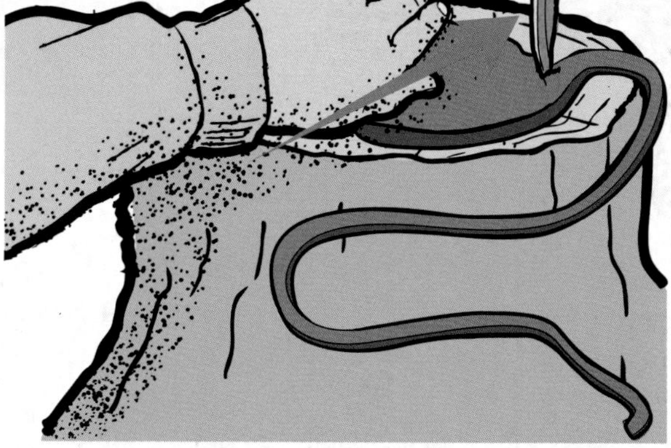

119 FIGHT OFF A WILD ANIMAL

Let's be real: Your odds of beating back a seriously pissed-off bear, mountain lion, or pack of coyotes aren't much better than finding a unicorn in an elk herd. But with a knife in hand, you've at least got a fighting chance. Of course, a sprinkling of fairy dust wouldn't hurt, either.

Robert Young Pelton has thought about this more than most. The war-zone journalist and best-selling author of *The World's Most Dangerous Places* owns DPx Gear and designs hard-use knives–one of which is a favorite of hog hunters who know a bloody thing about getting to the heart of the matter. "A quick kill requires a deep, open stabbing wound–ideally straight into the heart to drop systolic blood pressure and starve the beast's brain of oxygen," Pelton says. But that's not the only way to make a four-legged opponent think twice about taking a bite out of your hide.

FACE A MOUNTAIN LION "A mountain lion will grab prey with jaws and front paws to crush the neck," says Pelton, who has been stalked by big cats in East Africa and British Columbia. "Meanwhile, they're attempting to disembowel you with the rear paws." Forget killing such a kitty. Instead, Pelton says, "break up the attack and make the cat run off." Bear-hug the animal tightly to protect your head and organs, and stab at the eyes. Shove the blade into the mouth and throat, and jab as quickly and as often as you can.

FIGHT A BEAR Two strategies are common in accounts of people successfully fighting off a bear with a knife. First, the hand not holding the knife is used, often sacrificially, to stiff-arm the bear's head or jam a fist into its mouth. Second, the knife is used to stab the bear repeatedly–"savagely, desperately," Pelton suggests–around the neck and head.

CONFRONT CANIDS Coyotes and wolves will parry in groups and go for the rump or legs, so face the attacking animal head-on. Keep snarling jaws away from you and stab through the animal's side into the hard, knotlike heart. "And don't poke," Pelton says. "Imagine a spot 6 inches through the chest and strike hard." Lever the knife back and forth to create maximum tissue trauma, then remove it quickly for maximum blood loss.

FEATS of STEEL

KILL A BEAR WITH A KNIFE

Shortly before midnight on September 27, 2014, Brandon Johnson, 44, of Michigan, was helping a friend blood-trail a 525-pound black bear when it charged. The only weapon he had: an $8 flea-market knife. Here's the story, in his own words.

"A stick snapped, and I said to my friend Trevor, 'I think I hear it.' I took three steps to the left, and then . . . I remember lying on a plush mattress, staring at the stars, just kind of floating. That was the shock, I guess. When I snapped out of it, the bear's face was a foot from mine. My hands were around his muzzle as it came down in slow motion and latched onto the left side of my face. He knocked me down in the mud and had my jaw in his mouth. I had the knife in my right hand and I stabbed him in the face. I shoved my left arm as far as I could down the bear's throat, and stabbed and stabbed, hard and as fast as I could. All of a sudden, the bear was gone.

"I lay there on my back for maybe five minutes. Stay quiet, I thought Don't say a word. Then the bear came again, straight for my crotch. I locked my knees as he started biting at me. He batted my left arm away and opened his mouth so wide the pupils rolled up in his head. I thought, this is it. I heard a stick snap, but it was actually my left arm.

"All the while, I kept stabbing. After the bear broke my left arm, he had my left hand in his mouth, and when he spun, he twisted my wrist and hand all the way around inside the skin and snapped my thumb and ripped all the ligaments. The bear backed away and left me in the dark. I don't know how long I was there, but I could feel everything leave me–all the hope and the fight draining like water in a tub.

"Next, the bear ran straight in and climbed on my chest. I had just enough time to use my right hand to drape my broken left arm over my face before the bear opened his mouth again–like 10 inches wide, just unbelievable. At that moment, I knew: This is my chance. With all the strength I had left, I shoved the knife down his throat as far and as hard as I could. I broke two fingers.

"I pulled my hand back out and kept stabbing. Blood covered my eyes, so I wiped them with my sleeve, and I saw a three-quarter-inch stream of blood pumping out of the bear's face. It wasn't my blood in my eyes –it was his. That's when it hit me: I am going to kill this thing.

"It seemed the bear knew the knife was causing him so much trouble. He grabbed my right arm in his mouth and chomped down twice, breaking it. I could barely move by then. All I could do with the knife was wave it back and forth in a small arc in front of the bear. I just wanted to appear threatening. But when the bear saw it, he swatted my broken arms apart, hit me in the chest, grabbed my right calf, turned me around, and slammed me to the ground like a chew toy.

"After that, at last, he left for good."

Johnson was taken to the hospital for more than half a dozen operations on his injured arms and hands. His friends found the bear. Bleeding profusely, it had moved off about 45 yards, then turned around and laid its head on crossed paws.

AXES, HATCHETS & SAWS

BIT BY BIT

One man with one ax could girdle a large tree in a matter of minutes. He would strip the outer bark and inner cambium all the way around the trunk. Eventually the tree would die and fall, creating a small clearing in the woods. When the man had girdled and cleared enough trees, he had created a field for corn and beans. With his ax and all those logs, he would build a home, and barns, and a community. And when more people showed up than he liked, the man took his ax, and with a few friends he cleared a road through wilderness and moved to another forest, where he girdled another tree and planted another field and built another home. And this is how America was made.

It would be difficult to conjure up a hand tool more closely associated with the American experience than the ax. It was as critical to the survival of early settlers as the flintlock. It was as foundational to early American industry as the steam engine. And for hunters and anglers across the centuries, the ax has cleared trails and rivers and fed the fires of innumerable adventures. And it still does.

Possessing serious ax skills might seem to be somewhat old school in these modern times, but the ability to use an ax to buck logs, skin an elk, and fell a tree is what sets an outdoorsman apart. There's a certain air of self-sufficiency and capability apparent with the skillful swing of a full-size ax, but it only comes with practiced use—there is no app for an axman's skills.

The same could be said of hatchets, which are not merely sawn-off axes made for youngsters. Buy a $14.95 hatchet from the local big box conglomerate, and you'll get what you deserve. Pour a little more thought (and not a whole lot more money) into the purchase, and you'll get a tool that will cut firewood, clear canoe trails, and cleave an elk's pelvis. For you and your grandkids.

If there was ever an underappreciated outdoor tool, it would have to be the saw. Like the lumberman's ax, saws and saw skills have fallen from a position of highest regard. But for hunters, campers, and anglers, carrying a smart, modern hand saw helps make it easier to build fire, craft shelter, and enjoy the outdoors. That's a lot to ask of a hand tool. But not, as it turns out, too much.

AX & HATCHET DESIGN

→ IN THIS SECTION →

GET A GRIP:

STRAIGHT VS. CURVED HANDLES

HEADS UP

CHOOSE THE RIGHT BIT

HANDS ON:

GRAB THE RIGHT-SIZED TOOL FOR THE JOB

AXIS OF FORCE

HOW TO READ A HANDLE'S WOOD GRAIN

AX ANATOMY

KNOW EVERY PART OF YOUR TOOL

SPLIT & CHOP

THE SHAPES OF THINGS THAT CUT

HEADS

There's far more to ax and hatchet head design than a stout cutting edge. Most tools are made for a specific woodsmanship task: splitting log rounds, limbing trees, and cutting kindling, to name a few. Choosing the right tool for the job at hand not only makes the work go more quickly, but it makes it safer, too.

The general outlines of an ax or hatchet head are similar. The sharp edge is the bit, and the opposite end is the poll. The top corner of the sharpened edge is the toe; the bottom corner is the heel. The side of the head is called the cheek. How each element is designed and forged determines how the tool performs when you swing it.

AMERICAN FELLING AX

DESCRIPTION For dropping trees, a felling ax with a sharp, thin bit and tapered cheeks will penetrate across the wood grain. These axes are fitted with midweight heads for easy swinging. During the pioneering and settlement periods, scores of variations cropped up across American regions. This Dayton pattern is a classic.

BEST FOR General camp and forest work

HUDSON BAY AX

DESCRIPTION Developed for French fur traders in the 17th century, this is one of the oldest ax designs in North America. Typically fitted with a three-quarter-length handle, the smaller head excels at trimming branches, clearing trails, and cutting kindling.

BEST FOR Limbing, clearing, low-impact camp work

CAMPING HATCHET

DESCRIPTION One-piece forged hatchets for general purpose outdoor duty are a great compromise. They won't split a redwood, but they're inexpensive and super handy around a camp.

BEST FOR General camp work

SPLITTING AX OR HATCHET

DESCRIPTION Axes and hatchets made for splitting wood are ground to a concave, thin edge at the bit, but carry a broad section at the cheek to push wood apart far better than a typical head can.

BEST FOR Splitting and chopping

MAUL

DESCRIPTION The big, chunky head is made for splitting wood rounds, with a flat poll designed for pounding a splitting wedge. Typical maul heads range in weight from 4 to 8 pounds..

BEST FOR Splitting and chopping

A NEW GOLDEN AGE FOR AXES?

Like the burgeoning custom knife trade, an emphasis on craftsmanship and an artisan's approach has resulted in a flush of new handmade ax and hatchet makers. And prompted commercial brands to produce new lines of inspired tools.

CARPENTER'S AX OR HATCHET

DESCRIPTION Built with a long beard for ease in choking up on the handle, and a thin, straight edge for detailed cuts in dry wood, a carpenter's ax or hatchet works like a large, heavy knife.

BEST FOR Carving, hewing

BROAD AX

DESCRIPTION Designed specifically for squaring and shaping timbers for log construction, the broad ax head features a long, slightly curved edge and a blocky heel.

BEST FOR Squaring and shaping timbers for log construction

DOUBLE-BIT AX

DESCRIPTION Now mostly used in ax-throwing competitions, the double-bit was once a favorite of backcountry woodsmen, with one edge honed fine for felling trees and the other ground more bluntly for knocking off hard knots and limbs.

BEST FOR Throwing

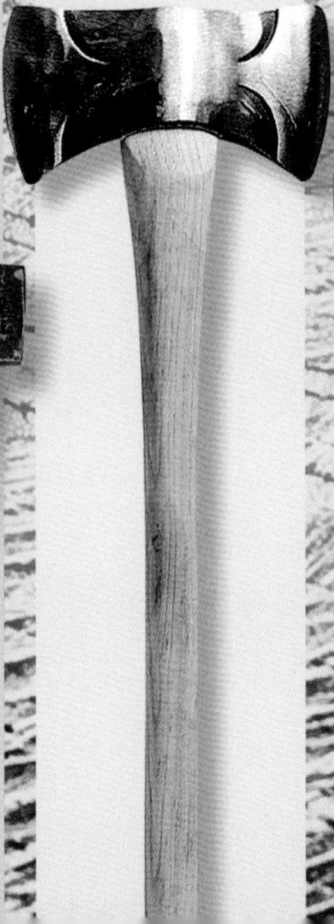

CARVING AX OR HATCHET

DESCRIPTION Used for hewing wooden bowls, spoons, and other objects, the carving ax's curved cutting edge extends well above the head's eye. It has a thick bit and a short handle that enables multiple holding options.

BEST FOR Carving, hewing

PULASKI AX

DESCRIPTION With a cutting edge on one side of the bit and a grubbing tool on the other, the Pulaski is designed for firefighting and trail building.

BEST FOR Firefighting and trail building

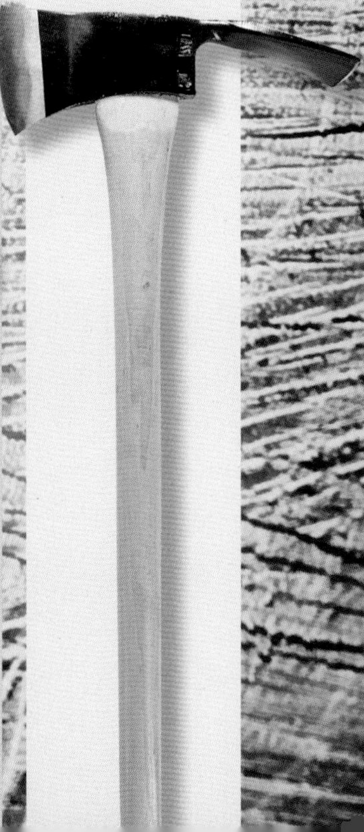

120 LEARN THE PARTS OF AN AX

Axes and hatchets share a common anatomy, and the various design elements dictate how well the tool will handle a particular job. It's important to match the ax or hatchet to the task at hand--or in two hands, perhaps. Fatter head cheeks, for example, split wood better than thin head cheeks, which excel at felling standing trees. Curved bits perform differently than straight bits. Many experienced hunters, anglers, and campers keep a variety of axes and hatches ready for work.

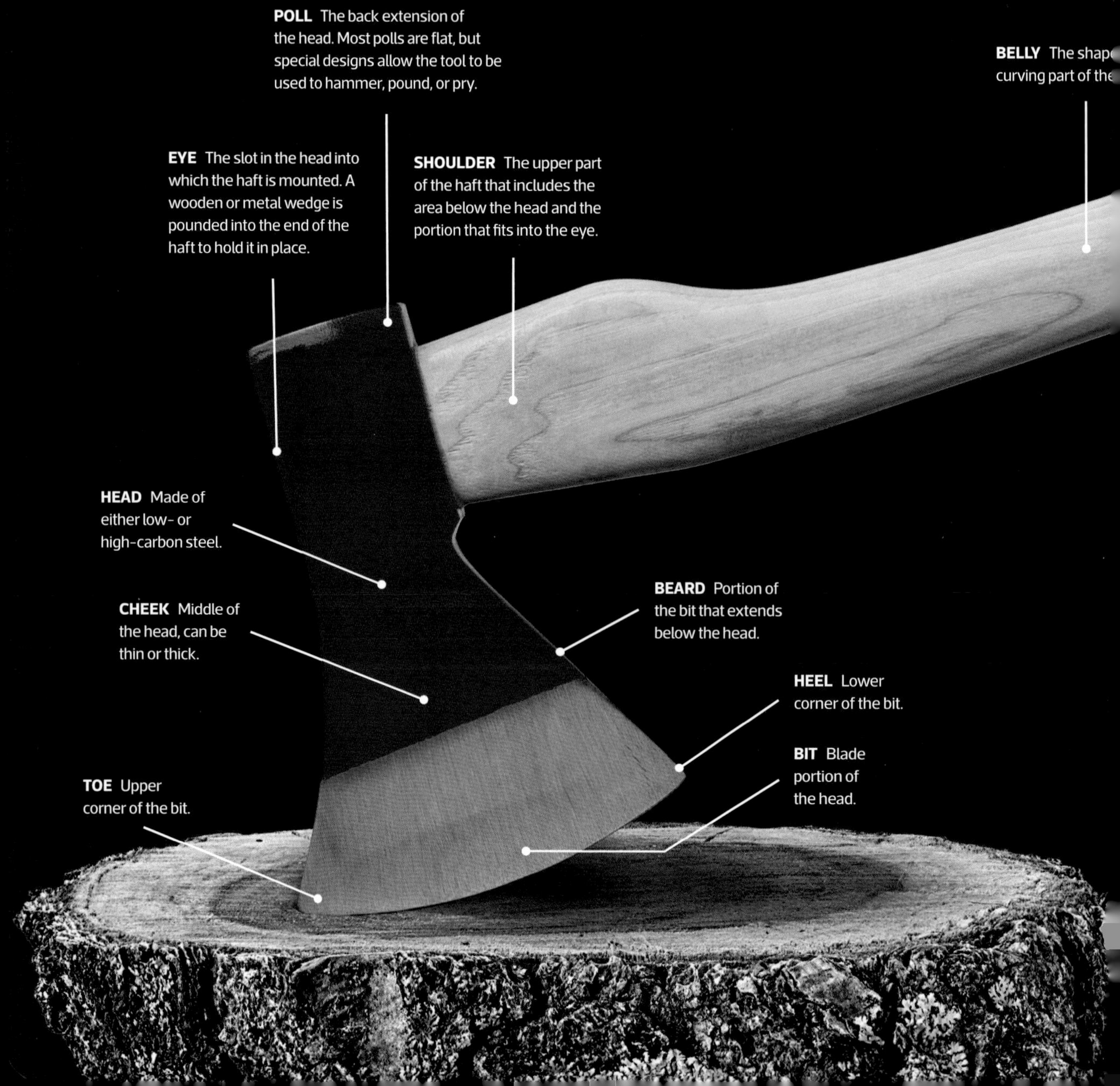

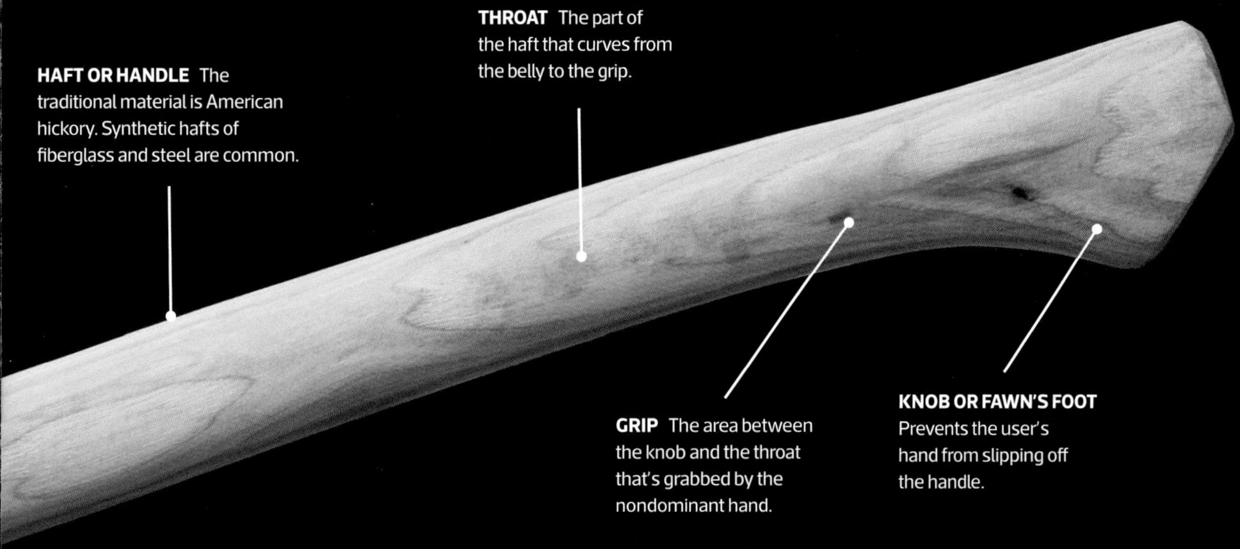

121 CHOOSE THE RIGHT HAFT FOR YOU

Straight or curved? Ax handles come in a wide variety of shapes, from ruler-straight hafts to various S-curves and sweeping bends. The shape of a handle affects the physics of the swing, and while the best choice is a matter of experience and opinion, there are guidelines to steer your decision.

Pioneering American woodsmen favored a straight ax handle. Double-bit axes require a straight handle so both edges can be used effectively.

Curved handles change the angle of your wrist and forearm in relation to the handle and the head. Many people prefer curved handles for their ease of gripping. But too much curve in a handle, especially at the bottom, can increase the chances of pivoting your wrist on the swing, which decreases both the force and accuracy of the strike. On many curved handles, a swollen knob at the end, called the "fawn's foot," provides additional purchase.

HAFTS

An ax's or hatchet's handle is the tool's transmission system, where power, finesse, and deft handling combine to allow the sharp edge to work most efficiently. It might seem like a secondary consideration to head design, but choosing the right handle will help the wood chips fly.

A FULL-SIZE AX Also called a "felling ax," it has a standard 36-inch length that allows more force to be driven to the head. Long-handled axes can be hard to control. Unless you're splitting wood or cutting down trees, an ax with a shorter handle is typically more efficient.

B HATCHET A hatchet's handle ranges from 11 to 13 inches, making for convenient carry. Hatchets aren't powerful wood choppers, but they are perfect for most general tasks. A wide variety of available heads means there's a hatchet for just about any job.

C BOY'S AX Despite the moniker, this is a full-size working tool, albeit about three-quarters the length of a full-size ax. The 28-inch length makes it easier to aim and swing, and the best choice for most ax work.

GRAIN AND GRIP

Most wood ax and hatchet handles are made of straight-grained American hickory or ash. It's critical that the grain in a wood handle be aligned with the axis of force, which is parallel to the handle itself. Synthetic handles, such as fiberglass, will last in harsh conditions, but avoid metal handles, which don't absorb shock well.

AX & HATCHET SKILLS

→ IN THIS SECTION →

HEAD TRAUMA: RETURN A BIT TO WORKING ORDER

WHAT THE BUCK? MAKE QUICK WORK OF DOWNED TREES

TIMBER! FELL A TREE WITH AN AX

GAME CARE: PROCESS AN ANIMAL WITH A HATCHET

122 FIX IT IN THE FIELD

Stuck in the woods with a dull ax or hatchet? You don't need a vise or grinding wheel to bring cutting glory back to your blade. Assuming you're savvy enough to carry a file and whetstone in the toolbox, here's how to sharpen the edge using the cold, hard ground as a workbench.

STEP 1 Drive a peg into the ground. Place a wrist-thick stick or log quarter four inches from the peg.

STEP 2 Place the poll of the head against the peg, resting the cheek on the log quarter so that the bit is slightly raised. File the blade with even strokes on each side.

STEP 3 Finish with a whetstone, using a circular motion to hone the edge.

123 TAKE YOUR BLADE TO THE SHOP

An ax or hatchet is a handy companion, but only if it's sharp. A heavily dulled blade needs a makeover best handled on a steady workbench. Pull on work gloves to protect your hands during this three-step process that produces a wood-eating edge.

RESTORE THE PROFILE Place the head in a vise with the edge facing up. Using a flat, single-cut mill bastard file turned perpendicular to the edge, file away nicks, gouges, and turned edges.

ESTABLISH A SECOND BEVEL Place the handle in the vise so the edge is horizontal. Hold the file to match the original bevel of the head and use long strokes across the entire edge from toe to heel. When you feel a burr forming on the edge, turn the ax around in the vise and repeat on the other side.

SHARPEN THE EDGE Now, file a 10-degree bevel into the edge, stroking the file until you raise a burr, then repeat on the other side. You can stop at this point, but for further honing, use a handheld sharpening puck with both a coarse and a fine side. Start with the coarse side. Oil the stone, hold the head in one hand, and hone with small, circular motions all along the cutting edge. Repeat with the other side. Switch to the whetstone's fine side and repeat the process.

124 RENEW YOUR EDGE ON THE JOB

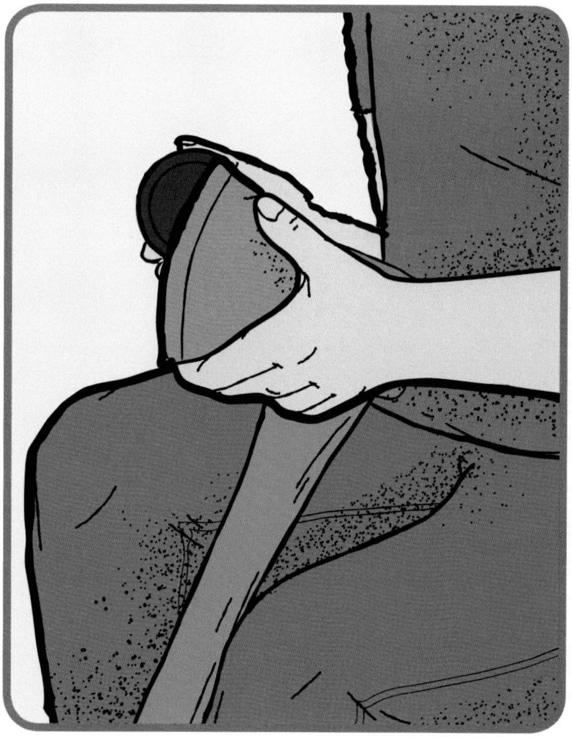

It's not hard to dull an ax or hatchet when working in the field. An errant stroke might send the ax glancing off toward a stone. Or a final stroke might bury itself in the ground. However they occur, nicks and dull spots make work more difficult and less safe. Touching up an ax or hatchet in the middle of a big job is not only simple, but it will make the rest of your cutting go much easier. To hone an edge when you're away from your shop tools, sit on a sturdy seat with your legs at a comfortable 90-degree angle. You can either place the end of the handle on the ground and brace the handle's shoulder against your knee or rest the ax head on your thigh. Point the edge away from your body and use a file or sharpening puck to keen the bit.

Consider wearing gloves, because your hands will be near the edge of the ax head. Like with other sharpening techniques, count your strokes so you can file the blade evenly on each side.

THE KNIFE I CARRY

WILL BRANTLEY, HUNTING EDITOR

I have a Buck General—the biggest damn thing they make—with a Cocobolo handle. My dad gave it to me when I was 12, and it was given to him by the widow of his best hunting buddy, Harold. Harold bought the knife, planning to carry it while elk hunting, but he got sick before he had the chance to head out west. It's too large to be a practical hunting knife, though I've used it to field-dress and skin a bunch of deer and one elk. I once killed an armadillo with it, too. I can't claim a similar achievement with any of my other blades.

125 BUCK A LOG WITH AN AX

You round a bend in the trail and groan: A fallen tree blocks the path. Your buddy's response is to stomp to the back of the truck, pull out the chainsaw, check the chain tension, futz around with premixed fuel, and try to find his ear plugs and safety glasses. By the time he walks up to the log with his chainsaw, you've bucked the tree into pieces ("buck" is the term for cutting wood that's fallen on the ground) with little more than an ax and attitude. Here's how.

STEP 1 Stand on top of the log and chop a V-notch into the side of it between your feet. Make three swings angling in from the right–the first one high on the log, then low, and then in the middle.

STEP 2 Repeat with swings angling in from the left–high, low, and middle. On that sixth and final stroke, flick your wrist slightly (an inch will do) the instant the bit bites wood. This will help toss chips out of the notch and prevent the ax from sticking.

STEP 3 Cut halfway through one side of the log, then turn around and chop another V-notch through the other side. You'll want the notches to be slightly offset so that the bit doesn't over travel into your legs on the final stroke.

126 FELL A TREE

The trick to downing a standing tree with an ax is to cut a pair of offset notches in the trunk. Chop the face cut first, notching to the midpoint of the tree. Move to the opposite side of the tree and chop a downward upper notch so that the point of the notch will reach the midpoint of the tree a few inches above the apex of the lower notch, creating a hinge. When done correctly, the tree will fall on the side of the lower notch.

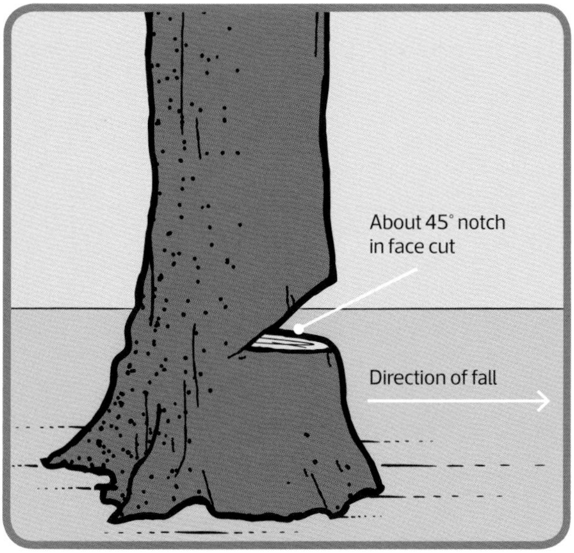

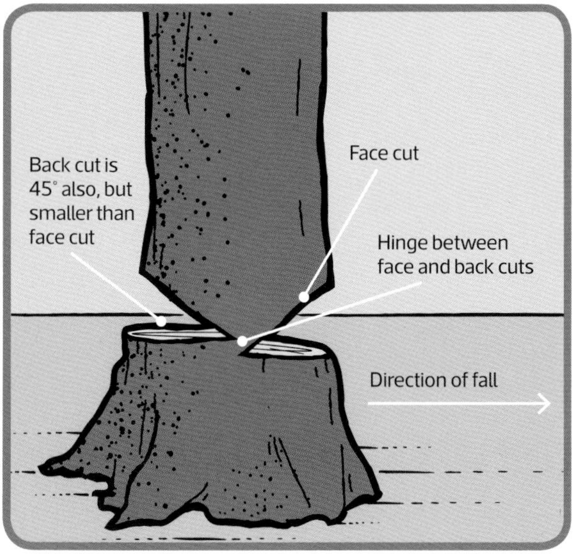

127 MAKE FIRE FUEL FROM WET WOOD

Forget scrounging for tinder fungus and bellybutton lint. If you have a hatchet and a log, you can render a round of sopping-wet wood into tinder, kindling, and fuel.

STEP 1 Find a downed, solid log no more than 10 inches in diameter. A coniferous wood such as pine or cedar works best due to its flammable resin, but any sound log will do. Remove a 12-inch section from the log.

STEP 2 Split the section into quarters. Lay one quarter on the ground, bark side down. Score the apex of the wedge with a pair of inch-deep cuts 4 inches apart. Use your hatchet to shave off thin, 4-inch-long dry wood curls and splinters. Pound these curls with the back of the hatchet to separate the wood fibers, then rub some of them between your palms to further separate the fibers. This is your tinder. You'll want two handfuls.

STEP 3 Split match-sized and pencil-sized pieces of wood from the wedge corners of a remaining quarter of wood. Break these into 6-inch pieces for kindling.

STEP 4 Continue to split the quarters, utilizing the innermost, driest pieces of the wood. Use these as small and large pieces of fuel.

128 FIT A NEW HANDLE

An ax or hatchet handle is a renewable resource that's easily replaced. In fact, many vintage tools can be refurbished with a fresh handle for another generation of cutting. Here's how.

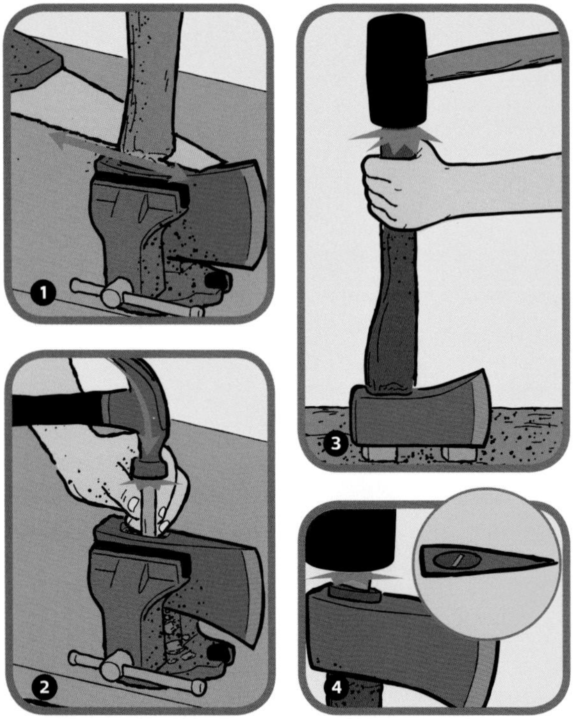

STEP 1 Place the head in a vise and use a hand saw to saw off the old handle as close to the head as possible.

STEP 2 Closely examine the top of the handle at the eye. If there are metal wedges, dig around them with a chisel and remove with needle-nose pliers. Use a handheld $^{1}/_{4}$-inch drill to drill out the wooden wedge and as much of the remaining handle wood as possible. When most of the wood is removed, knock out the remaining handle wood with a punch. Clean the inside of the eye with steel wool.

STEP 3 Pound the new handle into the head until it passes through the eye and extends about an inch past the top of the head. Apply carpenter's glue to the wedge slit in the top of the new handle and along the sides of a wooden handle wedge. Drive in the wedge. Saw off all but $^{1}/_{8}$ inch of the excess handle wood.

STEP 4 Pound in a steel wedge diagonally to the wooden wedge.

129 SKIN AN ANIMAL WITH A FLAY POLL

A flay poll is a rounded, polished poll forged or ground thinner than usual and found on hatchets and axes designed specifically for hunters. To skin a large animal with a flay poll, pull the hide away from the body as you stroke the poll through the connective tissue. The blunt, polished edge prevents cutting through meat or skin. Once the hide is removed, a head with a flay poll can used for gutting and cutting. Hold it in your fist with the edge pointing down, similar to how you would hold an ulu.

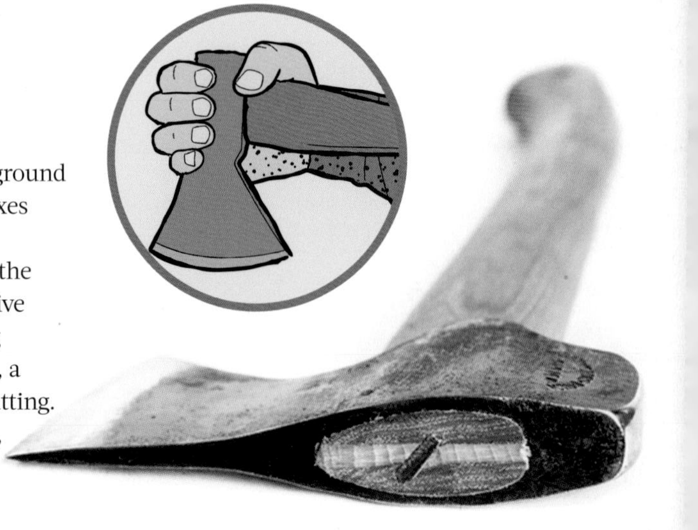

130 GIVE YOUR TOOL SOME TLC

Taking care of an ax or hatchet is a simple matter; ruining one is even simpler. If you want a rusted head on a worthless, dried out handle, just ignore these handy tips. If you'd prefer a working tool, read on. For starters, make sure the sheath is completely dry before replacing it on the head. Apply a bit of machine oil or grease to the head before long-term storage.

REMOVE RUST Tune up a rusty tool using steel wool or a wire brush to scour away scales and surface rust, then apply a thin coating of gun oil.

TIGHTEN A LOOSE HEAD Any play at all in an ax or hatchet head must be addressed swiftly. To firm up the connection, pound in a small metal handle wedge at a 45-degree angle to the wooden wedge.

GET A GRIP Check fiberglass and synthetic handles for any cracking or splintering. If the tool has a metal handle with a wrapped rubber grip, make sure the wraps remain tight.

REWORK WOOD A good wooden handle will last for decades if not longer, but you can extend the life and sweeten the grip with an occasional dressing of boiled linseed oil.

MACHETES & OTHER EDGED TOOLS

→ IN THIS SECTION →

MODERN MACHETES:
BEST TOOLS FOR EVERY JOB

HISTORY OF THE TOMAHAWK

BEYOND THE WHACK:
GET MORE OUT OF A MACHETE

LET FLY:
THE PROPER WAY TO HURL A 'HAWK

WILD CHILD:
WEIRD AND USEFUL MACHETE OFFSPRING

MACHETES

They were everywhere I looked: machetes tied to the waists of workers in the pineapple fields, machetes in the hands of old women with bundles of sticks on their backs, machetes lashed with baling wire to bicycles ridden by 8-year-old boys. In the mornings I awoke to the songs of antbirds and parakeets and the raspy hiss of workers sharpening machetes in the coffee groves outside my door. It was my first trip to Central America, and machetes seemed to be as common in rural Honduras as palm trees.

For centuries, the machete has been a fundamental tool of the agrarian working class. In Latin America and across the tropics, they are still a working implement for many and a means of gathering fuel for the kitchen fires that remain a primary means of cooking in rural areas. Such ubiquity and broad utility have given rise to a wide variety of machete blade designs–the African panga with its sweeping belly, the bolo with a weighty bulge to the tip, the double-edged colima.

Growing up in the South, I always kept a big blade handy to hold the vernal hordes–kudzu, poison ivy, bamboo, greenbrier–at bay. But those machetes were made of flimsy metal with cheap plastic handles. Thankfully, American bladesmiths have taken a note from our neighbors to the south, and rugged, high-quality machetes are now easy to find.

Choosing a machete requires thinking about your target: Hard wood or softer reeds and brush? Targeted chopping or blade-whirling trail clearing? The spectrum runs from long and thin to short and thick. Here's a breakdown by intended task.

NAME	JOBS	DESCRIPTION
A IMACASA PATA DE CUCHE	Tall grass, hanging vines, briars, and brambles	The "pig leg" is a common machete style across Latin America. Made by Imacasa of El Salvador, the 28-inch blade of 1075 high-carbon steel carries its weight evenly down a long, relatively narrow profile. It is one serious weed and greenbrier chopper, and it'll do a number on saplings and branches under two inches in diameter.
B CONDOR KNIFE & TOOL GOLOK	Kindling, small branches, saplings, and rough brush	A mashup of the traditional American-style machete and an Indonesian parang, the golok has a curved, weighted end good for chopping; its 14-inch length wreaks havoc on small limbs and rough brush.
C GERBER GATOR BRUSH THINNER	Hanging vines, dense low brush, and roots	A billhook-style machete is great for grubbing around tree trunks to rip out brush from the roots and for hooking overhead vegetation to bring it into cutting range. Others are better for clearing grass or general camp duties, but a billhook excels at bringing nearer the stuff that needs cutting.
D MY PARANG DUKU CHANDONG	Small pieces of firewood, tent stakes, meat, pineapples, and coconuts	The 12-inch blade might be a bit short for serious campsite clearing, but the 5160 carbon-steel blade is end-heavy for wicked chopping, and its curved edge works well for slicing chores. It's a bushcraft favorite: The raised grip of the handle helps prevent bashed knuckles during heavy use.
E TRAMONTINA 14-INCH BOLO	Tall grass, hanging vines, rough brush, and small trees	Originating in the Philippines, this design has a broad blade with a distinctive bulge at the end, adding weight to the forward part of the machete for powerful swinging. The hardwood handle is frequently sanded and filed to fit the user's hand.

131 SWING IT SAFELY

The attributes of a machete that make it such a useful tool–a sharp blade, a light swing weight, a long edge–also combine to make it dangerous to use if not wielded properly. Before swinging a machete, check your "field of swing." That's the space around you in all directions within reach of a machete in your hand with your arm fully extended. Make sure the field of swing is clear of vines, branches, and most important, people.

THE TOMAHAWK THEN & NOW

Generally lighter and slimmer than a hatchet, the tomahawk was largely used as a tool of combat. Developed by Native American tribes, tomahawks with stone heads were also prized as ceremonial pieces. In more recent times, tomahawks have been fashioned for extreme modern hand-to-hand combat, with sharpened and spiked polls. Other tomahawks are designed for breaching, excavation, and demolition, and are used by first responders in emergency situations.

ORIGINATION

The word "tomahawk" derives from the early Algonquin *tamahaac*. The first European explorers encountered natives with short, hatchetlike tools with stone heads. The introduction of metal to the New World shifted tomahawk design into a new sphere, including "smoke tomahawks" that had a cutting edge on one side of the head and a pipe bowl on the other.

EVOLUTION

Tomahawks saw a resurgence during the Vietnam War, when Peter LaGana designed his original Vietnam Tomahawk for the jungles of Southeast Asia. It proved deadly against enemy troops and was useful for clearing helicopter landing fields. The American Tomahawk Company licensed LaGana's design and now builds the LaGana Tactical Tomahawk, or VTAC (for Vietnam Tactical Tomahawk), with a drop-forged 1060 steel head and modified nylon handle. Useful for both combat and breaching, it has been used extensively by soldiers and mercenaries.

MODERNIZATION

Tactical tomahawks continue to evolve. Some are designed as survival tools, incorporating features such as prybars, wrenches, hammer pommels, and even fire-starting ferro rods. Others, like this United Cutlery M48 Tactical Tomahawk, retain their combat and rescue DNA. A fiberglass-reinforced nylon handle reduces overall weight for all-day carry, and a wide, upswept head of 2Cr13 stainless steel features a long beard for a secondary, choked-up hold. The breaching spike bashes through doors, glass, armor, Kevlar, and cinderblock

M48 TACTICAL TOMAHAWK
VIETNAM TOMAHAWK
SMOKE TOMAHAWK
M48
HAWK

132 STOCK UP ON SURVIVAL HAND TOOLS

The machete is the SUV of cutting tools, so it's no surprise that blade makers have riffed on the standard machete design to create a world of tools designed for survival, bushcraft, and general badassery. If you find yourself in a fix so fearsome you can't hack, bash, or cut your way out of with one of these next-level hand tools, there's a good chance you weren't coming home anyway.

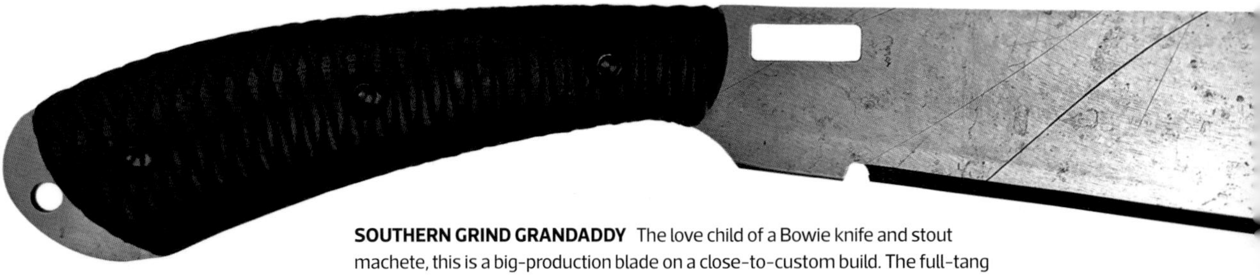

SOUTHERN GRIND GRANDADDY The love child of a Bowie knife and stout machete, this is a big-production blade on a close-to-custom build. The full-tang steel is cut from a reclaimed high-carbon sawmill blade and is differentially heat-treated so it can bend 90 degrees without splitting. It's set between tough G10 handle scales. Saplings, brush, kindling, watermelons, zombies—none stand a chance.

WOODMAN'S PAL Designed in 1941 by a Swiss national who settled in Pennsylvania, the Woodman's Pal has been built in the Keystone State ever since. A standard-issue tool of American soldiers from World War II through Desert Strom, it has a cutting edge and sickle hook that have also been used to build hunting blinds, clear shooting lanes, and open up countless campsites.

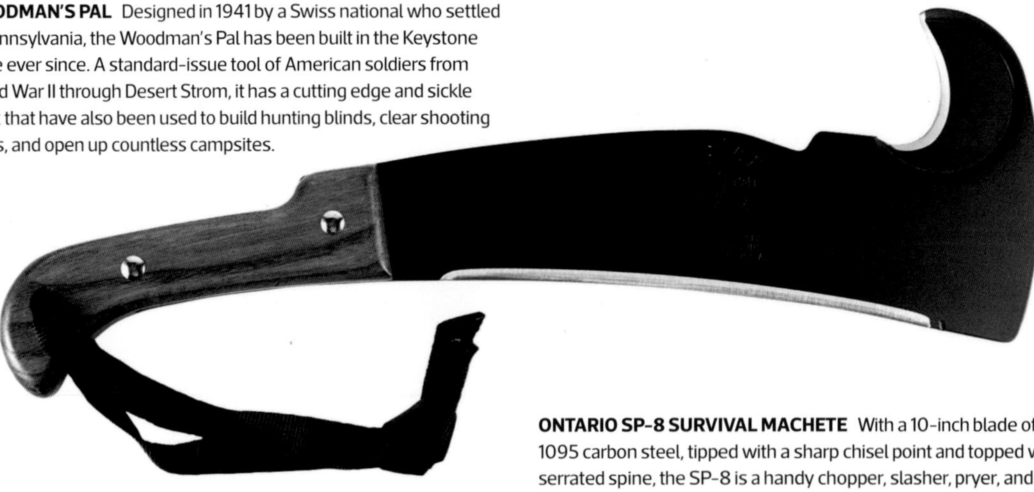

ONTARIO SP-8 SURVIVAL MACHETE With a 10-inch blade of 1095 carbon steel, tipped with a sharp chisel point and topped with a serrated spine, the SP-8 is a handy chopper, slasher, pryer, and digger. Weighing in at a pound and a half thanks to a quarter-inch-thick blade, it's not a light tool—then again, it's not designed for lightweight use.

TRUCKER'S FRIEND Despite its appearance, this is no gimmick. Instead, it's a well-built combination of hatchet, claw hammer, crowbar, grapple hook, and more, nicely sized for under-the-truck-seat storage. Who needs a set of hex sockets that doubles as a demolition tool? You and all your friends.

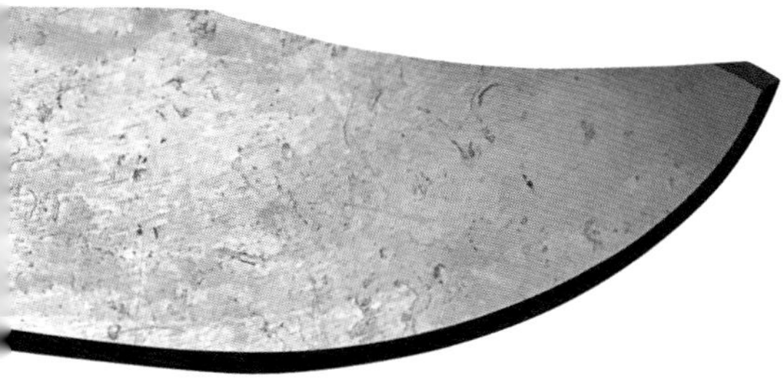

LEATHERMAN RAPTOR EMERGENCY MEDICAL TOOL This is the survival tool you hope you never need: a dedicated medical emergency device. The shears make quick work of bloody clothing, fresh bandages, and even tattered flesh; other features are designed to cut through seat belts and webbing, shatter windshields, and remove rings from swollen, snake-bitten hands.

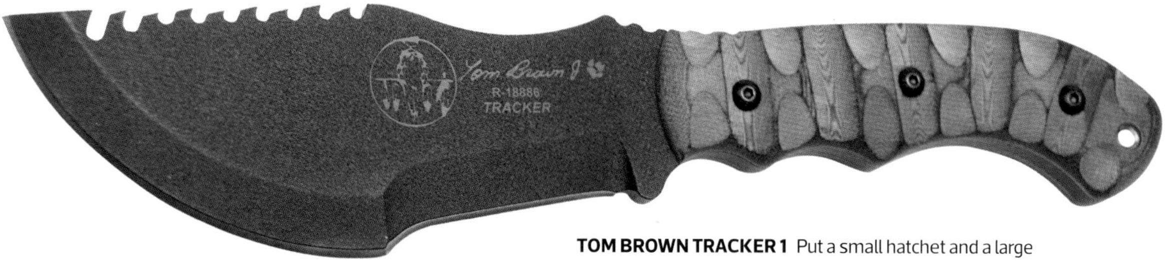

TOM BROWN TRACKER 1 Put a small hatchet and a large knife in a blender and this is what you'd get. The quarter-inch-thick 1095 tool steel blade sports two cutting edges: a weighted, beveled forward section for chopping and a carving blade that can be used as a drawknife.

133 SHARPEN THE BIG KNIFE

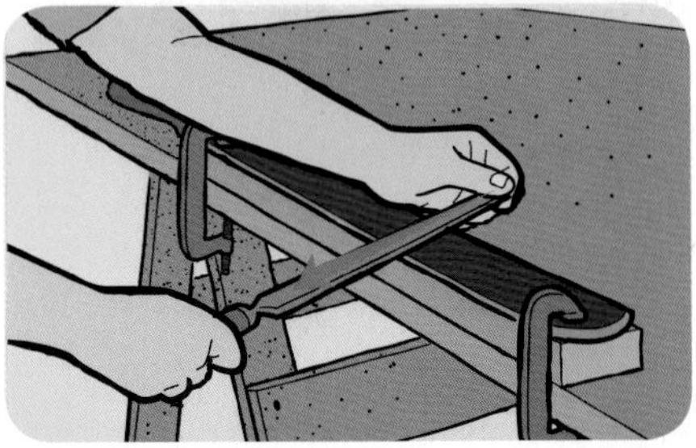

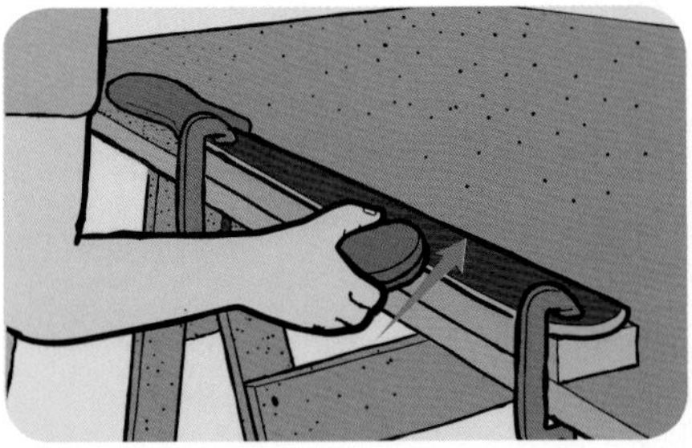

Few machetes come with a decent edge, so sharpening one is the first skill you'll need. Before you start, decide on an edge bevel angle. For cutting grasses, reeds, and small vines, a 20- to 25-degree angle works well. For heavier slashing and repeated chopping, file the machete edge to a 25- to 35-degree angle to keep it from rolling or chipping. If your machete has a thicker blade with a convex edge, follow the factory edge bevel by rolling the file to match the bevel.

STEP 1 Place a two-foot length of 2×4 or 4×4 on the edge of a workbench or table. Place the machete on top of the block with the edge facing you and use a C-clamp or ratchet bar clamp to secure both lumber and blade to the bench's surface.

STEP 2 Using a large bastard mill file (with cutting grooves in one diagonal direction), push the file into the blade from heel to tip. Use enough strokes to raise a burr on the other side of the blade, then turn the blade over and work the other edge.

STEP 3 Sharpening with a file will put a serviceable edge on a machete. If you want a finer edge, use a coarse bench stone to finish the edge while the machete is still clamped down firmly.

134 USE EVERY INCH

A machete is far more than just a chopping and whacking tool. Utilize the full length of the blade for a variety of tasks.

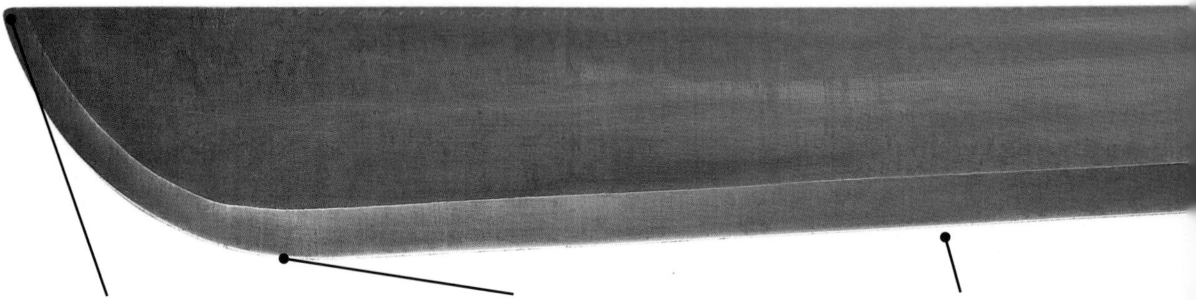

GET TO THE POINT Few machetes have a sharp point, but those that do can be used to drill fireboards or open up a big-game animal.

LEAD WITH AN EDGE This is where much of the work gets done, so designs vary. Slender machetes are used for grass clearing; those with weighted, bulging ends are suited for heavy chopping.

USE THE BIG MIDDLE The middle third of the blade can be used for bushcrafting and survival tasks. Hold the spine at either end and move it like a drawknife or spokeshave to carve spoons and tools or shave feathersticks and kindling.

135 HURL A 'HAWK

If you were really smart, you'd never throw a tomahawk in battle. Why give up one of the most devastating hand-to-hand combat weapons ever devised? But movie scriptwriters don't think that way, hence the innumerable scenes of whirling 'hawks being lofted by Native Americans, frontiersmen, zombie killers, and jungle warriors. That said, tomahawk throwing is serious fun, so much so that throwing competitions abound. Here's how to stick it.

STEP 1 Pace off five full steps from the target. Grasp the tomahawk handle in your dominant hand with a hand-shaking grip.

STEP 2 Roughly aim the tomahawk by lifting the top of the head so that it's in line with the bull's-eye. This helps to ensure that the blade points perfectly straight ahead (if it's turned to one side, the 'hawk will wobble in flight) and positions your hand for the windup.

STEP 3 Drop the tomahawk down along your hip. As the head passes by your leg, stop the swing and then raise the 'hawk back up toward your head as if answering a telephone.

STEP 4 Take a step forward with the foot opposite the hand that's holding the tomahawk and power the 'hawk forward for the release. Adjust your distance from the target as necessary.

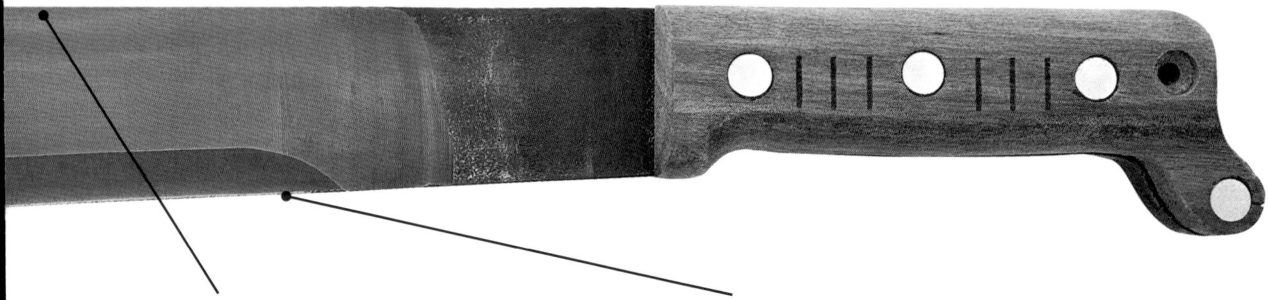

SAVE YOUR SPINE Forget saw-toothed spines. It's far better to carry a saw and have a straight, unsharpened machete spine for bashing open hickory nuts, mashing acorns for meal, and batoning larger pieces of wood.

HONE A KEEN SPOT Sharpen a couple-inch section near the handle to a finer edge for whittling and carving figure-4 trap triggers, gigs, and notches for lashing projects.

SAW DESIGN

→ IN THIS SECTION →

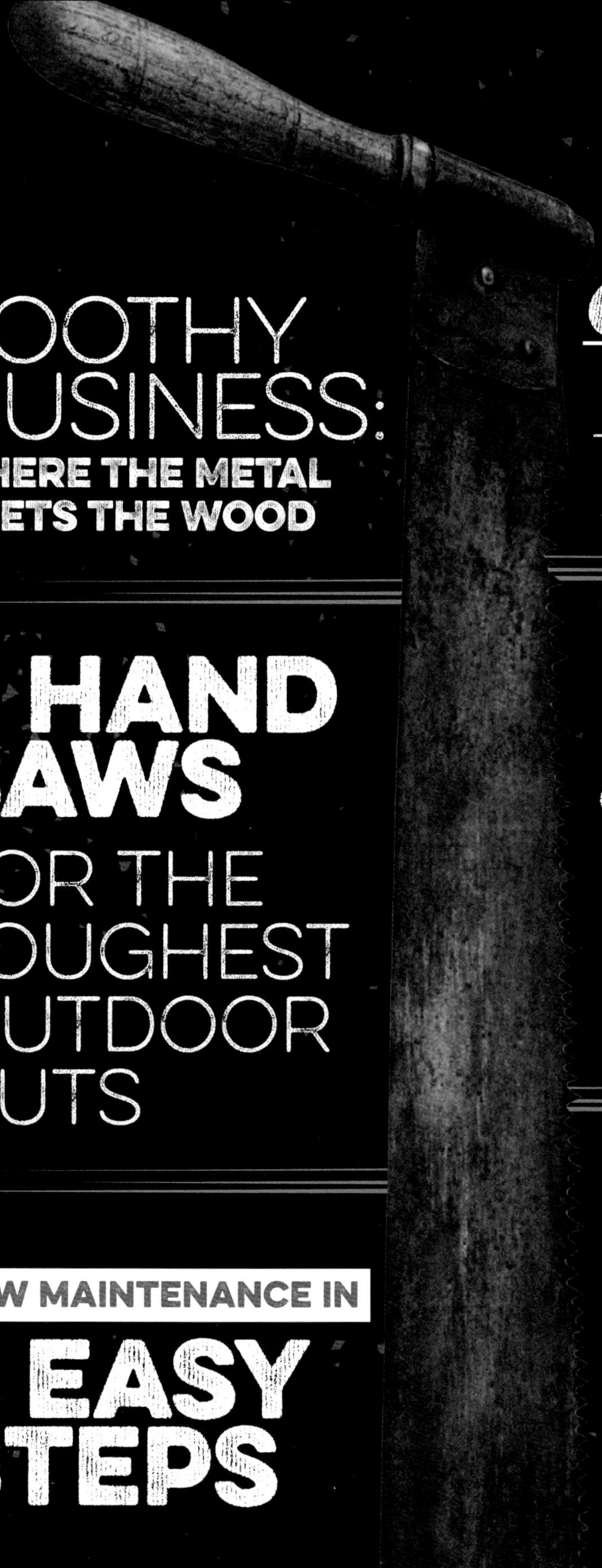

TOOTHY BUSINESS:
WHERE THE METAL MEETS THE WOOD

CROSSCUT CLASSICS
THE BLADES THAT MADE AMERICA

6 HAND SAWS
FOR THE TOUGHEST OUTDOOR CUTS

DOWN & (NOT) DIRTY:
BUCKING LOGS BY HAND

SAW MAINTENANCE IN
3 EASY STEPS

KERF THIS:
TALKING SAW LIKE AN EXPERT

136 CHEW THROUGH WOOD

The teeth of a typical crosscut saw are designed to perform three unique tasks: cut wood fibers, break wood fibers loose, and help remove sheared wood fibers from the cut to keep the saw moving efficiently. Working together, the teeth create a clean, straight cut through the wood. Here's the pertinent lingo.

KERF The cut made by a saw. The narrower the kerf, the more likely the saw will hang up in the wood during cutting.

CUTTER A sharpened cutting tooth, most often beveled on only one side. Cutters are set alternately so the saw cuts two parallel incisions in the kerf.

RAKER These flat-filed teeth don't cut fibers; instead they break the loose fibers free from the log and rake the kerf clean.

GULLET The scalloped space between cutters and rakers or groups of cutters. Cut wood fiber is stored in the gullets while the saw moves through the kerf; the fiber drops out of the gullet as it clears the wood at the end of the stroke.

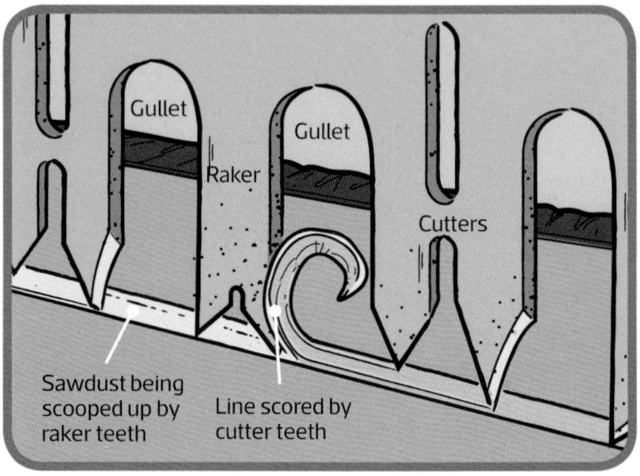

137 TAKE CARE OF YOUR TEETH

Dirt, rust, and sticky sap will make even the sharpest saw difficult to push and pull through wood. Clean a saw well after hard use.

CLEAN SAP AND PITCH Use a citrus-based cleaner to remove pitch deposits and sap streaks. Steel wool and a cleaning solution can attack hard-to-clean buildup. If all you have is soap and hot water, use steel wool with brisk strokes. Dry the blade completely after cleaning.

REMOVE RUST Steel wool and naval gel work wonders on saw rust.

PROTECT THE METAL Once clean, give the blade a wipe of light oil.

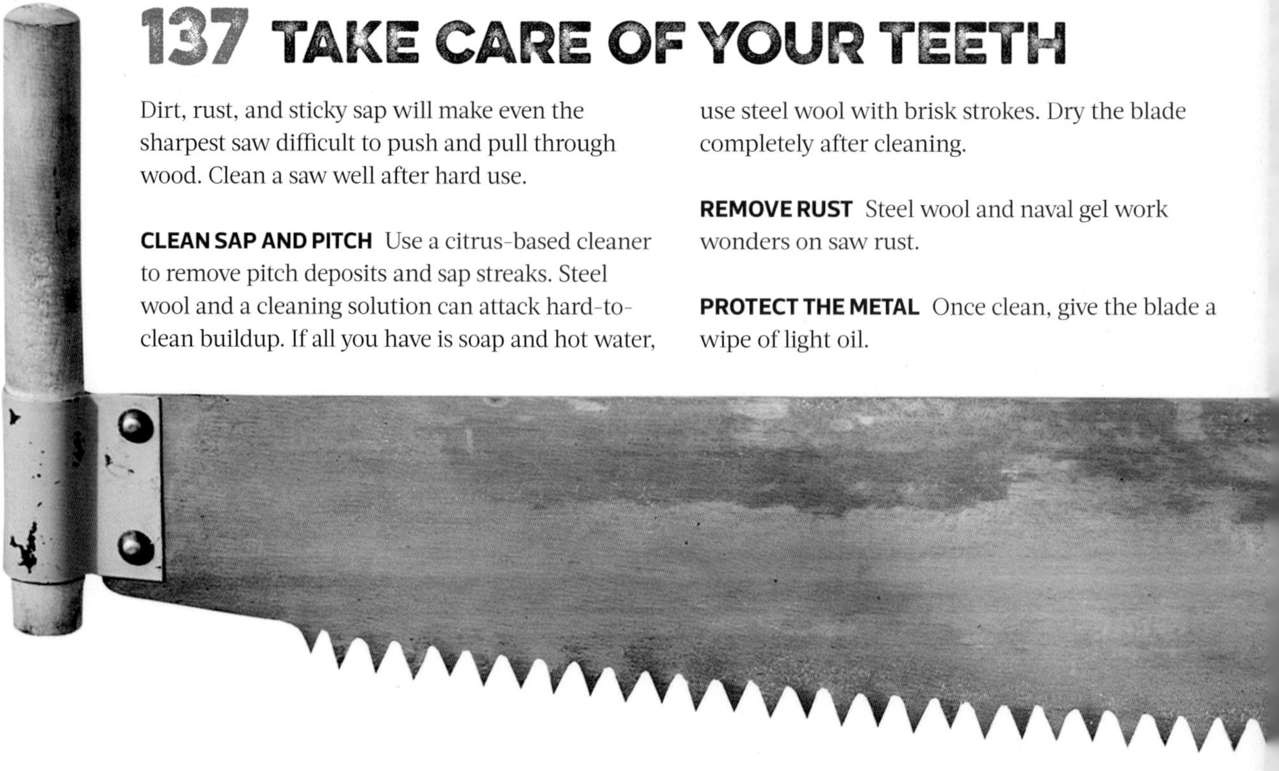

138 CHOOSE THE RIGHT TOOTH PATTERN FOR THE JOB

The golden age of crosscut saws in North America began in the 1880s–as pioneers and timber companies moved west–and continued until mechanized saws overtook hand saws in the early 1930s. Crosscut saws are still used to clear trails and fell timber, especially in wilderness areas. And collectors prize the various tooth patterns that evolved for different cutting conditions.

PLAIN TOOTH PATTERN Also known as the peg tooth pattern. A plain tooth saw includes only cutter teeth. This is the most common pattern for hand saws used for general outdoors tasks.

M TOOTH PATTERN An ancient pattern more than 500 years old, the M tooth pattern is the sport utility pattern of saw blades: It cuts wood fibers, breaks them loose, then pushes them out of the kerf.

GREAT AMERICAN TOOTH PATTERN Sometimes called a crown pattern, this one features groups of three teeth separated by gullets.

CHAMPION TOOTH PATTERN Two cutter teeth are set with cutting edges on alternate sides, with a raker and a gullet between them. Champion teeth are designed for hard, even frozen, wood.

LANCE TOOTH PATTERN A longtime standard in the American West, this pattern includes groups of four cutters separated by rakers, with a gullet on either side of the group. A lance tooth pattern absolutely eats through soft green conifers.

PERFORATED LANCE TOOTH PATTERN Similar to a lance pattern, but with bridges between the teeth to form the perforations.

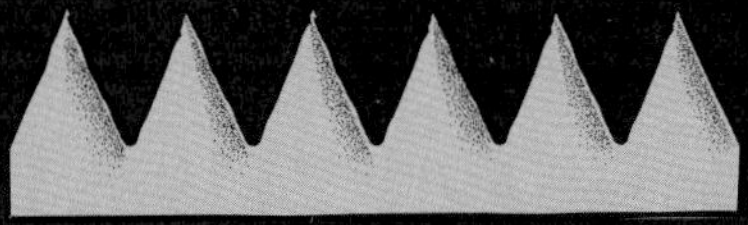

PLAIN TOOTH PATTERN

M TOOTH PATTERN

GREAT AMERICAN TOOTH PATTERN

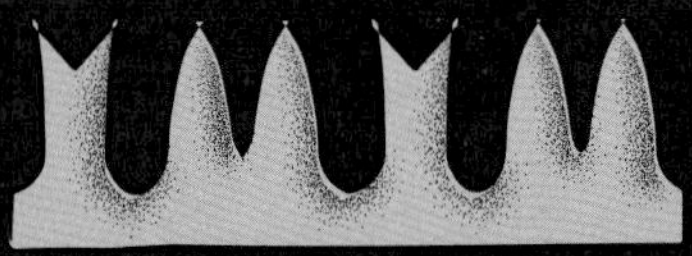

CHAMPION TOOTH PATTERN

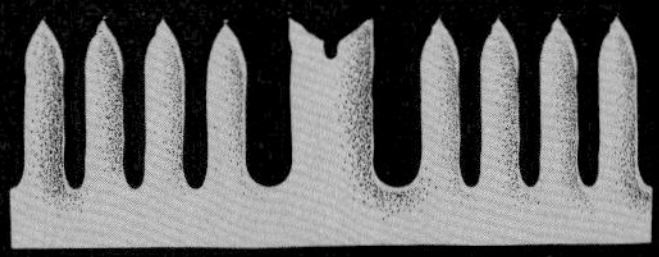

LANCE TOOTH PATTERN

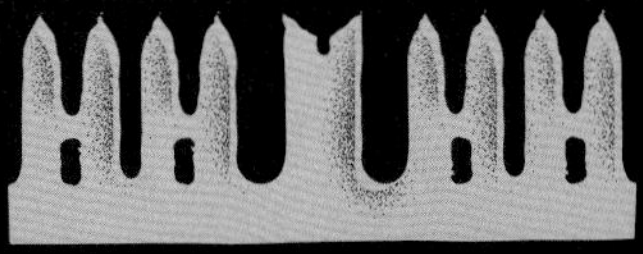

PERFORATED LANCE TOOTH PATTERN

139

BUCK A LOG WITH A SAW

Bucking means to cut a downed, delimbed tree into logs, either for firewood or to clear it from a trail. Bucking is a far more useful skill than even felling a tree, but it can be a dangerous task. Before attempting to buck any fallen tree, take a few minutes to make a plan. Figure out the binding pressures. Is the tree under tension or compression? Clear out any trees or branches that the downed tree may have fallen on; these can spring up with great force when pressure is released. Stand on the uphill side of the tree. And come prepared with a few plastic wedges to keep the kerf open for easy sawing.

IF THE TREE IS FLAT ON THE GROUND Cut from the top down, moving partway through the log. Then, either roll the log to continue the cut or lever the log up and shim it with a piece of wood in order to finish.

IF THE TREE IS SUPPORTED AT ONE END Make an initial cut from the bottom up, through approximately one-third of the log's diameter. The second cut is made from the top down to meet the first.

IF THE TREE IS SUPPORTED AT BOTH ENDS Make the first cut from the top down. Watch the cut closely. The second cut is from the bottom up.

140 GET A HANDLE ON HAND SAWS

Packable hand saws can be a huge help in the woods, whether you're cutting kindling for the fire, clearing shooting lanes for hunting stands, building blinds, or working on trails. Like any tool, you get what you pay for, so stay away from the cheap stuff. The good news: None of these saws will break the bank.

THE FOLDING PRUNER If what needs cutting involves bone, branches, or small limbs, the Bahco Laplander folding saw is the tool for the job, hands down. I have cursed many a folding saw that blew up as I dangled from half-erected tree stands. Never the Laplander. Unlike many folders, the specially designed teeth cut both ways. Unlike many folders, the blade is coated to keep friction to a minimum. And unlike many folders, the pivoting mechanism is stout enough that it will not blow up as you dangle from a half-erected tree stand.

THE SURVIVAL TOOL Wire saws tend to be gimmicky throwaways, but the 24-inch UST Sabercut Chain Saw is—as its name suggests—essentially a chain saw blade with handles. It's not as light as a survival wire saw, and it takes some calories to get it working. But it's a good solution as a packable woodcutter for both survival and regular camping uses.

THE IGLOO BUILDER You might not need a snow saw every day, but when you really need one, nothing else will do. The folding, curved blade of the MSR Basecamp Snow Shelter Saw sports specialized teeth that gnaw through packed snow and ice like an abominable snow beaver. Put up an emergency snow shelter, igloo, or backcountry ice bar in a jiffy.

THE MULE, TRUCK & ATV SAW A classic trail saw used by mule packers and horsemen, the 19-inch No. 20 Fanno Saw and Scabbard has a slightly curved blade for serious bite. The self-cleaning and self-feeding lance teeth clear wood from the kerf, and the wooden D-shaped handle is comfortable to hold and set at an angle for a strong sawing motion. Its stout leather scabbard enables lashing to a saddle or ATV rack. Pick one up at a packer supply shop.

THE PACKABLE WOOD CHIPPER I've cleared a country mile of shooting lanes with a pile of different hand saws, and nothing comes close to the 14.2-inch folding Silky Bigboy. Weighing just a pound, it's super light, tough, and easy to jam into a daypack. The cutting power of the Bigboy is almost hard to believe. It comes in four different models with varying tooth arrangements—opt for the curved blade with extra-large teeth. Write your name on it in big letters with a Sharpie.

THE BACKPACKER'S BUDDY Lightweight, tough, and easy to stow in a pack, the Minnesota-built Sven-Saw has been a trail staple for more than 50 years. The 21-inch model will cut through a 6-inch log in less than a minute. The blade folds into the handle to protect the teeth, and the whole thing can be easily rolled into a sleeping pad or crammed into a pack pocket.

141 SET YOUR SIGHTS

When bucking a log, accuracy trumps power. Each time the blade bites off-target, you've wasted time and energy. Focus on the specific spot you want to strike. Swing smoothly. Once you've established an accurate swing, you can add power and velocity.

CHAPTER 1: KNOW THE KNIFE

RANDALL MADE KNIVES
MODEL 25 – TRAPPER

EMERSON KNIVES
COMMANDER

TOPS KNIVES
FIELDCRAFT

BUCK KNIVES
MATT WOULD GO

SPYDERCO
SALT I YELLOW

CRKT HOMEFRONT

SOG SPECIALTY KNIVES & TOOLS
VULCAN TANTO

FIRSTEDGE RYAN HOOVER 4050-4055
HR-1 BACKUP/SELF-DEFENSE KNIFE

WHITE RIVER KNIFE & TOOL
M1 BACKPACKER

GUINEA HOG FORGE
DAMASCUS TUSK

TERRY L. VANDEVENTER
DAMASCUS

BILL BURKE
DAMASCUS

GERBER
GATOR PREMIUM FOLDER

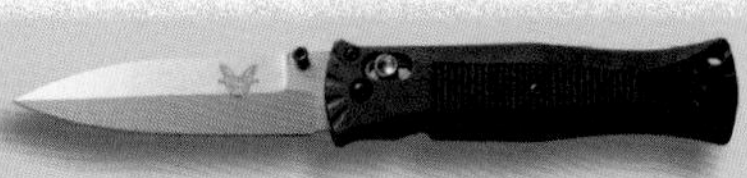
BENCHMADE
PARDUE MODIFIED SPEAR-POINT AXIS

CATTARAUGUS CUTLERY
VINTAGE SPEY KNIFE

BÖKER PLUS
HAWKBILL FOLDING KNIFE

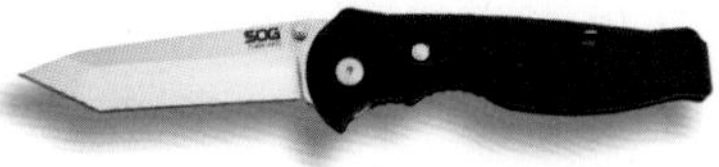
SOG SPECIALTY KNIVES & TOOLS
FLASH II FSAT8-CP

HELLE OF NORWAY
EGGEN

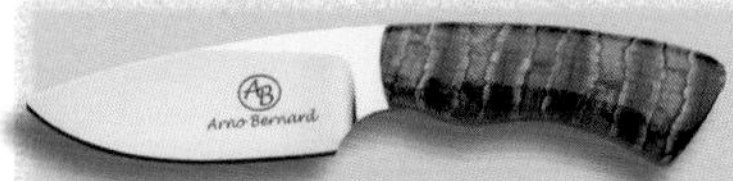

ARNO BERNARD
GECKO MAMMOTH MOLAR

SCHRADE
SURE-LOCK CLIP FOLDER

ONTARIO KNIFE COMPANY
RANGER SERIES RD7 BUSHCRAFT

SPYDERCO
MANIX 2 BLUE LIGHTWEIGHT

SPYDERCO
DELICA 4

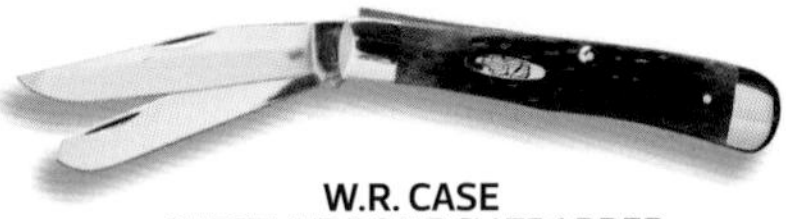
W.R. CASE
CHESTNUT BONE CV TRAPPER

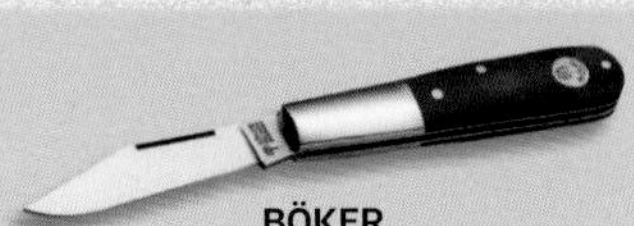
BÖKER
BARLOW CLASSIC

BUCK KNIVES
OPEN SEASON CAPER

OUTDOOR EDGE
FIELD-BONE

BARK RIVER KNIVES
NESSMUK

RANDALL MADE KNIVES
MODEL 1 – ALL-PURPOSE FIGHTING KNIFE

KNIVES OF ALASKA
ALPHA WOLF D2 – STAG

SCHRADE EXTREME SURVIVAL

HELLE OF NORWAY ODEL

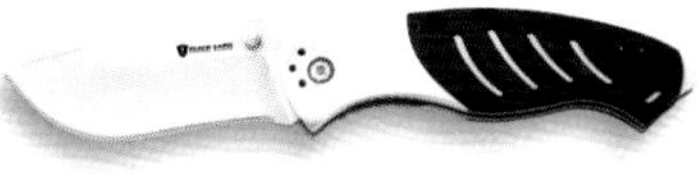

BROWNING
BLACK LABEL UNDISPUTED

GUINEA HOG FORGE
SPARROW HAWK

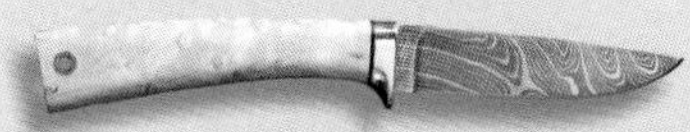

SCHMIDT KNIVES & FORGE
CUSTOM DESIGN

SCHMIDT KNIVES & FORGE
CUSTOM DESIGN

STEEL WILL
DRUID 255

OUTDOOR EDGE
GRIPLITE

BARK RIVER KNIVES
CLASSIC TRAILING POINT HUNTER

SPYDERCO
ENUFF LEAF FIXED BLADE

W.R. CASE
AMBER BONE STOCKMAN

CRKT
MINIMALIST WHARNCLIFFE

W.R. CASE
LEATHER HUNTER

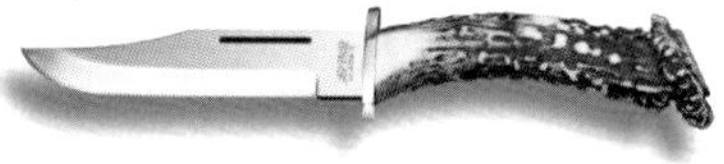

SILVER STAG KNIVES
DV6.0

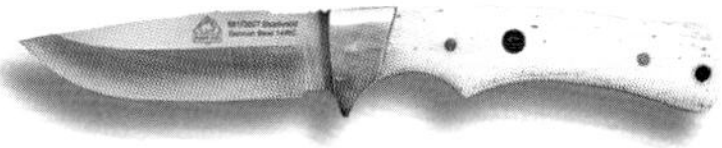

PUMA
SGB DEADWOOD CANYON

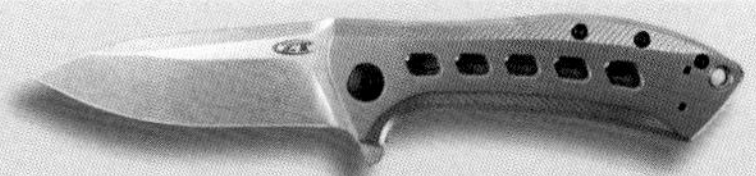

ZERO TOLERANCE 0801TI

OUTDOOR EDGE CONQUER

KERSHAW KNIVES LEEK 1660CF

W.R. CASE
BLUE BONE TRAPPER

BUCK KNIVES
CANOE

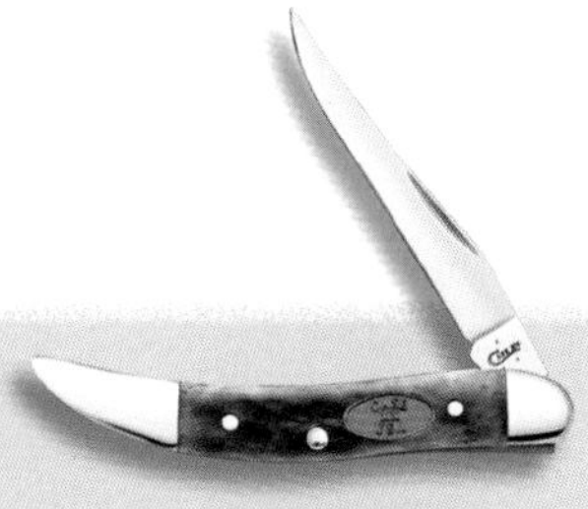

W.R. CASE
TEXAS TOOTHPICK

BROWNING
ESCALADE BIRD AND TROUT

CRKT
BIG EDDY II FILLET KNIFE

ONTARIO KNIFE COMPANY
OLD HICKORY 76-7" CLEAVER

SOG SPECIALTY KNIVES & TOOLS
TARGA

EMERSON KNIVES CQC-7BW

CRKT M16 SERIES

ONTARIO KNIFE COMPANY
U.S. MARINE CORPS OKC-3S BAYONET

ONTARIO KNIFE COMPANY
U.S. AIR FORCE ASEK SURVIVAL

BENCHMADE
USCG RESCUE & SURVIVAL KNIFE

HELLE OF NORWAY
ARV

CRKT KUK

COLD STEEL
SCOTTISH DIRK

COLD STEEL
TUFF LITE

MUELA
MOUSE

KA-BAR
BECKER NECKER

LEATHERMAN
WAVE

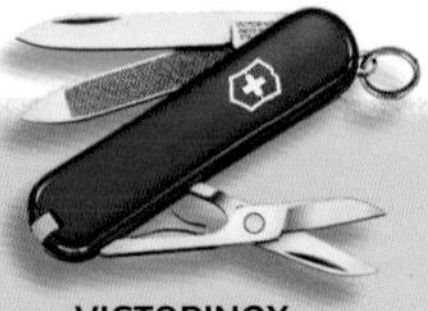

VICTORINOX
SWISS ARMY CLASSIC

VICTORINOX
SWISS ARMY SWISS CHAMP

CHAPTER 2: USE THE KNIFE

LOST PLANET FORGE
CUSTOM SEMI SKINNER

SPYDERCO
4-INCH PARING KNIFE

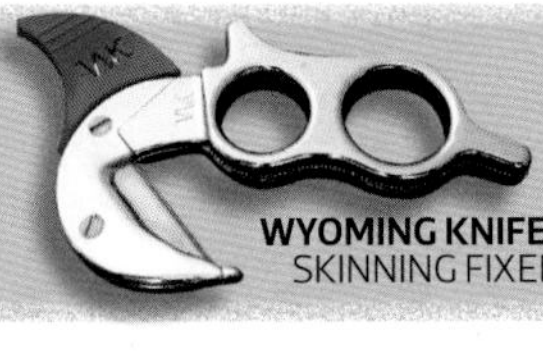

WYOMING KNIFE ORIGINAL
SKINNING FIXED BLADE

KERSHAW KNIVES
TASKMASTER GAME SHEARS

OUTDOOR EDGE
RAZORLITE EDC

MORAKNIV
GARBERG

TOPS/BUCK
CSAR-T

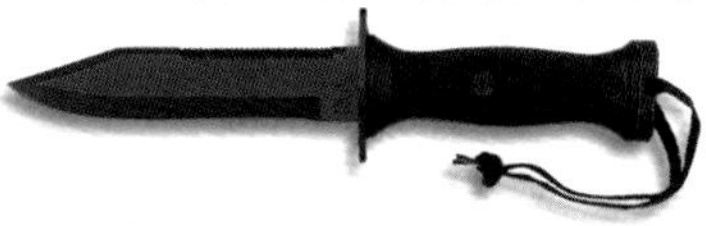

ONTARIO KNIFE COMPANY
U.S. NAVY ONTARIO MARK III

ONTARIO KNIFE COMPANY
U.S. ARMY M9 BAYONET

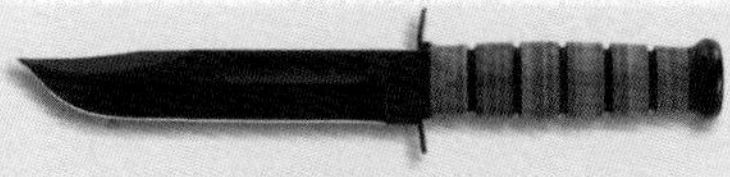

KA-BAR USMC

BENCHMADE
BALI-SONG

KNIVES OF ALASKA
MAGNUM ULU

EMERSON KNIVES
KARAMBIT FIXED BLADE

DPX GEAR
HEAT

MANTIS KNIVES
MT-9C TOUGH TONY

KERSHAW KNIVES
SHUFFLE

RANDALL MADE KNIVES
MODEL 2 – FIGHTING STILETTO

RANDALL MADE KNIVES
RAYMOND THORP

SCHMIDT KNIVES & FORGE
CUSTOM DESIGN

BEHRING MADE
CUSTOM DESIGN

VICTORINOX
SOLDIER

BURT FOSTER
DAMASCUS

SPYDERCO ENDURA 4

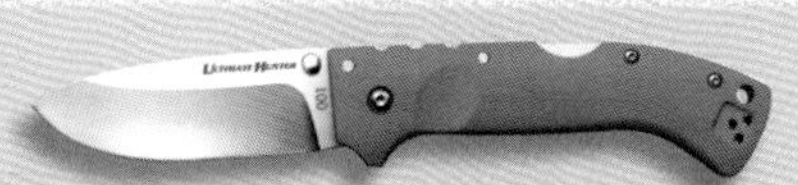

COLD STEEL
ULTIMATE HUNTER

BUCK KNIVES
ZIPPER KNIFE

OLD TIMER SHARPFINGER

DPX GEAR HEST 6 ASSAULT

BUBBA BLADE KNIVES
FLEX FILLET KNIFE

BUCK KNIVES
110 FOLDING HUNTER

OPINEL NO. 8

MORAKNIV
WOODCARVING JUNIOR

BENCHMADE 162 BUSHCRAFTER

FÄLLKNIVEN F1

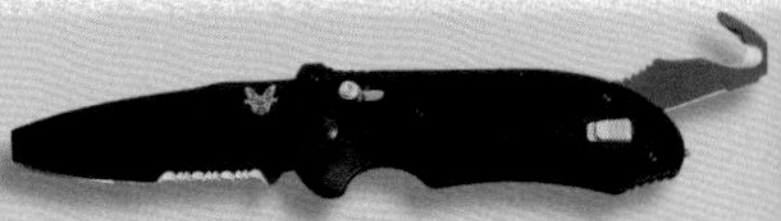
BENCHMADE AUTO TRIAGE

CHAPTER 3: AXES, HATCHETS & SAWS

COUNCIL TOOL
AMERICAN FELLING AX

L.L. BEAN
HUDSON BAY AX

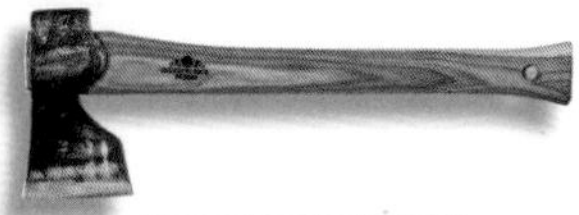
HELLE OF NORWAY
CARPENTER'S AX

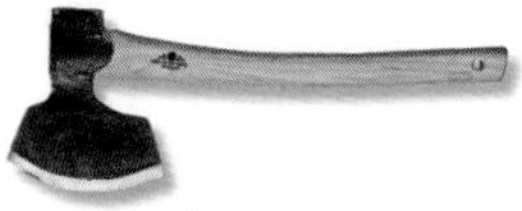
GRÄNSFORS BRUK
BROAD AX

COUNCIL TOOL DOUBLE BIT AX

IMACASA PATA DE CUCHE

CONDOR TOOL & KNIFE GOLOK

MY PARANG DUKU CHANDONG

WOODMAN'S PAL

ONTARIO KNIFE COMPANY
SP-8 SURVIVAL MACHETE

INNOVATION FACTORY
OFF GRID SURVIVAL AXE ELITE

MSR
BASECAMP SNOW SHELTER SAW

UST
SABERCUT CHAIN SAW

FANNO SAW NO. 20

D.H. RUSSELL CANADIAN BELT KNIFE

WEATHERFORD KNIFE CO. WESTERN SKINNER

LAGUIOLE ORIGINE GARANTIE T12

VICTORINOX EVOLUTION GRIP S18

W.R. CASE LEATHER MINI FINN HUNTER

FLEXCUT KN12

ESTWING CAMPING HATCHET

GRAND FOREST SPLITTING AX

RAZOR-BACK MAUL

GRÄNSFORS BRUK CARVING AX

BEN MEADOWS PULASKI AX

CONDOR TOOL & KNIFE AMALGAM

GERBER GATOR BRUSH THINNER

TRAMONTINA 14-INCH BOLO

SOUTHERN GRIND GRANDADDY

LEATHERMAN RAPTOR

TOM BROWN TRACKER 1

BAHCO LAPLANDER

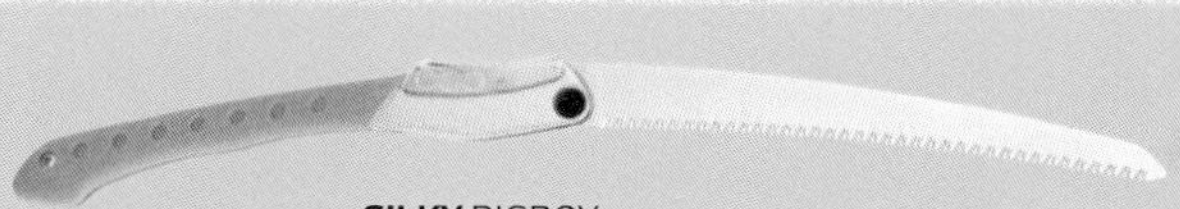

SILKY BIGBOY

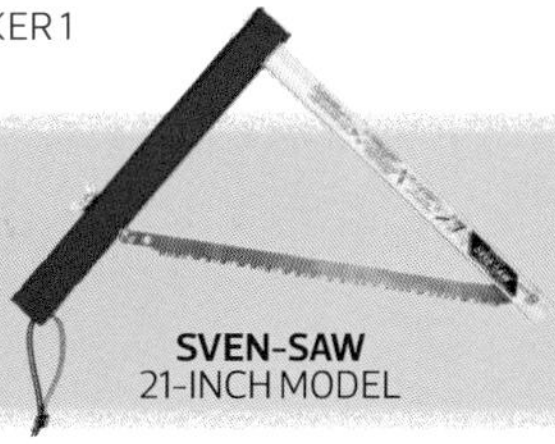

SVEN-SAW 21-INCH MODEL

D

E

F

G

H

ACKNOWLEDGMENTS

FROM THE AUTHOR, T. EDWARD NICKENS

I've had an unhealthy obsession with knives since I read about Jim Bowie's sandbar duel when I was a kid. And I've had a healthy respect for knives ever since my brother accidentally stabbed me in the leg while we were stupidly playing with knives in the back seat of our family's 1973 Ford Pinto station wagon. But it wasn't until I began reading the knife writings of David E. Petzal, *Field & Stream*'s longtime rifles and knife guru, that I more clearly understood what an exquisite, lifelong, and consuming passion knifery—to use a Petzal term—could be. Petzal writes about knives like Norman Maclean wrote about fire and rivers. So, thanks to my friend Dave for showing me how little I knew and fashioning a pathway to learning so much more. And much gratitude, as well, to Anthony Licata and Colin Kearns, the sage editors at *Field & Stream* who had a vision for the Total Outdoorsman concept and the incredible talent to make it real.

CREDITS

Photography courtesy of

Aaron Johnson: Knife Design subhead (photo courtesy of Randall Made Knives, Model 25–Trapper); **American Tomahawk Company:** The Tomahawk (The NEW LaGana Tactical Tomahawk); **Arno Bernard:** Design Class: Handle Materials (Mammoth [Gecko Mammoth Molar]); **Bahco:** 140 (The Folding Pruner [Laplander]); **Bark River Knives:** 013 (A2 [Nessmuck]), Design Class: Blade Profiles (Trailing Point [Classic Trailing Point Hunter]); **Behring Made:** 032 (Custom Design); **Ben Meadows:** Design Class: Know Your Ax and Hatchet Heads (Pulaski Ax); **Benchmade Knife Company:** Design Class: Blade Profiles (Spear Point [Pardue Modified Spear-Point Axis]), 021 (U.S. Coast Guard [USCG Rescue & Survival Knife]), 025 (Bali-Song), Survival subchapter (162 Bushcrafter), 117 (Auto Triage); **BLADE Show/BLADE® Magazine:** 033 (knife show); **Bobby Branton:** 024 (Che Che White Cloud and Paul LaCross); **Böker Plus:** Design Class: Blade Profiles (Hawkbill Folding Knife), 015 (Barlow Classic); **Browning:** 013 (154 CM [Black Label Undisputed]), 016 (Bird and Trout Knife [Escalade Bird & Trout]); **Bubba Blade Knives:** 074 (Flex Fillet Knife); **Buck Knives:** 013 (5160 [Matt Would Go]), 015 (Canoe), 016 (Caping Knife [Open-Season-Caper]), 020 (Tops/Buck CSAR-T), 060 (zipper knife), Camping subchapter (110 folding hunter knife); **Brooks Hansen:** 082; **Charles Harris:** 104; **Chuck Ward:** 014 (Ladder [Terry L. Vandeventer Damascus] & Geometric Mosaic [Bill Burke Damascus]); **Cold Steel Knife and Tool Company:** 016 (Field Dressing Knife [Ultimate Hunter]), 025 (Scottish Dirk), 026 (Teacup Practical [Tuff Lite]), Hunting and Fishing subchapter (Ultimate Hunter); **Condor Tool & Knife:** Ax & Hatchet Design subchapter, Machetes & Other Edged Tools subchapter (Amalgam), Design Class: Machete Types (Golok); **Corona:** 140 (RazorTOOTH Saw Raker Saw); **CRKT:** Designers Who Changed Everything: AG Russel and Ken Onion, 013 (AUS-8 [Homefront]), Design Class: Blade Profiles (Wharncliffe [Minimalist Wharncliffe]), 016 (Fillet Knife [Big Eddy II Fillet Knife]), 020 (CRKT M16 Series), 025 (Kukri [Kuk]); **Council Tool:** Design Class: Know Your Ax and Hatchet Heads (American Feeling Ax and Double Bit Ax); **Cutting Edge:** Design Class: Blade Profiles (Spey Point [Vintage Spey Knife]); **David R. Adamovich:** 024 (The Great Throwdini); **Dusan Smetana:** Author's Note; **DPX Gear:** 026 (Tiny EDC [Heat]); **Eddie Nickens:** 070; **Emerson Knives:** Designers Who Changed Everything: Ernest Emerson (Commander), 020 (Emerson CQC-7BW) 025 (Emerson Karambit Fixed Blade); **Esee Knives:** 093 (Izula-II fixed blade knife); **Estwing:** Design Class: (Camping Hatchet); **Fällkniven:** Blades that Matter: Fällkniven F1; **Fanno Saw:** 140 (The Mule, Truck & ATV Saw [No. 20]); **FirstEdge:** 013 (ELMAX [Ryan Hoover 4050-4055 HR-1 Backup/Self-Defense Knife]); **Flexcut Tool Company:** 102 (KN12); **Gerber Knives:** Design Class: Blade Profiles (Clip Point [Gator Premium Folder]), Design Class: Blade Grinds (Gator Premium Folder Clip Point), Design Class: Machete Types (Gator Brush Thinner); **Global Cutlery USA:** 043 (sharpening rod [stainless steel ceramic sharpener]); **Grand Forest:** Design Class: Know Your Ax and Hatchet Heads (Splitting Ax); **Grändsfors Bruk Sweden:** Design Class: Know Your Ax and Hatchet Heads (Broad Ax and Carving Ax); **Grohmann Knives:** Blades that Matter: D.H. Russell Canadian Belt Knife (Canadian Belt Knife); **Guinea Hog Forge:** 014 (Multibar Twisted "W" [Sparrow Hawk]), 036 (Scott McGhee); **Helle of Norway:** 013 (SANDVIK 12C27 [Odel]), Design Class: Handle Materials (Wood [Eggen]), 025 (Puukko [ARV]), Design Class: Heads (Carpenter's Ax); **Husqvarna:** Design Class: Know Your Ax and Hatchet Heads (Carpenter's Ax or Hatchet); **Industrial Revolution:** 018 (Morakniv Garberg); **Innovation Factory:** : 132 (Off Grid Survival Axe Elite); **KA-BAR:** Blades that Matter: KA-BAR USMC, 026 (Wicked Necklace [Becker Necker]); **Kershaw Knives:** Design Class: Handle Materials (Carbon Fiber [LEEK 1660 CF]), 016 (Game Shears [Taskmaster Game Shears]); **Knives of Alaska:** 013 (D2 [Alpha Wolf D-2 Stag]), Designers Who Changed Everything: Charles Allen, 025 (Ulu [Magnum Ulu]); **Laguiole:** Blades that Matter: Laguiole Knife (Origine Garantie T12); **Leatherman:** 132 (Raptor Emergency Medical Tool); **L.L. Bean:** Design Class: Know Your Ax and Hatchet Heads (Hudson Bay Ax); **Loctite:** 056 (bottle [primerless thread locker 243]); **Lost Planet Forge:** Knife Care subchapter (Custom Semi Skinner); **LovelessKnifeCollector.com:** Designers Who Changed Everything: R.W. "Bob" Loveless; **Machete Specialists:** Design Class: Machete Types (Imacasa Pata de Cuche and Tramontina 14-inch Bolo); **Mantis Knives:** 026 (Fighting Folders [MT-9c Tough Tony]); **Morakniv:** 099 (Morakniv woodcarving junior); **MSR:** 140 (The Igloo Builder [Basecamp Show Shelter Saw]); **Muela:** 026 (Skin a Little [Mouse]); **MY Parang:** Design Class: MAchetes (Duku Chandong); **Norton:** 043 (manmade oil stone [combination India stone], courtesy of Lost Planet Forge) ; **OfficialAlamo:** Bowie Knives (True-Blue Bowie, above [Searles-Fowler Bowie]); **Old Timer Knives:** Blades that Matter: Old Timer Sharpfinger; **Ontario Knife Company:** Design Class: Handle Materials (Micarta [Ranger Series RD7 Bushcraft]), 016 (Cleaver [Old Hickory 76-7" Cleaver]), 021 (U.S. Army [M9 Bayonet], U.S. Air Force [ASEK], U.S. Navy [Ontario Mark III], and U.S. Marine Corps [OKC-3S Bayonet]),132 (SP-8 Survival Machete); **Opinel:** Blades that Matter: Opinel No. 8; **Outdoor Edge:** Design Class: Blade Profiles (Drop Point [GripLite]), Design Class: Handle Materials (G10 [Conquer]) 016 (Boning Knife [Field Bone]), 109; **Permanent Collection of the Historic Arkansas Museum, Little Rock, Arkansas:** Bowie Knives (True Blue Bowie, below [Historical Bowie Knife]); **Portland Made Collective:** Designers Who Changed Everything: Tim Leatherman; **Protool Industries:** 132 (Woodman's Pal); **Puma Knife Company:** Design Class: Handle Materials (Bone [SGB Deadwood Canyon]); **Randall Made Knives:** 013 (O-1 [Model 1-All-Purpose Fighting Knife]), Blades that Matter: Arkansas Toothpick (Model 2-Fighting Stiletto), Bowie Knives (Raymond Thorp), Designers Who Changed Everything: W.D. "Bo" Randall; **Razor-Back:** Design Class: Know Your Ax and Hatchet Heads (Maul); **Schmidt Knives & Forge:** 014 (Random Twist [Custom Design], Raindrop or Pool and Eye [Custom Design]), Custom Knives subhead (Custom Design); **SharpByCoop Photography:** 038 (Knife Legends); **Schrade:** 013 (8CR13MOV [Shrade Extreme Survival]), Design Class: Handle Materials (Aluminum [Sure-Lock Clip Folder]); **Shutterstock:** cover, title page, contents, 002, 006, 007 (raw carbon steel & molten steel), 010, Design Class: Sheaths (knife in belt sheath), 016 (fur background), 018 (metal background texture & blade starting a fire), 021 (camouflage background texture), 022, 023, 024 (background texture), 025 (stiletto), 026 (background texture), Bowie knives (paper and wood background textures), 027, 029 (background texture), Designers Who Changed Everything: Tim Leatherman (Leatherman Wave knife), 032 (making a knife), 037 (flag illustrations), 039 (TSA photo, knife, & concealed knife) Use the Knife chapter opener, Gaining and Edge, 043 (top three photos, honing steel, guided sharpening device, powered sharpening device), 050, 051, 052, 053, 055, 056 (screws), 058, 063, 066, 068 (pig), 069, 072, 075, 076, 077, 079, 084, 085, 087, 089, 090, 091, Feats of Steel: Make a Shit Knife, 095, 098, 107, 108, 110, 111, 112, 117 (background photo), Feats of Steel: Kill a Bear with a Knife, index (hiking travel gear on wood backdrop, big military knife, bushcraft survival knife, knife on survival belt), Axes, Hatchets, & Knives opener and introduction, subchapter, 120, 123, 127, Design Class: Get a Grip on Handles, Ax and Hatchet Skills opener, 130, 131, 134, 135, Saw Design opener, 137, 139, Know the Knife opener, The Right Knife; **Silky:** 140 (The Packable Wood Chipper [Silky Bigboy]); **Silver Stag:** Design Class: Handle Materials (Stag [DV6.0]); **SOG Specialty Knives & Tools:** 013 (VG-10 [Vulcan Tanto]), Design Class: Blade Profiles (Tanto [Flash II FSAT8-CP]), 019 (Targa); **Southern Grind:** 132 (Grandaddy); **Spyderco:** 013 (H-1 [Salt 1 Yellow]), Design Class: Blade Profiles (Leaf [Enuff Leaf Fixed Blade]), Design Class: Handle Materials (Nylon [Manix-2-Blue-Lightweight]), Designers Who Changed Everything: Meet the Spyder Man (Sal Glesser), 044 (4-inch Paring Knife), 057 (Endura 4); **Steel Will:** Design Class: Blade Profiles (Straight-Back [Druid 255]); **Sven-Saw:** 140 (The Backpacker's Buddy [Sven-Saw 21-inch model]); **The William F. Moran Jr. Museum & Foundation, Inc.:** Designers Who Changed Everything: Bill Moran; **Tops Knives:** 013 (1095 [Fieldcraft]), 132 (Tom Brown Tracker); **United Cutlery:** The Tomahawk (M48 Hawk Tactical Tomahawk); **UST:** 140 (The Survival Tool [SaberCut Chain Saw]); **Victorinox Swiss Army:** 028 (Soldier), 029 (Swiss Army Classic, Swiss Army Swiss Champ, Wenger 16999 Giant, & Victorinox Soldier), 099 (Victorinox Evolution Grip S18); **Waterbury Publications:** Cover, Design Class: Separations (Spyderco Delica 4), Design Class: Sheaths (knife & sheath courtesy of Weatherford Knife Company), Knife Types subchapter (W.R. Case Chestnut Bone CV Trapper), 017 (Outdoor Edge RazorLite EDC), 026 (Kershaw Shuffle), Multi-Tools subchapter (Leatherman Wave), Custom Knives subchapter (Schmidt Knives & Forge), 035 (Burt Foster Custom Design), 036 (GHF wooden mockup & GHF test blade), Knife Care subchapter (props courtesy of Lost Planet Forge), 042 (whetstone courtesy of Lost Planet Forge), 043 (natural oil stone, water stone, diamond hone, courtesy of Lost Planet Forge), 047, 048, 057, Wild Kitchen subchapter (knife courtesy of Weatherford Knife Company [Western Skinner]); **White River Knife & Tool:** 013 (CPM S30V [M1 Backpacker]); **Wikimedia Commons:** 025 (Pesh-Kabz), Bowie knives (James Bowie portrait), 029 (Swiss Army Soldier Knife 1891), Feats of Steel: Avon Ralston, The Tomahawk (portrait and Smoke Tomahawk); **Work Sharp:** Original Knife & Tool Sharpener; **W.R. Case & Sons Cutlery Co.:** Design Class: Blade Profiles (Sheepsfoot [Amber Bone Stockman]), Design Class: Handle Materials (Leader Hunter), 015 (Blue Bone Trapper and Texas Toothpick), 099 (Leather Mini Finn Hunter); **Wyoming Knife Corporation:** Blades that Matter: Wyoming Knife (Original Skinning Fixed Blade); **Zero Tolerance:** Design Class: Handle Materials (Titanium [0801TI])

Illustration courtesy of

Conor Buckley: 01–03, 05, 06, Design Class, Three Modern Bowies, 31, 45, 46, 59, 64, 65, 67, 71, 73, 76, 78, 79, 92, 94, 96, 105, 114–116, 119, 122, 128, 133; **Hayden Foell:** 62, 81, 83, 124, 138; **Vic Kulihin:** 97, 113; **Liberum Donum:** 68, 125; **Dan Marsiglio:** 44, 80, 88, 106; **Christine Meighan:** 40, 41, 103, 118; **Raymond Larrett:** 86; **Shutterstock:** 37; **Lauren Towner:** 100, 126, 136.

All text by T. Edward Nickens, with the following exceptions: Ryan Arch 434; **Scott Bestul:** 242; **Phil Bourjaily:** 377, 390, 409; **Jacob Campbell:** 8; **Joe Cermele:** 119, 131, 137, 146-148, 150, 158, 162, 167, 168, 196, 444; **Eddie Crane III:** 68; **Kirk Deeter:** 89, 157, 178; **Joe Doss:** 55; **Bill Heavey:** 79; **Dave Hurteau:** 240, 254; **Tom Keer:** 200; **David Kretzschmar:** 133; **Anthony Licata:** 358; **Greg Martin:** 28; **Keith McCafferty:** 20, 22, 73, 77, 265, 271, 286, 300, 314, 322, 408, 431, 442, 443, 452, 457, 459, 463-465, 475, 485, 489, 491, 495; **John Merwin:** 98, 120, 153, 160, 207, 219; **David Petzal:** 237, 238, 251, 341, 373, 407; **Michael R. Shea:** 362; **Slayton L. White:** 205, 259, 380-381; **Kathy Zaborowski Richardson:** 9

weldonowen

President & Publisher Roger Shaw
SVP Sales & Marketing Amy Kaneko
Associate Publisher Mariah Bear
Project Editor J.T. Browning
Associate Editor Ian Cannon
Creative Director Kelly Booth
Art Director Allister Fein
Illustration Coordinator Conor Buckley
Production Director Michelle Duggan
Imaging Manager Don Hill

Waterbury Publications, Inc.,
Des Moines, IA
Creative Director Ken Carlson
Editorial Director Lisa Kingsley
Associate Design Director Doug Samuelson
Associate Design Director Becky Lau Ekstrand

Associate Editor Tricia Bergman
Production Designer Mindy Samuelson
Graphic Designer Ruby Hotchkiss
Photographer Emma Carlson
Copy Editor Gretchen Kauffman
Indexer Kevin Broccoli

PO Box 3088
San Rafael, CA 94912
www.weldonowen.com

ISBN 978-168188-368-7
10 9 8 7 6 5
2025 2024 2023 2022
Printed in China

FIELD & STREAM

Editor-in-Chief Colin Kearns
Group Creative Director Sean Johnston
Group Managing Editor Jean McKenna
Deputy Editor Slaton L. White
Managing Editor Margaret Nussy
Fishing Editor Joe Cermele
Hunting Editor Will Brantley
Shooting Editor John B. Snow
Senior Editor Natalie Krebs
Copy Editor Nicole Pakowsky
Photography Director John Toolan

Associate Art Director Russ Smith
Production Manager Judith Weber
Digital Director Nate Matthews
Special Projects Editor David Maccar
Executive Vice President Gregory Gatto
Group Editorial Director Anthony Licata
Online Content Editor Alex Robinson
Associate Online Editor JR Sullivan

2 Park Avenue
New York, NY 10016
www.fieldandstream.com